Earthly Signs

RUSSIAN LITERATURE

AND THOUGHT

Gary Saul Morson

Series Editor

Earthly Signs

Moscow Diaries, 1917–1922

MARINA TSVETAEVA

Edited, translated, & with an Introduction by

Jamey Gambrell

YALE UNIVERSITY PRESS · New Haven & London

The translator gratefully acknowledges a grant from the National Endowment for the Arts.

NATIONAL
ENDOWMENT
FOR 🌱 THE
ARTS

Set in Carter Cone Galliard type by The Composing Room of Michigan, Inc.
Printed in the United States of America by Vail-Ballou Press.

Library of Congress Cataloging-in-Publication Data
Tsvetaeva, Marina, 1892–1941.
[Prose works. English. Selections]
Earthly signs: Moscow diaries 1917–1922 / Marina Tsvetaeva ; edited, translated, and with an introduction by Jamey Gambrell.
p.   cm. — (Russian literature and thought)
Includes bibliographical references.
ISBN 0-300-06922-7 (alk. paper)
1. Tsvetaeva, Marina, 1892–1941—Translations into English.
I. Gambrell, Jamey.   II. Title.   III. Series.
PG3476.T75 A24   2002
891.71'4208 — dc21   2002004498

A catalogue record for this book is available from the British Library.

The paper in this book meets the guidelines for permanence and durability of the Committee on Production Guidelines for Book Longevity of the Council on Library Resources.

10   9   8   7   6   5   4   3   2   1

TO JOSEPH BRODSKY

who always insisted I persevere

CONTENTS

ACKNOWLEDGMENTS

Translators never work in a vacuum—one is always indebted to many people for assistance both concrete and general. There is one person in particular to whom I owe an incalculable debt; without him this translation would not have been possible. Alexander Sumerkin, editor of the first collected works of Marina Tsvetaeva (Russica Publishers), introduced me to Tsvetaeva many years ago. His wise, knowledgeable, unstinting, and patient help—and his friendship—have made this a far better book than it could have been otherwise.

Also high on my list is Sidney Monas, who convinced me to study Russian; his enthusiastic support and advice over the years have meant a great deal to me. Susan Sontag's generous response and her efforts in arranging the first publication of several pieces were tremendously encouraging and much appreciated. Jonathan Brent of Yale University Press continued that encouragement by publishing two essays when he and Frances Brent were editors of *Formations*.

I am grateful to many friends and colleagues who have contributed in more ways than they know, among them Kelly Haggart, Liza Knapp, Catharine Nepomnyashchy, and Carol Ueland; and to my parents, Jim and Helen Gambrell, who, though not Russian speakers, have helped elucidate all manner of obscure questions related to this book. And to my daughter Callie—just for being.

A fellowship from the National Endowment for the Arts provided crucial support for these translations.

Introduction
Jamey Gambrell

Marina Ivanovna Tsvetaeva was born in Moscow in September 1892, the daughter of Maria Alexandrovna Meyn and Ivan Vladimirovich Tsvetaev. Maria Alexandrovna came from a wealthy, educated family and was a gifted pianist. Marina's father already had two children from his first marriage; her younger sister, Anastasia, or Asya, as she was called, was born in 1894 (she died in 1993). Ivan Tsvetaev, the son of a village priest, was a classical philologist who taught at Moscow University and was curator of Fine Arts and Antiquities at the Rumyantsev Museum. He founded the Pushkin Museum of Fine Arts, based on a collection he acquired over almost a quarter of a century; The Alexander III Museum, as it was then called, opened in 1912, shortly before his death.

Tsvetaeva spent her early childhood in a large, comfortable house in the center of Moscow, close to the Pushkin monument; summers were spent in Tarusa, a town near the Oka River in Kaluga province. Marina was strong and healthy, but Asya was a sickly child and therefore (at least as Tsvetaeva perceived it) got more attention; their sibling rivalry continued for decades. By all accounts, the girls' mother was not inclined to expressions of maternal warmth: she was strict, demanding, and impatient. But she was obsessively involved in her daughters' education. From early childhood Marina and Asya were steeped in culture and the arts; they had governesses and tutors, and their mother read to them in several languages and took them to museums and the theater. Marina learned to read and began piano lessons with her mother at age four. In 1926, Tsvetaeva wrote of her childhood: "The dominant influence was that of my mother (music, nature, poetry, Germany). The passion for Jewry. One against all. Heroica. My father's influence was less obvious but no less powerful. (His passion for work, the absence of careerism, his simplicity, his single-mindedness.) Father's and mother's influence fused in a Spartan attitude to life. . . . The atmosphere of the house was neither bourgeois nor intellectual—it was 'chevaleresque.'"[1]

In 1902 the family moved to Europe because Tsvetaeva's mother had contracted tuberculosis. Marina and Asya attended a succession of boarding schools while their mother was treated in sanatoriums. These travels not only released Tsvetaeva from many of her mother's demands but allowed her to perfect her French and German and instilled in her an abiding love for German Romantic culture. The family returned to Russia in 1905; Maria Alexandrovna Meyn died in 1906, when Tsvetaeva was just thirteen years old.

Over the next four years Tsvetaeva studied in Russia and Paris, during which time her serious literary work began. She wrote poetry and translated Edmond Rostand's *L'Aiglon* into Russian. In 1910 she had a collection of her poems published; *Evening Album* attracted the attention of the well-known Symbolist poet and critic Valery Briusov, and the Acmeist poet Nikolai Gumilyov, who was married to the poet Anna Akhmatova. Gumilyov wrote that Tsvetaeva brought a "new and bold, sometimes excessively bold, intimacy" to Russian poetry. Although many of the verses were romantic and sentimental—as might be expected of an adolescent—one could sense the "inner originality of the young poetess," he added.[2] Briusov also approvingly noted Tsvetaeva's poetic gift and her "terrible intimacy" but added that her verse "at times becomes embarrassing, as though you'd peered impolitely through a half-closed window into someone else's apartment and witnessed a scene that outsiders should not see."[3] Fifteen years later, his relatively mild (and astute) caveats still rankled. In *A Hero of Labor,* written after his death, Tsvetaeva mercilessly dissected Briusov's work and his bureaucratic rise to the position of poetry commissar under the Soviet regime.

Evening Album also inspired the thirty-three-year-old poet and artist Maximilian Voloshin to seek out Tsvetaeva. The two became close friends. Voloshin introduced Tsvetaeva to literary Moscow, and she frequently visited his house in Koktebel, on the Crimean coast. It was there, in the summer of 1911, that eighteen-year-old Tsvetaeva met her future husband, the student Sergei Efron. Tsvetaeva and Efron were married in early 1912; that same year Tsvetaeva published her second collection of poems, *The Magic Lantern,* and gave birth to her daughter Ariadna (Alya). Money from her mother's family meant that Tsvetaeva was reasonably well off: she and Efron bought a house in Moscow and could afford help. They spent summers in Koktebel and Tsvetaeva devoted herself to writing. Her unswerving loyalty to Efron notwithstanding, she had affairs with the poet Sofia Parnok and Osip Mandelstam, among other. In both cases the affairs left a legacy of extraordinary poetry.

By the beginning of 1917, Tsvetaeva was expecting her second child (a daughter, Irina, was born in April), and Efron had been drafted into the Imperial Army. The October Revolution caught Tsvetaeva visiting Voloshin in the Crimea. She made it back to Moscow after a difficult, frightening journey, described in "October on the Train," which gave her a first glimpse of what the Revolution would mean: "My first vision of the bourgeoisie in the Revolution: ears hiding in fur hats, souls hiding in fur coats, heads hiding in necks, eyes hiding behind glasses. In the light of a sputtering match — a blinding vision of cowardly *hides*." Tsvetaeva made another trip south, this time with her husband, who had joined the White Army. She returned to revolutionary Moscow in late November, planning to move to Koktebel with the children, to be closer to Efron. But by that time travel was no longer possible. Tsvetaeva would have no word of her husband for three years, and it was four before they met again. During those years, Alya became her mother's closest friend and confidante. She was an extraordinarily precocious child, though at the time of the Revolution she was barely five years old.

◖◗

For Tsvetaeva, as for tens of millions of Russians, the Revolution irrevocably shifted the vicissitudes of private life onto the plane of historical tragedy. At age twenty-five Tsvetaeva found herself nearly destitute, alone with two small children and with no profession by which to support herself. She lived hand to mouth, selling off her belongings and trying to feed her children and keep warm in a city plagued by chaos, famine, and severe fuel shortages. Throughout Russia, life had been turned upside down. The new order was foreign to her: she was outspoken, impractical, and had no sympathy for the Revolution and no tolerance for any sort of rigid ideology; in addition, her husband was in the opposition. She was neither accepted nor at home in Soviet Russia.

Tsvetaeva's comfortable life was over. "I've taken the year 1919 a bit exaggeratedly," she wrote in "Attic Life:" "The way people will understand it a hundred years from now: not a fleck of flour, not a speck of salt (clinker and clutter enough and to spare!), not a speck, not a mote, not a shred of soap!—I clean the flue myself, my boots are two sizes too big—this is the way some novelist, using imagination to the detriment of taste, will describe the year 1919." Things got worse as the year progressed. Toward the end of 1919, unable to feed Alya and Irina, Tsvetaeva placed them in an orphanage outside Moscow. Alya became ill, and Tsvetaeva brought her home to nurse her back to health. In February 1920, not yet three years old, Irina died of starvation in the children's home.

Despite all the hardships, panic over Alya's illness, and guilt about the death of Irina, to whom she had always been curiously indifferent (if not downright abusive, as some evidence suggests), this was a productive period for Tsvetaeva. Between 1917 and 1921 she wrote a number of long verse dramas, several *poemy* (long, sometimes epic-length poems), and hundreds of short lyrics that she eventually collected in *Mileposts I, II, The Swans' Encampment*, an homage to the White Army, and *Craft*. She also kept detailed diaries, which she later drew on in prose essays. During these difficult years, her own, utterly unique voice emerged, and along with it a good deal of her major poetry. She described the arduous daily quest for the necessities of life in diaries later incorporated into "Attic Life": "I didn't note the most important thing: the gaiety, the keenness of thought, the bursts of joy at the slightest success, the passionate directedness of my entire being—all the walls are covered with lines of poems and NB! for notebooks."

In May 1922 Tsvetaeva and Alya left Russia for Berlin to rejoin Efron, who was living in Prague. She plunged into the whirlwind of Berlin's émigré literary life, quickly arranging the publication of two collections, *Psyche* and *Craft* (both in 1923). Before she could even be reunited with her husband, she became involved with her publisher, Abram Vishniak. During the same period she struck up an intense friendship with the poet Andrei Bely (who wrote enthusiastically about her versification) and began an epistolary romance with Boris Pasternak that would last more than a decade. After two months in Berlin, the family moved to a small village outside Prague with no running water. Her son, Georgy (known as Mur), was born in 1925. The family eked out a meager living on Marina's publications and stipends that the Czechoslovak government provided to Russian émigré students and intellectuals.

Tsvetaeva's time in Czechoslovakia also proved extremely prolific: she composed most of the 150 lyrics contained in *After Russia,* which is widely considered her finest collection and which marked a new stylistic maturity. As Simon Karlinsky, the eminent Tsvetaeva scholar and biographer writes, "In terms of language and versification, the poetry of [*After Russia*] is a staggering accomplishment — a synthesis of meaning, word and verbal music which the Russian Futurist poetry strove for and so rarely achieved to such a degree."[4] Some of Tsvetaeva's best known long *poemy* were also written at this time, including *The Swain* and *The Pied Piper* (both based on fairy tales), and the extraordinary *Poem of the Mountain* and *Poem of the End,* both inspired by another affair, one that almost ended her marriage.

In November 1925, the family moved to France; for the next fourteen years Tsvetaeva would live in and around Paris. She was initially well received by the émigré community in Paris, but relations soured over the next few years. Although her anti-Bolshevik credentials were well established by works like *The Swans' Encampment,* her poetics were too radical and idiosyncratic for Paris's conservative émigré elite. Many considered her difficult poetry deliberately obscurantist and her emotional intensity hysterical. Furthermore, her article attacking the well-known émigré critic Georgy Adamovich cost her many supporters and publishing opportunities, as did an open letter to Vladimir Mayakovsky during his visit to Paris in 1928. Anything Soviet was anathema to the émigré community, and Tsvetaeva's public praise for the poetry of Pasternak and Mayakovsky, whom she saw as the greatest living Russian poets, effectively placed her in the enemy camp.

Despite the antipathy her independent positions often elicited, she published regularly in many of the leading journals and newspapers of emigration and participated in public poetry readings and literary discussions. But the family lived in poverty, and Tsvetaeva's day-to-day life in France, as in Czechoslovakia and postrevolutionary Moscow, was a study in contrasts: the everyday grind of cooking, cleaning, and child care under much less than comfortable circumstances was intercut with exalted flights of poetic creation. Among the latter was her epistolary love affair with Pasternak and Rainer Maria Rilke in the summer of 1926.[5]

（ ）

Much has been written on the role that Tsvetaeva's love affairs played in her life and poetry. Whether they were realized in the flesh or merely epistolary, with men or sometimes with women, the pattern was the same. No one ever described that pattern better than Sergei Efron, in an anguished letter to Max Voloshin, written from Prague, when Tsvetaeva's obsession with Konstantin Rodzevich (which inspired *Poem of the End*) had brought the couple close to separation. Efron's letter is worth quoting at some length, because it eloquently summarizes the emotional core of both woman and poet:

> Marina is a woman of passions. . . . Plunging headfirst into her hurricanes has become essential for her, the breath of life. It no longer matters who it is that arouses these hurricanes. Nearly always (now as before) — or rather always — everything is based on self-deception. A man is invented and the hurricane begins. If the insignificance and narrowness of the hurricane's arouser is quickly revealed, then Marina gives way to a hurricane of despair. A state which facilitates the appearance of a new arouser. The important thing is not *what* but *how*. Not the essence or the source but the rhythm, the insane rhythm. Today — despair; tomorrow — ecstasy, love, complete self-abandon; and the following day — despair once again. And all this with a penetrating, cold (maybe even cynically Voltairean) mind. Yesterday's arousers are wittily and cruelly ridiculed (nearly always justly). Everything is entered in the book. Everything is coolly and mathematically cast into a formula. A huge stove, whose fires need

wood, wood, and more wood. Unwanted ashes are thrown out, and the quality of the wood is not so important. For the time being the stove draws well — everything is converted to flame. Poor wood is burnt up more quickly, good wood takes longer.

It goes without saying that it's a long time since I've been any use for the fire.[6]

(( ))

The 1930s mark a sharp decline in Tsvetaeva's poetic output. She turned increasingly to prose — perhaps partly in an attempt to earn a living. In a sequence of autobiographical pieces she explored her prerevolutionary childhood; she wrote essays on Pushkin and her contemporaries, including Pasternak, Mayakovsky, Mandelstam, Andrei Bely, Voloshin, Mikhail Kuzmin, and the artist Natalia Goncharova. Meanwhile, Sergei Efron's political views had taken a radical turn. As the decade wore on, he became more involved in the Eurasian and returnee movements, which were widely (and correctly) suspected of ties to the Soviet secret service (NKVD). As a result, conservative journals refused to publish Tsvetaeva; liberal papers, reacting to her "monarchist" poems and previous publications in anticommunist papers, also kept her at a distance.

By the mid-1930s Tsvetaeva's family was pressuring her to return to the Soviet Union. Her relations with her husband and daughter were extremely tense. Efron, she wrote to her Czech friend Anna Tesková, "has completely buried himself in Soviet Russia, can see nothing else, and sees in Russia only what he wants to see."[7] She did not want to go, however, even after Alya left for Moscow in March 1937. Despite her tendency to invent and romanticize personal relationships, often to disastrous effect, Tsvetaeva was entirely clear-headed on the subject of the USSR. Unlike her husband, she had lived under the Soviet regime and knew the nature of the beast she had left behind in 1922. "Go to Russia?" she presciently wrote to Tesková, "I won't be gagged merely by being unable to publish my work, I won't even be allowed to write it."[8]

Tsvetaeva of course knew of her husband's pro-Soviet sympathies — the former White officer had changed his views right under her eyes. However, despite the view prevailing in the Paris émigré community at the time, there is little reason to believe that she had any knowledge of her husband's activities on behalf of the NKVD — until he was interrogated by French officials in connection with the murder of Ignaty Reiss, a Soviet defector, in September 1937. Efron fled. It is known that Tsvetaeva accompanied him part way to Le Havre after that interrogation; he "disappeared" before they arrived at the port and made his way to Russia with the help of the Soviet authorities.

Tsvetaeva was now left with no choice: she would have to return to Moscow. After Efron's flight, all but her closest friends avoided her. She was excluded from literary gatherings, and most publications were closed to her. Nonetheless, she and Mur did not leave France for another year and a half. They lived off a small stipend from the Soviet consulate while Tsvetaeva meticulously reviewed, copied, and annotated her letters and poems. Most of her archive, deposited with friends in Paris, seems to have been lost in a flood during the war; fortunately, she also gave a packet of manuscripts (including copies of the correspondence with Rilke) to Basel University, and these have survived. On June 12, 1939, Tsvetaeva and her son finally set sail from Le Havre.

(( ))

In her last letter to Tesková before leaving for Russia in 1939, Tsvetaeva wrote: "Goodbye! What comes now is no longer difficult, what comes now is fate."[9] Fate did not take long to loose its terrible storm. Back in Moscow, Tsvetaeva learned that her sister, Asya, was in the camps. Barely two months after her return to Moscow, Alya was arrested. Efron's arrest — by the organization for which he had worked — followed in early October.

After Efron's arrest, Tsvetaeva and Mur were forced to leave the NKVD dacha outside Moscow where the family had been staying.[10] Tsvetaeva had no income and no place to live. Old acquaintances shunned her, afraid of contact with a wife of an "enemy of the people," and an émigré to boot. She and her son stayed for a time in one room with Efron's sister while Tsvetaeva looked for work as a translator. She wrote some poetry after her return, but the lion's share of the considerable literary energy she could still muster went into translations of English and German folk ballads (including Robin Hood), and poems by

Federico García Lorca, Charles Baudelaire, and the Georgian poet
Vazha Pshavela. Most of the work and assistance Tsvetaeva did get
(translations, and the right, for a few months, to take her meals at the
well-provisioned Writers Union retreat in Golitsyno, outside Moscow)
are directly traceable to Pasternak's intervention. But there was only so
much Pasternak could do.

When the Germans invaded the Soviet Union in June 1941, Tsvetaeva was torn as to whether to leave Moscow with the many writers being evacuated. But as the summer passed and the bombing raids over
Moscow increased, her panic grew. Maria Belkina, the young wife of a
Soviet literary critic (who was seven months pregnant at the time) remembers her last meeting with a near hysterical Tsvetaeva not far from
the Writers Union Club, just after an air raid in August 1941:

> Her first words were: "What, you haven't evacuated yet? That's
> madness! . . . You should run from this hell! It keeps coming, com-
> ing and nothing can stop it, it sweeps away everything in its path,
> destroys everything. . . . You must run. . . ." She grabbed my hand
> and it was such a passionate monologue and such a whirlwind flight
> into her heights. . . . There was France, and Czechoslovakia, and
> the death of Pompeii, and the trumpet before the Last Judgment,
> and graveyards, graveyards, and ashes, and the cry of a newborn
> child, which clearly referred to me. . . . She was on the brink, she
> was a live bundle of nerves, a clot of despair and pain. Like a bare
> wire in the wind, a flash of sparks and a short circuit.[11]

It was in this state that Tsvetaeva left Moscow on August 8. She and
Mur were evacuated by boat along the Volga to Elabuga, a small town
on the Toima and Kama rivers. Those with more clout in the Writers
Union were evacuated to nearby Chistopol. In Elabuga, Tsvetaeva
rented a room for herself and Mur from a local couple and went to
Chistopol to try and have her residence permit changed; she looked for
work there and even applied for a job washing dishes at the writers' cafeteria. There was some reason to hope that she would receive permission
to move, according to contemporaries Belkina interviewed. But Tsvetaeva was beyond hope. She returned from Chistopol to Elabuga.

On August 31, while Mur and her landlords were out of the house,

Tsvetaeva hanged herself. She left three notes: two of them were pleas to others to take care of her son and see that he studied, and the third was to Mur himself: "Murlyga!" (a diminutive), she wrote, "forgive me, but it would only have gotten worse. *I am seriously ill,* this is no longer me. I love you madly. Understand that I couldn't live any more. Tell Papa and Alya — if you see them — that I loved them to the last minute, and explain that *I had reached a dead end.*"[12] Tsvetaeva was buried in an unmarked grave in the Elabuga cemetery. Mur, who was sixteen at the time, was indeed helped by many — including Akhmatova and Alexei Tolstoy. He eventually made his way back to Moscow to study but was evacuated again to Tashkent, where Belkina ran into him on the street in 1942. He was drafted into the army in 1943 and killed in combat in July 1944.

Alya survived seventeen years in the camps and exile, returning to Moscow in 1955. She fought for the rehabilitation of her mother's poetry, carried out the difficult work of sorting through Tsvetaeva's archive, deciphering the diaries and preparing texts for publication. She lived to see a volume of Tsvetaeva's verse published in the Soviet Union and died in 1975. Alya was buried in Tarusa, where, as one of Tsvetaeva's biographers, Viktoria Schweitzer writes,

> Long before her death, contemplating the fact that she was unlikely to be buried in her beloved Tarusa, [Marina] had asked for a stone with an epitaph. . . .
>
> Here Marina Tsvetaeva
> would have liked to lie.[13]

Earthly Signs

When Tsvetaeva left Russia in 1922, she carried with her hundreds of verses composed during the harrowing but poetically fruitful years since the Revolution. She also brought with her to the West the numerous diaries and poetic notebooks she had kept religiously since the fall of 1917. She immediately proposed a book based on them to Abram Vishniak, editor of the émigré publishing house Helicon, which had earlier accepted some of her poetry. In a letter of February 17, 1923, to

Roman Gul,[14] written from Mokropsy, the village outside Prague where she and Alya had moved in August 1922, she described the broad outlines of the book, which was to be called *Earthly Signs:*[15] "It's a book of *notes* (everyday life, thoughts, conversations, dreams, rev[olutionary] Moscow — a sort of psychic chronicle), 2) unified by years (from 1917 to the end of 1918) and my essence: everything boils down to a common denominator, 3) between 4–5 signatures (at the standard 40,000 letters per signature), but the book itself will come out longer, for there are a lot of short notes, I often start with a new line break. All in all, a certain *latitude with paper* is required."[16]

Vishniak was apparently eager to publish the prose but asked Tsvetaeva to cut political matter, because Helicon exported books to the Soviet Union.[17] This enraged the poet, and she withdrew her proposal. In early March she again wrote to Gul, vividly outlining both the contents of the proposed book and her reaction to Vishniak's request.

Mokropsy, night of new March 5–6, 1923.[18]

. . . A couple of words about business. Helicon answered, marvelous conditions . . . but: *outside of politics.* I answered in turn. Moscow 1917–1919 — what was I doing, rocking in a cradle? I was 24–26 years old, I had eyes, ears, hands, legs: and with these eyes I saw, and with these ears I heard, and with these hands I chopped (and wrote!), with these legs I walked the city markets and gates from morning to night — where did these legs not take me!

There's no *politics* in the book: there is *passionate* truth: the partisan truth of cold, of hunger, of anger, of the *Year!* My youngest girl died of hunger in a children's home — that's also "politics" (the home was Bolshevik).

Oh, Helicon and Co.! Esthetes! Don't want to stain their hands! I'm writing him definitively, I'm begging: let me go in peace. I'm writing that I regret that he won't be the one to publish it, but that I *cannot* cripple the book.

The "politics" in my book: 1) a trip to a requis[ition] station (a *red* one), officer-Jews, Russian Red Army soldiers, peasants, the train car, robberies, conversations. 2) My job at "Narkomnats" (pure humor! A bit terrifying.). 3) Thousands of small scenes: on lines, squares, at the markets (the impression on the street when the Tsar was shot, for instance), market prices — the everyday life of revol[utionary] Moscow. Also: encounters with White officers, impressions of the Oct[ober] Anniversary (the first and second), thoughts on the assassination attempt against Lenin, reminiscences about a certain Kanegisser (Uritsky's murderer). This is the "politics." And outside of that — everything: dreams, conversations with Alya, meetings with people, my own soul — all of me. This isn't a *political book,* not for a second. This is a living soul in a dead noose — but alive nonetheless. The background is gloomy, but I wasn't the one who invented it. . . .

Gul tried to help Tsvetaeva find another publisher, and she laid out the contents of the book to him again in May. By that time, she envisioned a much larger book consisting of two volumes, one of which would contain her daughter's notebooks. In this letter and another, to Alexander Bakhrakh,[19] written around the same time, Tsvetaeva defends her work from the simplistic political reaction she predicts it will provoke.

> Prague, 27 new May 1923.
>   . . . My book will be called *Earthly Signs* and this (spring 1917-autumn 1919) will be Vol. I. Then follows Vol. II. — A Child's Notes — which could also be ready by autumn. Now listen even more carefully, this is *important.*
>   *Earthly Signs,* Vol. I (1917–1919), which I am now copying out — consists of *my notes. Earthly Signs* Vol. II (1917–1919) — of *Alya's notes,* at first written down by me, later in her own hand: a sort of diary. There has never been a book like this *in the world.* It's her letters to me, descriptions of Soviet life (the street, market, nursery school, lines, the countryside, etc. etc.), dreams, reviews of books, of people — the precise and full life of a six-year-old child's soul. One could reproduce a facsimile of the handwriting. (All her diaries are available.)
>   Gul, this *isn't* a Black Hundreds book,[20] it's deeply truthful and extremely contradictory: turned down by Gosizdat it would also be turned town by Diakonova's publishing house (Black Hundreds?)

This is a book of living life and truth, that is, politically (i.e., in terms of lies) it is certain to fail utterly. In it there are charming c[ommun]-ists and impeccable wh[ite gu]ards, the former will see *only* the latter, and the latter — *only* the former. (. . .)

In the letter to Bakhrakh she reiterated her feelings:

The danger shoals of this book are: counter-revolution, hatred of the Jews, love of the Jews, glorification of the rich, vilification of the rich; despite an undoubted White Guard attitude, certain irreproachable living communists are given their full due of admiration. Yes, and also a fierce love for Germany and ridicule of the bovine patriotism of the Russians during the first year of the war.

In a word, the publisher, like my own rib cage, should be able to encompass EVERYTHING. Here, everyone is involved, everyone stands accused, everyone is acquitted. This is a book of TRUTH. There.

Everyone will tear this book to pieces (with their teeth!), everyone . . . except for a few genuine unprejudiced persons who know that TRUTH IS A TURNCOAT.[21]

None of Tsvetaeva's attempts to publish *Earthly Signs* as a book met with success, and in 1924 she began to break up the material into separate sketches that were published in émigré periodicals in Czechoslovakia, France, and elsewhere. The first such piece was "Excerpts from the Book *Earthly Signs*," in the Prague-based journal *Volia Rossii,* in 1924. Over the next three years, Tsvetaeva published another nine prose pieces originally intended as part of *Earthly Signs.* They appear in this book in the approximate order of the events' chronology rather than by the date of publication. In addition, the present volume contains her 1925 essay portrait of the poet Valery Briusov. *A Hero of Labor,* occasioned by Briusov's death in October 1924, describes the same period and clearly draws heavily on contemporary diaries.

In this book Russia during the period of War Communism comes alive through a multitude of voices. Equally in evidence throughout are the passion and the 'cold, penetrating, Voltairean mind' that Efron would later describe to Voloshin — in this case directed toward the tragic and absurd realities of the time.

In the fall of 1917 Tsvetaeva traveled to the Crimea to visit her sister, Anastasia, and to look for lodgings, since she had plans to move there with her children. As a result, she was not in Moscow when the provisional government fell and Soviet power was declared. The first part of "October on the Train" recounts Tsvetaeva's train trip from the Crimea to Moscow just days after the Bolshevik revolution. Contradictory accounts of events in Moscow printed in the provincial papers she bought along the way turned the two-and-a-half day trip into a nightmarish delirium: Tsvetaeva was afraid she would find her husband and children dead or missing. "Should God grant this miracle — leave you among the living, I shall follow you like a dog," she wrote. (On returning to Russia in the 1930s, Tsvetaeva noted in the margins of "October on the Train": "and here I am, following him — like a dog [21 years later].")

They were all well, however, and she and Efron immediately returned to the Crimea, where they visited the poet Max Voloshin. In a short scene that epitomizes the unreality of that time, she contrasts the tumult of the days following the Revolution with the unhurried, unchanging existence of the local Tatars, who seem to her to live outside time. The fragments of dialogue she heard on her second return trip to Moscow — arguments about God, the bourgeoisie, and the Bolsheviks — vividly convey the growing social tension in the country.

"Free Passage" tells the story of her visit to a requisition station in the countryside in September 1918 in search of food, an increasingly scarce commodity in the capital. With the help of friends, Tsvetaeva arranged a sham "business trip" to study folk embroidery in Tambov province, a pretext that permitted her to travel and allowed her to "import" one and one half poods of grain (about fifty lbs.) to the capital. Tsvetaeva took fabric, matches, and soap to trade, but she was hopeless at bargaining with the peasant women. She ended up trading some of her rare goods for wooden dolls and amber, rather than for the flour and lard she and her family needed.

The requisition station was inhabited by an unsavory cast of characters, including bands of marauding soldiers, an ideological Bolshevik, and a petit bourgeois opportunistically turned communist. Most memorable was a wily young peasant soldier whom Tsvetaeva saw as the reincarnation of Stenka Razin, the seventeenth-century Cossack hetman who plundered barges on the Volga River, raided Persia, led a rebellion against Moscow, and was eventually executed. Tsvetaeva had an infallible ear for all levels and modulations of Russian: the direct speech ranges from Russian newly bastardized by Marxist jargon to the poetic peasant dialect of the young soldier she calls Stenka Razin.

Like many women of her class, Tsvetaeva had never held a job prior to the Revolution—furthermore, she was temperamentally unsuited to service. In "My Jobs" Tsvetaeva gives a humorous account of her short-lived attempt to work at the People's Commissariat of Nationalities (known as Narkomnats) in the winter of 1918–19. Her lodger, Henryk Sachs, a Polish Communist who was a personal assistant to Feliks Dzerzhinsky, arranged this job for her. He helped Tsvetaeva on many occasions, though she made no secret of her feelings about the Bolsheviks and her support of the White Army.[22]

The job—which consisted of copying newspaper articles onto filing cards—brought her into contact with all the nationalities of the new Soviet Union. She met people as diverse as an Esperantist disillusioned by the communists' lack of interest in his internationalist mission and a young woman, an ardent Orthodox believer, who dreamed of assassinating Lenin.[23] Tsvetaeva accepted the job, she writes, because Narkomnats was located in the house that served as a model for the Rostov home in *War and Peace* (later the location of the USSR Writers Union); an account of the trip down to the hellish basement kitchen for ersatz tea therefore becomes a fantasy on Natasha Rostova and how different the heroine's fate would have been had she met Pushkin instead of Pierre.

"Attic Life" portrays Tsvetaeva's grueling daily existence in the hungry year of 1919, a portrait that is confirmed by many contemporary accounts. Tsvetaeva and her daughters occupied two rooms on the top floor of her former home, the rest of the house having been allocated to other people, in keeping with new Soviet housing policy. Most of the day was taken up with treks back and forth across Moscow in search of food and attempts to keep warm by burning the remaining bits of furniture and even the staircase banister. Tsvetaeva's resources dwindled as she sold off the few salable items she possessed. In contrast, the aphoristic essays "On Love" and "On Gratitude" are abstract, lyrical, and exalted in tone. But many of Tsvetaeva's meditations, particularly those on gratitude, were inspired by the hardships she both witnessed and endured during those years.

"Excerpts from the Book *Earthly Signs*," the piece she first published, is also the most fragmentary and reads rather like pages lifted verbatim from a diary. It consists of short notes and observations that are not organized by any single theme or narrative—numerous phrases and observations recur in other essays. Both "The Death of Stakhovich" and "A Hero of Labor" give subtle accounts of the postrevolutionary literary and artistic scene through portraits of individuals. The former, largely elegiac and nostalgic in tone, records Tsvetaeva's brief acquaintance with Aleksei Aleksandrovich Stakhovich (1856–1919), the famous Moscow Art Theater actor and friend of Stanislavsky. "A Hero of Labor" is a trenchant, humorous essay on Valery Briusov, the Symbolist poet turned literary commissar. Tsvetaeva's "On Germany," coming as it did in the wake of World War I, was not only a hymn to the great traditions of German literature, but a protest against the narrow-mindedness of Russian nationalism. "From a Diary" consists of seven vignettes drawn from postrevolutionary life, most of them both humorous and bittersweet.

The diary and notebook pieces of *Earthly Signs* break off in early 1920, shortly before the death of Irina, Tsvetaeva's younger daughter.

(( ))

The works in this book have been recognized as a significant source of biographical material on Tsvetaeva and have been quoted by all her biographers. They are also important to any student of Tsvetaeva's poetry, as they provide considerable insight into her poetic syntax, often elucidating the genesis of linguistic and thematic tropes found in condensed, telegraphic form in poems of the same period.

Tsvetaeva's portraits of life in postrevolutionary Moscow, however, are an extraordinary historical document in their own right. They could well be placed in the honored Russian tradition of urban sketches (especially of Moscow) popularized in the late nineteenth and early twentieth century by Vladimir Giliarovsky.[24] Tsvetaeva manages to combine what Briusov called her "terrible intimacy" with astute observation in a way that sometimes strangely recalls Walter Benjamin's *Moscow Diary,* though as a foreigner with no Russian, Benjamin walked through the Moscow streets in something of a socio-semantic fog. Tsvetaeva, on the other hand, was an insider, a discerning and knowledgeable eyewitness to what was one of the most turbulent periods of the twentieth century.

Most of the pieces translated here were subtitled "notes" or "from a diary." The diary genre gave Tsvetaeva license to ignore standard considerations of narrative development — as she once said, she was incapable of inventing an original plot. These pieces are multilayered tableaux vivants constructed from a variety of fragments separated typographically by asterisks or bullets. Keenly observed sketches of character and place developed with a fine wit and devastating sense of irony are intermingled with aphoristic meditations, childhood memories, notes, and reflections on all manner of subjects, from the Sovietization of the Russian language to the price of potatoes and the nature of poetry and love. Tsvetaeva uses snippets of conversation (some with her daughter, friends, and colleagues, some overheard in public), street scenes, bits of letters, quotations from newspapers, and poetry (often in French or German). The raison d'être of each fragment is usually evident: it may adhere to a narrative logic or delineate a single thought. What results from this patchwork technique is a complex, constantly shifting linguistic landscape that creates the illusion of narrative movement — the energetic equivalent of plot.

The diary, indeed, provided Tsvetaeva with its own sort of structure, one that most nearly approximated the alternating leaps, lags, jumps, digressions, and backtrackings of thought. The genre allowed for loops back in time, flashbacks that enrich rather than interfere with the present tense verisimilitude of the text. In "My Jobs," to give one example, Tsvetaeva's offer of help to a woman carrying a heavy package to the former governor-general of Moscow, now imprisoned by the Bolsheviks in Moscow's Butyrskaya prison, leads to memories of a childhood encounter with the man, who had been an acquaintance of Tsvetaeva's father. By the time Tsvetaeva returns to the street scene and bids the woman farewell, not only has the lost world of prerevolutionary Russia been vividly evoked but a wrenching contrast between past and present has been tactfully established without resort to political rhetoric. The diary format also corresponded most aptly to the disjunctions of the historical moment, and accounts for the cinematic feel of many episodes. One suspects that even had Tsvetaeva been a master of plot construction, she might have chosen this genre.

Tsvetaeva's early prose grew out of her poetry notebooks, so it is hardly surprising that she used poetic techniques in her prose. In "Excerpts from the Book *Earthly Signs*," Tsvetaeva notes that her approach to poetry and prose consists of trying to make the latter function according to the rules of the former.

> Poetry and prose:
>
> In prose too much seems superfluous to me, in poetry (genuine) everything is necessary. Given my attraction to asceticism of the prosaic word, I could end up with a skeleton.
>
> In poetry — there's a certain innate measure of flesh: less is impossible.

This inclination "to asceticism of the prosaic word" underlies the sometimes eccentric jumps from subject to subject or fragment to fragment in Tsvetaeva's diary work. The poet is continually paring down the text and seems fully aware of the effect this produces. She refuses to "flesh out" her prose, dispensing with what she sees as the "superfluous" verbiage of transitions and atmospheric descriptions. At times she does in fact leave nothing but the skeleton frame. As Joseph Brodsky wrote in his eloquent essay on Tsvetaeva's prose:

> Prose for Tsvetaeva was nothing but the continuation of poetry by other means. . . . Everywhere — in her diary entries, essays on literature, fictionalized reminiscences — that is just what we encounter: the resetting of the methodology of poetic thinking into a prose text, the growth of poetry into prose. Tsvetaeva's sentence is constructed not so much in accordance with the principle of subject followed by predicate as through the use of specifically poetic technology: sound association, root rhyme, semantic enjambment, etc. That is, the reader is constantly dealing not with a linear (analytic) development but with a crystalline (synthesizing) growth of thought.[25]

These synthesizing techniques are already abundantly evident in the early, diary works. In "Free Passage," for instance, Tsvetaeva meets a young Russian soldier just returned from a requisition roundup ("Esenin, but without the pettiness," she notes), whom she immediately christens Stenka Razin. There follows a disquisition on Razin: the historical Stepan Razin; the folk hero Razin of the popular song[26] and of Tsvetaeva's own poem "Stenka Razin," written in spring 1917; and the young soldier, whose name we never learn.

Tsvetaeva conjures up an image of the Russian folk hero — and of Russia itself — based entirely on linguistic associations with his name, inserting, along the way, an amusing aside on the Russian word *belokur*, which means "fair" or "blonde": "*My* Razin (the one in the song) is tow-headed [*belokur*] with red highlights. (By the way, a stupid loss of the letter d: tow-headed [*belokudr*], white curls [*belye kudry*]: both wild and white. But what is *belokur*? White chickens? [*belye kury*]? A sort of tailless word!) Pugachev is blackness, Razin is whiteness. And the very word itself: Stepan! Hay, straw, the steppe. Could a Stepan possibly be swarthy? But: Razin! Sunrise, straits — strike, Razin! Where it's spacious, it's not black. Blackness — is thick."[27] This passage is quite typical of Tsvetaeva's wordplay and the way she uses it to construct characters.

The image of the spacious Russian steppes elicited by the name of Stenka Razin is then enlarged into a vision of the pagan, pre-Christian Russia with which Tsvetaeva herself identifies. Again, she arrives at this vision by synthetic rather than analytic means: Stenka Razin leads naturally to mention of the Persian princess who, according to legend and popular song, he throws overboard into the Volga. The Persian princess, as a pagan, presumably offers Razin the adventure of conquering a new space, a new territory; Tsvetaeva reads poems to her peasant Razin, including one of her own about Stenka Razin. Both identifying with and distinguishing herself from the Persian princess, she offers herself to the young soldier (who in earlier passages had expressed his disdain for the Russian clergy) as the embodiment of a pre-Christian Russia as exotic as any Persian land. The image could have come straight out of Pushkin's long narrative poem *The Gypsies:* "Stenka Razin, I am no Persian princess, there is no double-edged cunning in me: neither of

Persia nor of the one who does not love. But neither am I Russian, Razin, I'm *pre*-Russian, *pre*-Tatar, pretemporal Russ——and I reach out to you! Straw-headed Stepan, listen to me, steppes: there were covered wagons and there were nomad camps, there were camp fires and there were stars. Do you want a nomad tent—where through the hole shines the biggest star?"[28]

In response, Tsvetaeva's "straw-headed Stepan" tells her the folk story of the city of Kitezh, which chose to be poetically submerged in a flood of silver water–sound streaming from the ringing of its church bells rather than surrender to the Tatars. As Tsvetaeva and "Stenka Razin" take leave of each other, the poet gives Stenka a ring ("serebrianyi perstenek") that synthesizes her identification with the Persian princess ("Persiianochka") and Stenka's story of "the town that drowned in its own [silver] ringing." Although an actual ring, the gift is clearly linguistic in origin: it merges the Persian princess with Stenka Razin and the legend of Kitezh in a single word, *perstenek,* a silver "signet ring." "Stenka Razin, I'm no Persian princess, but I'll give you a ring—silver—as a keepsake" ("Sten'ka Razin, ia ne Persiianochka, no perstenek na pamiat'—serebrianyi—ia Vam podariu").

(())

Earthly Signs represents Tsvetaeva's earliest attempts at prose. With time, her writing matured, becoming more adeptly structured, more focused, less aphoristic, less fragmented. Its peak came perhaps with the childhood memoirs of the mid-1930s, such as "The House at Old Pimen," "The Museum Opening" "The Devil," and her unforgettable portraits of the poets Maximilian Voloshin, Andrei Bely, and Osip Mandelstam, among others. The entire range of her future prose output can be seen in fledgling form in *Earthly Signs,* however: aphoristic literary essays, autobiographical memoirs or sketches, and portraits of family, friends, and literary peers.

The importance of prose to Tsvetaeva's oeuvre grew throughout the seventeen years of her emigration, particularly as her lyrical output began to diminish. Whereas in poetry Tsvetaeva attempted every possible genre and voice, from short lyrics to historical dramas in verse, from an autobiographical first person to a mythical third person, in prose she never strayed all that far from the diary. She did not turn to fiction. The few pieces she refers to as stories, such as "A Mother's Tale" (1935) were for the most part thinly veiled fictionalized autobiography. No matter how many characters she introduces, Tsvetaeva herself is always the narrator, the organizing consciousness.

(( ))

Tsvetaeva is not easy reading, even for educated native speakers of Russian. She confronts readers with a Joycean profusion of idioms and styles, ranging from the metaphorical speech of fairy tales and the circumlocutions of peasant dialect to a high literary diction steeped in Greek and Roman myths, the classics, and German Romanticism. She used almost all the classic Russian meters, adding her own innovations, and she made original use of Russian folk rhythms. Her subject matter draws on an equally diverse range of literary, historical, and folkloric sources. As Voloshin once said, ten poets coexisted in Tsvetaeva. Similarly, much of *Earthly Signs* could be considered a dramatic monologue — in which the speaker assumes or inhabits a variety of voices.

Tsvetaeva's considerable emotional and poetic force relies on the multiple associations arising phonetically and semantically from a complex interaction of strong root meanings, inflection (Russian has six cases and three genders), verbal aspect (which often conveys tense in Russian), the absence of definite and indefinite articles, and an extremely flexible system of noun, verb, and adjective formation that makes use of prepositional prefixes, suffixes, and participial adjectives — and renders the concept of neologism virtually moot. In short, as Brodsky wrote, the logic of her poetic language derives from the specific physical texture and structure of the Russian word.

The effect is a spectacular linguistic density. Frequently, discursive meaning must be teased out of incantatory, even hypnotic phonetic sequences that unfold in a syntax that can seem impacted, impenetrable. Reading Tsvetaeva sometimes feels like witnessing language in a primordial, undiluted form. In an almost biblical sense, the Word is the vehicle of creation; engendering both subject and emotion, it is the incarnation of the spirit.

Tsvetaeva is a poet of the ear rather than of the eye: visual images are rare in her poetry and her prose is rarely descriptive. In *Poem of the Air* she wrote:

[To be] the ear — is to be
Pure spirit . . .

. . . .
    Is it pure hearing
or pure sound
that propels us? . . .

Ukhom — chistym dukhom
Byt' . . .

. . . .
    Chistym slukhom
ili chistym zvukom
dvizhemsia? . . .

For her, the question is rhetorical: the ear (*ukho*), hearing-pitch (*slukh*), spirit (*dukh*), and sound (zvuk) are all blood brothers in the kinship system of the Russian language.

The breath (*dykhanie*) and the soul (*dusha*) inhabit the same branch — actually the roots — of this genealogical tree. Tsvetaeva's lines — poetic and prosaic — are frequently punctuated by the intake and exhalation of the breath, which functions not only as a metrical device or caesura but as an autonomous grammatical and semantic element on a par with words. Breath generates sound, of course, but it is also denoted by silent dashes, which Tsvetaeva uses liberally in both her poetry and prose. These are not simply pauses, however, metrical breathers or rest periods occupying the interstices of a poem. In Russian a dash is an equal sign standing in for the unwritten verb "to be"; it is also used instead of quotation marks to introduce direct speech. Breath-silence for Tsvetaeva is a mutable element, in constant expressive movement, since it contains all the nuances of being.

In "On Love" Tsvetaeva writes that "the complete concurrence of souls requires the concurrence of the breath, for what is the breath, if not the rhythm of the soul? And thus, in order for people to understand one another, they must walk or lie side by side." Or read poetry together, she might have written. Further on in the same piece she says: "[The heart] is always first to sound the alarm. I could say: it is not love that makes my heart pound, but my pounding heart that makes love. The heart: it is a musical rather than a physical organ."

Breath-poetry is the rhythm of the soul; and the breath of the soul plays the heart-organ, kindling love — and more poetry. Spiritual and physical passion have the same vocabulary, they speak the same language and are often indistinguishable. Soul, poetry, and emotion merge in an erotic cycle that played out dramatically again and again in Tsvetaeva's poetry and her life — as Sergei Efron described in his letter to Voloshin.

( )

Tsvetaeva's prose lives by the same principles as her poetry, if somewhat less intensely. This creates constant challenges — not to say moments of utter despair — for the translator. Even such casual remarks as her musing on *belokúr* versus *belokúdr*, quoted above, are so intimately tied to specific Russian words that they cannot be approximated in English; the translator therefore reluctantly resorts to notes. One particularly challenging problem in *Earthly Signs* is how to render the many types of direct speech. Tsvetaeva had a keen ear and an extraordinary ability to convey the subtleties of urban, rural, peasant, and middle-class diction as well as the educated speech of the intelligentsia to which she belonged. Peasant dialect, with its reliance on what are essentially poetic tropes, presents the most intractable difficulties, even when one manages to unravel its folkloric logic and understand the basic sense. Postwar American English has no equivalent to draw on. I have opted for discursive clarity and where possible have sought to suggest an uneducated, rural speech that has roots in the language of proverbs and fairy tales.

Inevitably, much of the associative and phonetic richness of Tsvetaeva's prose is lost in translation, an unavoidable sacrifice to accuracy and narrative sense. But great wealth remains. And sometimes the translator can find ways to approximate, at least by analogy, the textures of Tsvetaeva's language, and the way in which she often moves from sound to sense.

Tsvetaeva herself offers the best advice to translators. In the introduction to her own translation of Rilke's "Letters to a Young Poet," she wrote:

> And today I want Rilke to speak — through me. In the vernacular, this is known as translation. (How much better the Germans put it — nachdichten! Following in the poet's path, paving anew the entire road which he paved. For let "nach" be — (to follow after), but — dichten! is that which is always anew.) Nachdichten — to pave anew the road along instantaneously vanishing traces. But translation has another meaning. To translate not only *into* (the Russian language, for example), but also transport *across* (a river). I translate Rilke into the Russian tongue, as he will some day translate me to the other world.
>
> By the hand — across the river.[29]

Every translation, like every poem or novel, is a voyage of sorts. My hope is that I have managed to read these earthly signs well enough, to follow Tsvetaeva's path closely enough, to repave enough of her singular road, for English readers to be translated across the river.

Asya and Marina Tsvetaeva with Aleksandra Ivanovna Dobrokhotova,
Nervi, 1903

Asya and Marina Tsvetaeva, 1905

Sergei Efron and Marina Tsvetaeva, Autumn 1911

Tsvetaeva's daughters, Ariadna (Alya) and Irina Efron, ca. 1919

Tsvetaeva and her son Georgy, ca. 1930

M. I. Tsvetaeva

M. Tsvetaeva, S. Efron, & Alya. Czechoslovakia, 1922

October on the Train
Notes from Those Days

Two and a half days — not a bite, not a swallow. (Throat tight.) Soldiers bring newspapers — printed on rose-colored paper. The Kremlin and all the monuments have been blown up. The 56th Regiment. The buildings where the Cadets and officers refused to surrender have been blown up. 16,000 killed. By the next station it's up to 25,000. I don't speak. I smoke. One after another, travelers get on trains heading back.

Dream (November 2, 1917, nighttime).

We are escaping. A man with a rifle comes up from the cellar. I take aim with my empty hand. He lowers the rifle. A sunny day. We are climbing on some debris. S. is talking about Vladivostok. We are riding in a carriage through the ruins. A man with sulfuric acid.

LETTER IN A NOTEBOOK

If you are still alive, if I am to see you again — listen: yesterday, approaching Kharkov, I read *Yuzhny Krai*. 9,000 killed. I cannot tell you about this night because *it's not over yet*. Gray morning now. I'm in the corridor. Try to understand! I'm riding, and I'm writing to you and right now I don't know . . . but here follow words that I cannot write down.

We are approaching Oryol. I'm scared to write to you the way I want to — I'm afraid I'll burst into tears. This is all a terrible dream. I try to sleep. I don't know how to write to you. When I'm writing, you are there — since I'm writing you! — and then, oh! the 56th Regiment, the Kremlin. (Do you remember the huge keys you used to lock the gate for the night?) But most important, most important, most important — you, you yourself, with your self-destructive instinct. Could you actually stay at home? If everyone stayed home, you would go out alone all the same. Because you are irreproachable. Because you can't stand for others to be killed. Because you are a lion, giving away a lion's share: to give life — to everyone else, rabbits and foxes. Because you are selfless and balk at self-preservation, because "me" is not important for you, because I knew all of this from the first moment!

Should God grant this miracle — leave you among the living, I shall follow you like a dog.

The news is vague, I don't know what to believe. I read about the Kremlin, Tverskaya Street, the Arbat, the Metropol Hotel, Voznesensky Square, the mountains of corpses. In yesterday's (the 1st) issue of the SR newspaper *Kurskaya Zhizn* I read that disarmament had begun. Other papers (today's) write of fighting. I'm not allowing myself the will to write now — but I've imagined a thousand times how I'll walk into the house. Will it be possible to enter the city?

Soon we'll be at Oryol. It's about two in the afternoon now. We'll be in Moscow at 2 in the morning. And if I walk into the house — and there's no one there, not a soul? Where shall I look for you? Perhaps the house is no longer there? I keep feeling — this is a terrible dream. I keep expecting that any second now something will happen and there won't have been any newspapers, nothing. *That I'm dreaming, that I'll wake up.*

Throat tight, as if fingers are squeezing it. I keep loosening my collar, pulling on it. Seriozhenka. I've written down your name and I can't write any more.

(( ))

Three days — not a word with anyone. Only with soldiers, to buy newspapers. (Terrifying rose-colored sheets, sinister. Theatrical death posters. No — Moscow colored them! They say there's no paper. There was, but they used it all up. (To some that's all there is to it — to others — it's a sign.)

Finally — someone speaks: "What's wrong Miss? You ain't even taken a bite of bread the whole trip. I been on the train with you since Lozovaya. I keep watching and thinking — when's our young Miss there going to eat? Then I think, there, she's getting some bread now — no — writing in that book again. What are you now, studying for an exam or something?"

I, vaguely: "Yes."

The speaker is a workman, black eyes, like coal, a black beard, something of an affectionate Pugachev. A bit eerie, and pleasant. We talk. He complains about his sons: "They're infected with this new life, they've caught this mange. You, Miss, you're a young person, you're likely to see things different, but to my way of thinking — all these red rabbles, these obscene freedoms — it's nothing but a temptation of the Antichrist. He's a Prince, and his power is great, he's just been biding his time, waiting till the right hour's come — gathering his strength. You come to the countryside now — life there's gray, the women are gray-haired. 'A devil,' people say, 'a clown.' Look — he's playing with cabbage stalks, tossing them in the air. But what kind of clown is he when he's a born prince, the light created. You can't fight him with cabbage stalks, you'll be needing the angelic hosts . . ."

A fat officer squeezes into the compartment with us: a round face, mustache, about fifty years old, a bit vulgar, foppish.

"I have a son in the 56th Regiment! I'm terribly worried. All of a sudden I think — what the devil if . . ." (For some reason I calm down immediately.) "And he's no fool either; why should he want to go into the thick of it?" (My calm passes instantaneously.) "He's an engineer, and bridges, well, it doesn't much matter who you build them for — a tsar, or a republic — as long as they hold up!"

I can't hold back: "My husband's in the 56th."

"Hu-usband!? You're married? Well, I'll be. I'd never have thought! And here I thought, Miss, you were finishing high school. In the 56th regiment is he? You must be worried sick."

"I don't know how I'll make it."

"You'll make it! And you'll see each other. Mercy me, with such a wife — how could he go into the shooting! Your husband wouldn't do himself in. He's very young then too?"

"Twenty-three."

"There now, you see! And you're still worried! Well, I can tell you, if I were 23 and had such a wife I wouldn't . . . But then again, here I am 53 and don't have anywhere near such a wife and I still . . ." (That's the whole point! I think to myself. But just the same, for some reason, clearly recognizing the ridiculousness of it all, I calm down.)

《 》

The workman and I arrange to ride from the station together. And although it's not at all on the way for either of us — he's going to Taganka and I'm going to Povarskaya — I continue to plan it out: a deferral of the next half hour. (In half an hour we'll be in Moscow.) The workman is a bulwark, and for some reason I fantasize that he *knows everything;* even more, that he is himself of the princely host (not without reason Pugachev!) and that precisely *because he is the enemy* he will save me (S.). Has already saved me. And that he sat down in this compartment deliberately — to protect and reassure — and that Lozovaya is beside the point, he could simply have appeared in the window — amid the steppes, in stride with the train. And that in the station in Moscow he'll turn to ashes.

《 》

Ten minutes until Moscow. It's already beginning to grow light. — Or is it just the sky? My eyes used to the darkness? I'm afraid of the road, of the hour in the cab, of the approaching house (of death — for if he's been killed, I'll die). I'm afraid to hear.

Moscow. Blackness. You can enter the city with a pass. I have one, not the right one at all, but it doesn't matter. (It's for the return trip to Theodosia: I'm the wife of an ensign.) I call a cabby: the workman has of course vanished. I ride. The cabby talks, I drift, the pavement bumps along. People with lanterns approach three times. "Pass!" I proffer my pass. They give it back without looking. The first bell. It's about 5:30. It's gotten lighter. (Or does it only seem so?) Empty streets — emptied of habitants. I don't recognize the route, I don't know it (we're taking a detour) — the feeling is that time is to the left, the way a thought sometimes is in the brain. We're headed somewhere *through* someplace, and for some reason there's a smell of hay. (Maybe, I think, this is Haymarket Square and that's why there's — hay?) There's a slight rumbling from the outposts: someone will not surrender.

Not a thought — about the children. If S. is no longer, then neither am I, and neither are they. Alya won't live without me, she won't want to, won't be able to. As I won't without S.

(( ))

The Church of Boris and Gleb. Ours, the one in Povarskaya.* We turn into a side street, ours — Boris and Gleb Lane. The white house of the church secondary school — I always called it a "Volière": a connecting gallery and children's voices. And on the left, the old-fashioned green house standing at attention (a town governor once lived there and policemen stood in front.) Yet another house. And ours.

The steps opposite two trees. I get out. I take my things out. Detaching themselves from the gates, two men in semi-military uniform approach. "We're the house security guard. What can we do for you?"

"I'm so and so and I live here."

"We don't have orders to let anyone in at night."

"Then please call the maid from apt. 3." (Thought: now, now, now they'll say it. They live here and they know everything.)

"We're not your servants."

"I'll pay."

They go. I wait. I'm not alive. I am the legs on which I stand, the hands with which I hold the suitcases (I didn't set them down, it turns out). And I can't hear my heart. If not for the cabby's call, I wouldn't have realized I'd been waiting a long time — a monstrously long time.

"Well then Miss, what'll it be, will you let me go or not? I still have to go to Pokrovskaya St."

"I'll pay you extra."

The quiet terror that he'll up and leave: my last bit of life is with him, the last bit of my life *until* . . . However, setting down my things, I open my purse: three, ten, twelve, seventeen rubles . . . I need fifty. Where will I get them if . . . Footsteps. The sound of one door and then another. The entry door opens now. A woman in a scarf, a stranger.

Not giving her a chance to speak, I ask:

"Are you the new maid?"

"Yes."

"Has the master been killed?"

"He's alive."

"Wounded?"

*There's another one on Arbat Square. (M.Ts.)

"No."

"But how? Where has he been all this time?"

"In Alexandrovsky with the Cadets. What a terrible fright we've had. Praise God, the Lord had mercy. Only they've got awfully thin. Right now they're on N-sky St. with friends. The little ones are there and the Master's sisters . . . *All* healthy, well and safe, just waiting for you."

"Would you have 33 rubles to pay the cabby?"

"Goodness gracious, of course—we'll just bring in your things." We bring in my things, let the cabby go, and Dunya offers to accompany me. I grab one of two loaves of Crimean bread to take with me. We go. Ravaged Povarskaya St. Cobblestones. Potholes. The sky grows a bit lighter. Bells.

We turn into a side street. A seven-story house. I ring. Two people in fur coats and hats. In the striking of a match—the gleam of a pince-nez. The match right in my face.

"What is it?"

"I've just arrived from the Crimea and I want to see my family."

"But this is unheard of—bursting into a house at 6 in the morning!"

"I want to see my family."

"You'll get there all in good time. Come back around 9 o'clock and then we'll see."

At this point the maid steps in.

"What's wrong with you gentlemen, they have little children, heaven knows how long it's been since they've seen each other. I've known them a long time, I'll vouch for her—she's a trustworthy soul, has her own house on Polyanka."

"Just the same, we can't let you in."

At this point, unable to restrain myself: "And who are *you?*"

"We're the house security guard."

"I'm so and so, the wife of my husband and the mother of my children. Let me in, I'll go in anyway."

And, half admitted, half pushing my way through—I fly up six flights—to the seventh.

◖◗

(And so it has remained with me, my first vision of the bourgeoisie in the Revolution: ears hiding in fur hats, souls hiding in fur coats, heads

hiding in necks, eyes hiding in glass. A blinding — in the light of a striking match — vision of mercenary *hides*.)

(( ))

From below, the voice of the maid: God bless! I knock. They open.
"Seriozha's sleeping? Where's his room?" And, a second later, from the
threshold "Seriozha! It's me! I just arrived. The people downstairs are
vile. But the Cadets won all the same! Are you here or not?" It's dark in
the room. Having reassured myself:
    "I traveled three days. I brought you some bread. I'm sorry it's stale.
The sailors are vile! I met Pugachev. Seriozhenka, you're alive and . . ."

(( ))

The evening of the same day we leave for the Crimea: S., his friend
G-tsev, and I.

(( ))

A LITTLE PIECE OF THE CRIMEA

Arrival in Koktebel in a mad snow storm. The gray-haired sea. The
enormous, almost physically burning joy of Max V. at the sight of Seriozha alive. Enormous loaves of white bread.

(( ))

The apparition of Max V. on the steps of the tower, with a volume by
Taine on his knees, frying onions. And while the onions are frying, reading aloud to S. and me, the destinies of Russia tomorrow and beyond.
    "And now, Seriozha, there will be such and such . . . Remember."
    And softly, carefully, almost rejoicing, he shows us picture after pic-
ture. Like a kind magician revealing his secrets to children, he relates the
course of the entire Russian Revolution five years in advance: the terror,
the Civil War, the executions, the military outposts, the Vendée, the
atrocities, the loss of godliness, the unloosed spirits of the elements,
blood, blood, blood . . .

《 》

With G-tsev to get bread.

A cafe in the Otuzy. Bolshevik appeals on the walls. Long-bearded Tatars at the tables. How slowly they drink, how sparingly they speak, how imposingly they move. Time has stopped for them. The 17th century — the 20th century. Even the cups are the same, dark blue, with cabalistic signs, no handles. Bolshevism? Marxism?

Scream your lungs out, posters! What do we have to do with your machines, your Lenins, Trotskys, your new-born proletariats, your decaying bourgeoisie . . . We have Ramadan, Mullahs, grapes, a dim memory of a great queen . . . This is the boiling sediment at the bottom of these gilded cups. We — are outside, we — are above, we — are a long time ago. It's for you — to be, we — have passed. We — are once and forever. We — are not.

《 》

Moonlit twilight. A mosque. The herds of goats return. A girl in a raspberry skirt down to the floor. Tobacco pouches. An old woman, gnawed like a bone.

The sculpturesqueness of ancient races.

《 》

In the train compartment (the return trip to Moscow, Nov. 25.)
"Breshko-Breshkovskaya's a bastard too! She said 'you have to fight!'"

《 》

"To destroy more of the poor classes and live blissfully again themselves!"

《 》

"Poor Mother Moscow, clothing the entire front! We can't complain about Moscow! The papers cause all the trouble. The Bolsheviks are right when they say they don't want to spill blood, they're keeping an eye on things."

(( ))

In the compartment air — so thick you could cut it with a knife — three words resound: bourgeois, Junkers, bloodsuckers.

(( ))

"So their business will be better!"

(( ))

"Our revolution's young, but in France theirs is old, stale."

(( ))

"A peasant, a prince, what's the difference — their hides are all the same!" (I, thinking to myself: but some are only out to save their own hide — that's the whole point).

(( ))

"The officer, comrades, is the number one bastard. In my opinion, he's of the very lowest education."

(( ))

Across from me, on the bench, sleeps a downcast, emaciated, prudent Vikzhel.
"God, comrades, was the first revolutionary!"

(( ))

"You're from Moscow, right? We don't have any of those types in the south."
(An ensign from Kerch)

(( ))

An argument about tobacco.
"A lady, and she smokes! Everybody's equal, sure enough, only it don't do for a lady to smoke. Her voice gets rough from the tobacco, and her mouth smells like a man's. A lady should suck on candies, spray herself with perfumes so she'll have a sweet fragrance. Or else a young

gent'll pay his compliments, and there you are breathing the same man's smell — ugh!

"If there's anything the masculine sex can't stand to abide, it's a man's smell. What do you say Miss?"

I: "Of course you're right, a bad habit!"

Another soldier: "But I think, er, that is, comrades. the female sex ain't got nothing to do with it. I mean, the smoke goes in your throat — and everybody's throat's the same. Tobacco — bread, what's the difference? So what if young gentlemen won't love them, maybe it's better — lots of brothers run around wagging their tails. LOO-ove! Dogs — not love! And whoever falls in love — it's with the soul, and he'll take her no matter what the smell, he'll even roll the cigarettes himself. I'm right, ain't I? What do you think Miss?"

I: "Right. My husband always rolls my cigarettes. And he doesn't smoke himself."

(I'm lying.)

My defender — to someone else: "So she ain't a Miss after all. Hey brother, you blundered! And your husband, he'd be a student or something?"

I, remembering caution: "No, well, just my husband . . ."

The other one, explaining the situation: "That means they live off their capital."

My defender: "You'll be going to him then?"

I: "No, I'm going for the children, he stayed in the Crimea."

"What — you have your own dacha in the Crimea?"

I, calmly: "Yes, and a house in Moscow." (I made up the dacha.)

— Silence —

My defender: "You sure are brave, little Missus. Come, you don't really want to admit to such things now do you? These days a body's so afraid, he's happy to bury his house, his money, even himself in the ground with his own two hands!"

I: "Why bury oneself? There'll come a time when others will bury us. And anyway, this isn't the first time it's happened: self-buriers. They used to bury themselves alive in the ground — to save their souls. And now it's to save their bodies."

They all laugh, and I laugh too.

My defender: "And how come your husband ain't with the simple people?"

I: "No, he's with *all the people.*"

"I don't quite get you."

I: "As Christ commanded: neither poor, he said, nor rich: but all men and Christ in every one."

My defender, joyfully: "That's it, thou art not guilty of thy princeliness, and thou art not guilty of thy poverty . . ." (a bit suspiciously) "And you Ma'am . . . you wouldn't be a Bolshevik?"

Someone else: "What kind of Bolshevik when they have their own house?"

The first one: "It don't mean nothing, lots of them are in the educated class — gentry too, merchants. More and more it's the gentry that go over to the Bolsheviks . . ." (Glancing, unsure.) "And she has short hair."

I: "That's the fashion nowadays."*

A sailor unexpectedly breaks, rather, bursts into the discussion.

"Comrades, you ain't thinking this thing out straight, you ain't got no consciousness. It's these booklearned ones, this gentry, these damned Junkers that have filled Moscow with blood. Bloodsuckers! Bastards!" (To me): "And you, comrade, some advice: less talk about Christs and dachas in the Crimea. Those times are over."

My defender, scared. "Oh — she's just young. What kind of a dacha could they have — a little shack on three legs, like I've got in the country . . ." (Appeasingly): "Look how cheap her boots are . . ."

(( ))

About this sailor. Constant obscenities. The others (he's a Bolshevik!) are silent.

Finally, I ask him, sweetly, "Why do you swear so? Do you really enjoy it?"

---

*The fashion came later. For Russia it came along with typhus, i.e., in '19 or '20; for the West I don't know from or with what, in '23 or '24. (M.Ts.)

The sailor: "I'm not swearing, comrade — it's just a saying of mine."
The soldiers roar with laughter.
I, pensively: "A bad saying."

( )

This very same sailor, by the open window in Oriol, in the tenderest voice: "What a lovely breeze!"

( )

Alya (4 years old)
"Marina, you know Pushkin didn't say it right! He said:

Guns fire from the wharf
Calling the ships to join them

But it should be:

Guns *fire from the house.*"

(After the uprising)

Alya's prayer during and since the uprising:
"Save us Lord and grant us grace: Marina, Seriozha, Irina, Liuba, Asya, Andriusha, the officers and not-officers, the Russians and not-Russians, the French and not-French, the wounded and not-wounded, the healthy and not-healthy — all friends and strangers."

Moscow, October–November 1917

Free Passage

Prechistenka St., the Dame Chertova Institute, now the Department of Visual Arts.

I swear on the river Styx that had I lived a hundred and fifty years ago, I would definitely have been made a Dame of the Saint Catherine Order! (I'm here to get a pass to Tambov guberniya "to study hand-made embroidery," that is, to get wheat. Free passage — transport — of 1½ poods.)

《 》

The road to Usman Station, Tambov guberniya.

Boarding in Moscow. At the last minute — as though hell had opened wide: a clanking and whistling. I: "What's that?" A man, gruffly: "Quiet! Quiet! It's plain you haven't traveled!" A woman: "Lord, have mercy on us!" Terror, as if faced with oprichniks, the whole car — quiet as the grave. And, indeed, despite our tickets and permissions, we are all thrown out a minute later. It turned out that Red Army soldiers needed it.

At the last second, N., his friend, his mother-in-law and I end up back on the train nonetheless, thanks to my pass.

《 》

I begin to realize, tragically, that we are traveling to a requisition center . . . almost in the role of requisitioners. The mother-in-law has a son — a Red Army soldier in the requisition detachment. They promise all kinds of good fortune (up to and including pork lard). They threaten all kinds of misfortune (up to and including murder). The peasants are hostile and they sometimes set the trains on fire. The mother-in-law comforts us:

"I've already been there three times, and God was merciful. Poods of white flour. The peasants are furious — well, of course. Everyone takes care of his own. After all, they're robbing them blind. I already told my

Kolka, I said to him: You should fear God! You're not from a noble family, but still, you had enough, you had respect. How can you just leave someone with nothing? Well, *you've* seized this grand power—there's no denying it—so use it, rule to your heart's content! You were born under a lucky star. Because you see, Miss, each of us has our own fate. Oh, so you're not a Miss after all? Well, there go my plans! I'm also in the matchmaking business. What a groom I could have found you! Where's your husband? No news? And two children? That's bad, bad!

"So I tell my son: Take it at half-price, that way you won't be upset and he won't be resentful. Otherwise, what is this? It's just highway robbery. Ree-ally! You follow me, Miss? (why do I keep saying 'Miss'— you're in worse shape than a widow! Neither husband's wife, nor friend's life . . .) so, you follow me, ma'am: he's a young fellow, in his prime, when else can you have your fun, if not when you're young? He can't get it through his head that if you pick the bush clean, your plate will be lean. You have to use common sense when you milk a cow— squeeze, but don't squeeze dry. That's right.

"And the way they treat me at the center—I swear you'd think I was some Dowager Empress! One bows, the other scrapes. My Kolka gets on well with the head of the detachment—they're classmates, both from the same high school, they finished fourth year, they did. Then Kolka went to work in an office, and the other one just went to town. Pals, they are. And then this change up and happened, he came up from the bottom, the bubble went straight to the top. And he got my Kolka to work with him. Sugar! Lard! Eggs! They're all but swimming in milk! It's my fourth trip."

(())

From train conversations:

"And it will go on like this, until it stops: from legions—one Husband, from the darkness—one Wife."

(())

"In Moscow, comrades, there's a church—the Angel of the Great Soviet."

(( ))

A nighttime argument about God. The soldiers' hatred of icons and love of God. "Why kiss a piece of wood? If you want to pray, pray all by yourself!"

A soldier — to an officer (a former lycée type, parted hair, can't pronounce his r's.)

"And you, comrade, what faith do you adhere to?"

From the darkness, the answer: "I am the spiritualist of the socialist party."

(( ))

The Usman Station. Going on twelve midnight.

Arrival. A tea house. Groaning tables. Revolvers, machine-gun cartridge belts, leather gear everywhere. They're cheerful and offer us something to eat. We, the guests of honor, are all bootless — on our way from the station we almost drowned. For the mother-in-law, however, they come up with a pair of the owner's ankle boots.

The proprietresses: two spiteful, terrified old ladies. Servility and hatred. One of them says to me: "What would you be then — their acquaintance?" (Winking at the mother-in-law's son.) The son: a Chichikovian face, cornflower blue, piggish eye slits. You feel that the skin beneath his hair is bright pink. A mix of Dutch cheese and ham. He's insolently formal with his mother: he says "Mamasha," uses the polite "You" form and then says: "Well and to blankety-blank with you."

I go unnoticed, thank God. The mother-in-law, when making introductions, lets slip a vague: "in the old days I had an acquaintance with their relatives . . ." (It turns out that about fifteen years ago she sewed for my uncle's wife. "I had my own shop . . . I kept four seamstresses . . . All nice and proper. And then — my husband did me in: he died!"). In short, I don't exist — I'm *with* . . .

Having eaten and drunk their fill, our two companions go off with the others, to sleep in the train car. The mother-in-law and I (she's the mother-in-law of my friend N., the one who talked me into this trip) settle down on the floor: she sleeps on the proprietresses' pillows and feather bed; I sleep right on the floor.

(())

I wake up from a hard blow. The matchmaker's voice: "What is it?" A second boot. I jump up. Pitch dark. The ever louder stomp of feet, laughter, oaths. A resonant voice from the darkness: "Don't worry, Mamasha, it's just the requisition detachment come to search the premises!"

The strike of matches.

(())

Shouts, cries, the clinking of gold, the bareheaded old ladies, slashed feather beds, bayonets . . . They ransack everything.

"Take a good look behind the icons. Behind the saints. The gods like gold too!"

"But we . . . we don't have anything . . . Son! Father! Be a father!"

"Shut up, you old bitch!"

The flame of the candle stub dances. On the wall — the huge shadows of Red Army soldiers.

(())

(It turns out that the proprietresses of the teahouse had long been on the list. The son was just waiting for his mother to arrive: this was something like fleet maneuvers or a military parade in honor of the Dowager Empress.)

(())

The search lasts until dawn: every time I wake up it's the same scene. In the morning, sitting down to a cup of tea, I have the sobering thought: "they could poison us. Quite simply. Add something to the tea, and the deed's done. What do they have to lose? The money's gone — the game's up. And if they get the firing squad — well, we all have to die anyway!"

And, having firmly convinced myself, I drink.

(())

That very morning we move on. I wasn't the only one who had this thought.

⟨ ⟩

The oprichniks: a Jew with a gold ingot hanging from his neck, a Jew — who's a family man ("if God exists, he doesn't bother me — if not, it also doesn't bother me"), a "Georgian" from Triumphal Square, in a red Circassian hat, who would slit his mother's throat for ten kopecks.

⟨ ⟩

My two companions left to go to the former estate of Prince Viazemsky: ponds, gardens . . . (A massacre notorious for its brutality.)

They left and didn't take me with them. I remain alone with the mother-in-law and my own soul. Neither of them are any help. The former is cooling toward me, the latter (in me) is already at boiling point.

⟨ ⟩

With the teapot to the station for boiling water. A twelve-year-old "aide-de-camp" of one of the requisition officers. A round face, impertinent blue eyes against white sheep's curls — a smartly cocked cap. A mix of Cupid and a lout.

⟨ ⟩

The mistress (the wife of the oprichnik with the ingot) is a tiny (midget!) Jewess, the swarthiest of creatures, who "just adores" gold things and silk cloth.

"Are those platinum rings you have on?"

"No, silver."

"So why do you wear them?"

"I like them."

"Don't you have any gold ones?"

"Yes, I do, but I don't really like gold: it's crass, obvious . . ."

"Oh, what do you mean! Gold is the most precious metal. Yossi told me that all wars are fought over gold."

(I think to myself, "as is every revolution!")

"And, may I ask, do you have your gold things with you? Maybe you'd part with something? Oh, don't you worry, I won't tell Yossi, it'll just be between us women! Our own little secret!" (She giggles wantonly.) "We could set up a kind of *Austausch*." (Lowering her voice): "I

mean, I've got good stores set by . . . and I don't always tell Yossi everything! . . . If you need lard, for instance — I could get you lard, if you
need pure white flour — I can get pure white flour."

I, timidly: "But I don't have anything with me. Two empty baskets
for wheat . . . And ten lengths of rose-colored chintz . . ."

She, almost cheeky: "And where did you leave your gold things?
How can you leave gold behind and just take off?"

I, distinctly: "I not only left my gold, but . . . my *children!*"

She, amused: "Ach, ach, ach! You're so funny! Are children so valuable? Everyone leaves their children nowadays, they set them up somewhere. What children, when there's nothing to eat?" (Sententiously):
"There are shelters for children. Children are the property of our socialist Commune . . ."

(I think to myself: "just like our gold rings . . .")

( )

Having convinced herself of my gold insolvency, she tells her story
breathlessly. Before — she was the owner of a knitting atelier in "Petrograd."

"Oh, what an apartment we had. A little gem, not an apartment!
Three rooms and a kitchen, and a storage room for the servant. I never
allowed the maid to sleep in the kitchen — it's not hygienic, hair can fall
in the pots. One room was the bedroom, another was the dining room,
and the third, sky blue — was the parlor. I had very important cus-
tomers, you know, I dressed the best women in Petrograd in my jackets . . . Oh, we made a very good living, we had guests every Sunday:
and there was wine, and the best produce, and flowers . . . Yossi had a
whole smoking set: a little filigreed table from the Caucasus, with all
kinds of pipes and things, and ashtrays, and match boxes . . . We
bought it second-hand from a factory owner . . . We played cards and, I
assure you, the sums were no joking matter . . .

"But everything had to be left behind: we sold off all the furniture,
hid a few things . . . Of course, Yossi's right, the people can't languish in
the fetters of the bourgeoisie any longer, but still, with an apartment like
that . . ."

《 》

"But what are you doing here, when it's raining, when all your people are out on requisition? You're reading?"

"Yes . . ."

"What are you reading?"

"Marx's *Capital,* my husband won't let me have any novels."

《 》

Usman Station, Tambov Gub., where I've never been and never will be. Thirty versts on foot over cut fields, in order to barter chintz (rose-colored) for grain.

《 》

Peasant women.

Sixty huts — one response: "No, no, there's nothing at all, we don't sell, we don't barter. Whatever there was — the comrades took. Lord knows how we'll stay alive ourselves."

"But I'm not taking anything for free and I'm not paying with Soviet money. I have matches, soap, chintz . . ."

Chintz! The magic word! The first (after the serpent!) passion of our foremother Eve. The blazing of eyes, clearing of foreheads, stretching of hands. Even the great-grandmothers won't leave me alone, toothless lips spray: "A little bit of chintz would do nicely! For a shroud!"

And so I find myself in a suffocating ring of grandmothers, great-grandmothers, girls, young ladies, girlfriends, granddaughters. On my knees before the basket — I rummage. The basket is tiny — I'm exposed.

"Is the soap perfumed? Do you have any plain soap? How much are the matches? Does the chintz wear good? Manka, Manka, you could make a blouse! How many lengths did you say? Te-en! There's not even eight here!"

Fondling, smelling, pulling, smoothing, watch it — or they'll test it with their teeth.

And suddenly, one of them bursts out: "Look at the color! The color! Just like Katka got for a skirt last week. Another one of them from Moscow was selling. Damask — like silk! It gathers so even . . . Mama, Ma-manka, should we take it? Merchant lady, how much do you want for a length?"

"I'm not selling for money."

"You're not se-elling? How's that, you're not selling?"

"That's the way it is. You all know — money isn't worth anything."

"What do we know? We live in the dark. Another girl who came said that money's good in Moscow."

"Go there and see for yourself."

(Silence. Side glances at the chintz. Sighs.)

"What would you be needing then?"

"Wheat, lard."

"La-aaard? No, we don't have any lard. What lard! We eat everything dry ourselves. How about some honey?"

(A lightning vision of myself, covered with dripping honey, and from this vision, almost rage!)

"No, I want lard — or wheat."

"And how much, if you want wheat, will you take for the chintz then?" (By the way, it isn't chintz at all, but purebred, rare, rationed, rose-colored damask.)

I, immediately growing timid: a half pood (they taught me to say three!).

"A haaa-lf pood? There's no such price. What is this chintz you've got, silk or something? The color's beautiful, that's all. Look at it, it rubs off, it'll all wash out."

"How much will *you* give for it?"

"Your goods — your price."

"I already said: half a pood."

Ebb-tide. Whispers . . .

I look around the cottage: everything's brown, as if made of bronze: the ceilings, floors, benches, cauldrons, tables. Nothing superfluous, everything eternal. The benches seem to have grown into the walls, rather — to have grown out of them. And the faces match: brown! And the amber necklaces! And the necks themselves! And on all this brown-ness — the last blue tint of a late, woman's summer. (A cruel expression!)

(()

The whispers go on and on, my patience stretches — and bursts. I get up — and, dryly:

"Well then, are you taking it or not?"

"Now, if it was for money — it might be possible. But judge for yourself, what do we have?"

I scrape my things together (three pieces of soap, a packet of matches, ten lengths of sateen), and fasten the basket with a stick.

At the door: "So long!"

Twenty steps. Bare feet in pursuit.

"Merchant, ma'am, hey there?"

Not stopping: "Well?"

"Do you want seven pounds?"

"No."

And moving on, passing by five cottages in fury, I enter the sixth.

(()

Sometimes it's different: we've agreed, the grain is poured out, laid out and — at the last second: "The Lord only knows where you're from. We'll just have more troubles from you! And her hair's short . . . Be on your way and good health to you . . . We don't need none of your chintz . . ."

(()

And sometimes it goes this way:

"You see, our life's a mystery to you city folk. You think we get everything for free? That this wheat here falls from the sky like rain? Live in the village a little, work at our work, then you'll find out. You Moscow folk are lucky, the bosses give you everything. The chintz here, and the tea, were they also free?"

" . . . Give us a box of matches, so we have something to remember you by."

(()

And I give them, of course. Out of arrogance, out of fastidiousness, as Christ never commanded to give: I give — along the straight road to hell!

(( ))

For the cry: "the chickens aren't even laying," I'm ready to strangle not only all their chickens, but them as well — all of them! — ten generations back.

(I don't hear any other reply.)

(( ))

The market. Skirts — piglets — pumpkins — roosters. The reconciling and enchanting beauty of women's faces. All are dark-eyed and all are wearing necklaces.

I buy three toy wood women, attach myself to a real-live woman, barter with her for her necklace of dark amber wheels, and leave the bazaar with her — that is, with nothing. On the way I find out that she "went out with a soldier on Our Lady of Kazan day" — and now . . . She's expecting, of course. Like all of Russia, for that matter.

Back at home. The owner's ire at my new amber. My loneliness. To the station for boiling water, the girls: "Oh, Miss has gone and put on amber! Shame, shame!"

(( ))

Washing the boor's wife's floors.

"Scrub that puddle some more! Hang up the hat! You're not doing it right! You have to follow the grain of the boards! What, do they do it differently in Moscow? You know, I simply can't wash floors — my lower back hurts, you see! You've probably been doing it since childhood, isn't that right?"

I silently swallow tears.

(( ))

In the evening they pull the chair out from under me, I eat *my* two eggs without bread (at the requis. station, in Tambov gub.!)

I write by moonlight (black shadows from the pencil and my hands).

There's a *huge* ring around the moon. A steam-engine pants. Branches. Wind.

(( ))

Gentlemen! All my friends in Moscow and everywhere! You think about your own lives too much! You don't have any time to think about mine — but you should.

(( ))

The mother-in-law: a former seamstress, a dauntless, garrulous match-maker from Zamoskvoreche ("my husband did me in — he died!"). The boor, a Communist with a gold ingot hung around his neck; a petit-bourgeois Jewess, the former owner of a knitting shop; a gang of thieves in Circassian hats; suspicious, gloomy muzhiks, *someone else's* bread (even the Communist conscience can't bring itself to sell anything for money *here*).

I'm a pariah all round: to the boor's wife I'm "poor" (cheap stock-ings, no diamonds), to the boor "a bourgeoise," to the mother-in-law — a "former person," to the Red soldiers — a proud, short-haired young lady. Closest to my heart (at a distance of 1000 versts!) are the peasant women, with whom I share an identical weakness for amber and bright-colored skirts — and an identical kindness: like a cradle.

(( ))

"Lord Almighty! Kill to death him who has sugar and lard!"
(A local saying).

(( ))

"Nothing was more docile than our city!"
(A muzhik's story on the road to Usman. Couldn't it be said of all Russia?)

(( ))

Today the oprichniks chopped up the telegraph pole for firewood.

(( ))

The mistress bends over for something. A pile of gold falls out of her bosom, the gold coins roll across the room with a ring.

Those present look over — and then quickly avert their eyes.

( )

First thing in the morning — off for a bit of piracy. "You, wife, sit at home, make kasha, and I'll bring back some butter for it! . . ." Just like a fairy tale. They return around four o'clock. Our Kaplans run a kind of cafeteria. (The mistress: "It's convenient for them, and useful for Yossi and me." The "goods" are free — the meals are paid). There doesn't seem to be any wine. Lard, gold, cloth, cloth, lard, gold. They come in tired: red, pale, sweaty, irritated. The mistress and I rush to set the table. Soup with rooster, kasha, crepes, fried eggs. They eat silently at first. Under the caress of lard and butter foreheads smooth out, eyes grow moist. After piracy — the divvy: of impressions. (The material divvy takes place on the spot.) Merchants, priests, village kulaks . . . This one has so much cloth . . . That one has a barrel of cooking oil . . . This one has thousands in tsarist money . . . And another time — there's just a rooster . . .

Ruzman (the family man) is good-natured. On detecting some kind of forbidden (hidden) fruit, like a sack of flour, he is the first to sympathize:

"Ay, ay, ay! And such a big family! It's true, you can't feed your own seven children, wife, grandmother and grandfather on pure air!"

He's something of a connoisseur as well: thus, anything cunningly concealed and long-resistant arouses admiration in him.

"That Mikishkin is such a fox, such a fox! He should be in charge of liquidating the banks! And just where, do you think, did he embalm his money?!"

I get into the spirit of it easily (the eighth day!), I'm used to it and already share (lyrically!) their triumphs and woes. The mistress — worried by her husband's long absence — now says to me: "Our Yossi hasn't gone and betrayed us has he?"

I'm in the very middle of a fairy tale, *mitten drinnen*. The brigand, the brigand's wife, and I, the brigand's wife's maid. Of course, I might grab an axe . . . But most likely, successfully strewing my 18 pounds of wheat

among the 80 patrol detachments, I'll burst merrily into my Boris and
Gleb St. kitchen and right away — without stopping to catch my breath
— will exhale in verse!

( )

They're asking us along on a requisition. (As dukes, in the olden
days, invited you on a hunt!).

"Put your matches down! . . . (How many boxes do you have left?
What! You gave a whole three boxes away for nothing? Ay, ay, ay, how
impractical you are!) Come with us, you'll bring back a whole trainload
of flour without any matches. You won't have to do anything with your
own hands — I give you my word of honor as a communist: you won't
even have to lift your little finger!"

And the mistress, jealously (not of me, of course, but of the imagined
"goods"). "Ach, Yossi, it's not possible! Who will wash the dishes for me
tomorrow when I go to the market for yeast!"

(The only "produce" purchased in this family.)

( )

How many rewashed dishes and the already twice-washed floor! The
feeling that I've been definitely relegated to slavery. The good-for-noth-
ing mother-in-law, in line with the mistress, mistreats me. Neither hide
nor hair has been heard of my treacherous Theseuses for the second
week now (some Naxos I found!).

So far I have: 18 lbs. of wheat, 10 lbs. of flour, 3 lbs. of lard, some amber and three dolls for Alya. They're threatening us with the patrol detachments.

( )

I explode from laughter and anger. The evening passed as usual. People came, went, joked, smoked, planned the next day's raids, tallied the
current ones. In short: peace. And suddenly: thunder. God! Who began
it — I don't remember. I only remember my own voice:

"Gentlemen, if he doesn't exist — then why do you hate him so
much?"

"Who said we hate the Lord God?"

"Or else you love him too much: you talk about him incessantly."

"We talk about him because a lot of people still believe in that nonsense."

"And I'm number one! Born a fool and I expect I'll die a fool."

(The mother-in-law explodes.)

Levit, condescendingly: "You, Madame, are a completely understandable phenomenon, all our mamashas and papashas were believers" (he shrugs his shoulders in my direction) . . . "but that the comrade here at such a young age and still having the opportunity to take advantage of all the cultural blessings of the capital . . ."

The mother-in-law: "So what if she's from the capital? You think everyone in Moscow is a heathen, do you? In Moscow alone we have four score forty churches, and monasteries, and . . ."

Levit: "The remnants of the bourgeois system. We'll melt your church bells down into monuments."

I: "To Marx."

A sharp glance: "Precisely."

I: "And to the murdered Uritsky. By the way, I knew his murderer."

(A twitch. I sustain the pause).

" . . . Of course—we played in the sand box together: Kanegisser, Leonid."

"I congratulate you, comrade, on such playmates!"

I, finishing: "A Jew."

Levit, boiling: "Well, that doesn't have anything to do with it!"

The mother-in-law, not understanding: "Who did the kikes kill?"

I: "Uritsky, the head of the Petersburg Cheka."

The mother-in-law: "How do you like that! What, was he a kike too?"

I: "A Jew. From a good family."

The mother-in-law: "Well, so they squabbled among themselves. That's rare with kikes, it is, with them it's usually the opposite, they cover for each other—blood is thicker than water, I tell you!"

Levit, to me: "Well, and what comes next, comrade?"

I: "Then there was the attempt on Lenin. Also Jewish (addressing the host, politely)—the same last name as you: Kaplan."

Levit, answering for Kaplan: "And just what are you trying to prove?"

I: "That Jews, like Russians, come in all kinds."

Levit, jumping up: "I don't understand, comrade: either there's something wrong with my ears, or there's something wrong with your tongue. You are now at the requisition base, Usman Station, at the home of an active member of the RCP, Comrade Kaplan."

I: "Under a portrait of Marx . . ."

Levit: "And nevertheless, you . . ."

I: "And nevertheless, I. Why not exchange views?"

One of the soldiers: "That's right, what the comrade is saying. What kind of free speech is it if you can't even hiccup the way you want! And the comrade didn't say anything special anyway: only that a kike knocked off another kike, we know all that anyway."

Levit: "Comrade Kuznetsov, I ask you to take back your insult!"

Kuznetsov: "What insult?"

Levit: "You were so bold as to refer to an ideological victim — as a kike?!"

Kuznetsov: "Now comrade, calm down, I'm a member of the C-ist Party myself, and if I said kike — well that's just a habit of mine!"

The mother-in-law to Levit: "What're you so worked up about, deary? What's the big deal — "kike." All Moscow says kike — and none of your prohibition decrees will help! A kike's a kike, because they crucified Christ!"

"Chriii-ssst?!!!"

He lashed like a whip. As if he himself were lashing a whip. As if he had been lashed with a whip. He jumped up. The nostrils of his hook nose flared.

"So those are your convictions, are they, Madame? So that's the kind of goods you're collecting in the countryside? And that goes for you, too, comrade! Spreading propaganda, are we? Arranging a few pogroms? Shaking up Soviet power? I swear I'll have you! . . . In a hundredth of a second I'll have you . . ."

"You don't scare me! What do you think I got my son for? Himself, he's a genuine Bolshevik, a better one than you'll ever be! Huh! Flown off the handle hasn't he! A shame my Kolka isn't here, or else I'd teach you how to hiss like a snake at a respectable widow! Fifty years I've been on this earth . . . and such shameful behavior, I've never . . ."

The mistress: "Madame! Madame! Calm yourself! Comrade Levit was joking, the comrade always jokes that way! Now, judge for yourself . . ."

The matchmaker, waving her away: "I don't want to judge, and I don't want to joke. I'm sick of your new life! When we had Nikolasha — we always had our bread and kasha,* and now for the same kasha — God forgive me — we have to slog through mud for 30 versts like a mutt with his tongue hanging out."

One of the soldiers: "Nikolasha and kasha? Hey there, Mamasha! . . . And isn't it time for us to go home, guys? We have to go to Ipatovka at first light tomorrow."

《 》

N. and the son-in-law returned. They brought flour, and they're cheerful. My share is a half pood. Tomorrow we leave. We leave, if we can get on the train.

《 》

Stenka Razin. Two St. George Crosses. A round face, cunning, freckled: Esenin, but without the pettiness. He just returned, along with all the other fine fellows, from the requisition. I see him for the first time.

"Razin!" It wasn't I who said it: the heart rang out! (The heart! A bell! Only there aren't any bell ringers!)

I'll qualify that: *my* Razin (the one in the song) is tow-headed [*belokur*] with red highlights. (By the way, a stupid loss of the letter d: tow-headed [*belokudr*], white curls [*belye kudry*]: both wild and white. But what is *belokur*? White chickens? [*belye kury*]? A sort of tailless word!) Pugachev is blackness, Razin is whiteness. And the very word itself: Stepan! Hay, straw, the steppe. Could there possibly be swarthy Stepans? And Razin! Sunrise over the sound — strike, Razin! Where it's spacious, it's not black. Blackness — is thick.

He's Razin — *before* his beard, but already with a thousand Persian girls! And he immediately rushed at me, joyous:†

---

*"When the Bolsheviks came to power, no more bread and no more flour." A Moscow saying from 1918. (M.Ts.)

†The entire meeting, except for the first few words, was one on one. (M.Ts.)

"You're from Moscow, comrade? Of course, of course I know Moscow! I've seen Moscow from those very seven hills! When I was still just a tiny tyke I learned a poem about Moscow:

Glorious city, ancient city,
You contain within your bounds,
Markets, mansions, palaces,
Whole villages and towns . . .

"Moscow — she's the mother of all cities. It all started with Moscow — the kingdom and all."
I: "And it ended with Moscow."
He, understanding and laughing:
"You're right about that.

Moscow, Moscow, Moscow,
Town of golden-headed days
Now you're lost and gone astray.

"I celebrated Easter in Moscow once. When that Ivan the Great bell sounded — and in answer — each of them churches came back in its own voice — all pell-mell, then together, in front, in back — I couldn't tell whether it was the iron that was ringing, or something in me. I went crazy — I swear! I'll never forget that one."

(( ))

We're talking about churches, about monasteries.
"You're insulted, comrade, when people curse the priests, you praise the monastic life. I ain't saying nothing against it: if you can't get along with people — then go on off into the forest. You wouldn't save a soul in this world anyway, and you'd probably ruin four score forty in the bargain. But now, honestly, is that really why they become priests and monks? They do it for their belly, for the sweet life. Same as us going on requisition — I swear to God! And what does God have to do with it? God gets sick to his soul when he sees that kind of saintliness. He'd destroy His world if he could! No, don't go hiding behind God! God is light: your blackness goes right through him. He's none the blacker for you, nor you the whiter for him. And I ain't against God, comrade, but

against his servants: unfaithful hands! How many people have slipped through those hands and then He's lost 'em! Not everybody can reason things out. Take my father now, for example — as soon as this persecution started, he reckoned right away: they're laying blame on the healthy head instead of the sick one. The priests, rats' tails everyone of 'em, wrecked everything, and now they're taking God to the gallows. God isn't responsible for the priests' belly. And people themselves, father says, are to blame too: they didn't respect the priest and so he stopped respecting himself. But how can one respect him? I know their kind inside out, Miss. Who's the number one thief: the priest. Glutton? The priest. Sinner? The priest. When he gets drunk — but you're a lady, so it wouldn't be decent to spell it out."

"Well, what about monks, hermits?"

"No use talking about the monks, you know yourself. They talk about fasting, but their tongues lick meat and milk thoughts off their lips. Crack open his skull and you won't find nothing but smoked and marinated what-have-you, girls and cherry liqueurs. That's all there is to their faith! The monkish life! The saving of souls!"

"But in the Bible, do you remember? With one righteous man I can save Sodom? Or haven't you read it?"

"I ain't exactly read it myself, I have to admit. When I was a youngster I spent more time chasing pigeons, getting up to no good with the boys. But my father — he's a great churchman." (Becoming inspired): "Wherever you open that Bible there — he can rattle off a dozen pages in a row with his eyes shut . . .

"I wanted to say something else, comrade, about the monks. Nuns, for instance. Why does every nun make eyes at me?"

I think to myself: sweetheart, how could one *help* but. . . .

He, getting worked up: "Prances, dances, her eyes like wells. Where are you pulling me with those eyes, anyway? How could you be praying all the time after that? If you have mischievous blood — then don't go to the monastery, if your blood's prayerful — then keep your eyes down!"

I involuntarily lower my eyes: a moralizing Razin. (Out loud): "Tell me about your father instead."

"Fa-ather! My father's a great man! What do they write in those books? Marx, for instance, and the Gracchus brothers. Who ever saw them? I bet they're all foreigners: your tongue twists just saying the names, and there's no patrimony. Three thousand years ago — and behind seven seals and seven blue seas, across three score lands, in the fourth, it's not hard to pass yourself off for great! But maybe they're just made up? That guy (a wave toward the wall Marx) . . . shaggy old Long Beard over there — did he really exist?"

I, without blinking: "They invented him. The Bolsheviks up and invented him. On the road from Berlin — you know? They thought him up, put a jacket on him, a beard, fluffed up his mane, and pasted him on all the fences."

"You're a brave one, Miss."

"As are you."

(He laughs.)

" . . . But you wanted to tell me about your father?"

"My father. My father — was a neighborhood watchman of tsarist times." (I think: just as though he watched the tsarist time!) . . . "A great, man, I tell you. Wish I could follow him with a pen around the clock and write everything down. His words are like stone weights. He talks about tablets, great powers, dawns. Sends shivers down your spine, I swear! He blows the samovar coals up at night, puts on his horn-rimmed glasses, opens up his big book — and sets up a storm with those pages." (Lowering his voice) . . . "He knows *all* destinies. *When* things will happen. Who will receive what, what's been prepared for whom, he doesn't spare anyone. He foretold the Tsar's end. Even though he respected the Tsar like God. And now he says: 'You can skin me and eat me alive, but this regime won't last more than seven years. It's a snake, and it'll shed like a snake skin . . .' He's writing a book: *Russia's Tears*. He's filled up eight note books with oilcloth covers. Doesn't show them to anyone, not even to me . . . All I know is: *Tears*. He sits up every night till cock crow."

(( ))

Two St. George Crosses; he saved the standard.

"What did you feel when you saved the standard?"

"I didn't feel anything! If there's a standard — there's a regiment, no standard — no regiment!"

He bought a house in Klimachi at auction for 400 rubles. Robbed a bank in Odessa — "pockets full of gold!" Served in the Tsarevich's regiment.

"He got out of the train car: skinny, handsome, and he asked in such a pathetic little voice: 'And where may I walk now?' 'The automobile's waiting for you, Your Highness.' Lots of soldiers cried."

(())

I recite him my poems: "To the Tsarevich," "To the Tsar on Easter," "Purebred Steeds."

"Who made those up? Not one of the simple folk, that's for sure. What a rumble! Just like thunder rolling over! 'Slop-stall.' They'd really give it to him for that stall bit, wouldn't they? I reckon he wrote it in memory, didn't he? They killed his father, killed his mother, killed his brothers, killed his sister — and he up and started writing. You don't write like that from the good life! Miss, could you write me down that poem about the stall?"

"You'll get caught."

"Me?!!" His expression shifts from inspired to crafty. "Me?? — get caught? The trap hasn't been set yet that could catch me. Not set, not invented. I've got four gold watches, right here, Miss." (Hands on pockets!) "Check if you like! And they all run on different times: one on Moscow time, the next on Petersburg, the third on Ryazan, and this one here" (pounding his chest with his fist) "is on Razin time!"

"Shall I recite you a poem about Stenka Razin? The same person wrote it. Listen."

The winds left to sleep with the golden dawn,
The night approaches — like a mountain of stone.
And with his princess . . .

I speak like someone drowning — no, like a fish choking on its own sea. (A talking fish . . . Hmm . . . Well, it happens in fairy tales.)

After the mother-in-laws, matchmakers, wheat, rubbish pails, revolvers, Marxes — this ray (voice), hitting this blue (eyes!). For I read straight into his eyes: like gazing! Into the wild blue yon: gone!

Stenka Razin!

( )

Stenka Razin, I am no Persian princess, there is no double-edged cunning in me: neither of Persia nor of the unloving. But neither am I Russian, Razin, I'm *pre*-Russian, *pre*-Tatar, pretemporal Russ — and I reach out to you! Straw-headed Stepan, listen to me, steppes: there were covered wagons and there were nomad camps, there were camp fires and there were stars. Do you want a nomad tent — where through the hole you see the biggest star?

But . . .

"But you, there, Miss, write a bit larger: I don't read handwriting too good."

He watches the appearance of the letters with childlike delight (I print the letters, of course).

"Dee, em . . . And there's *yat* just like a church with a dome."

"Are you from a village yourself?"

"From the outskirts!"

( )

"And now, Miss, for your troubles, I'll tell you a story — about an underwater city. I was still little, about eight, when my father told it to me.

"It seems that somewhere in our Russian land there's a lake, and at the bottom of that lake — there's a city buried with churches, towers, markets, barns and all. (Sudden laugh). Only there's no fire towers: if you've gone and drowned you ain't gonna burn! And it seems this city drowned in a special circumstance. The Tatars came to our land, they began collecting tributes: crosses of pure gold, bells of pure silver, the fruit of honest flesh and blood. City after city, like ears of grain, bowed down to the Tatars: rattled their keys and fell on their knees. But there was one prince, you see, he wasn't one to bow. 'I won't give away my sanctuary — better my blood should flow, I won't give away my Pomoga even if they chop off my arms and legs.' He hears — the army isn't far off: there's a great stomping. He calls all the town's bell ringers, orders them to ring their bells with all their might one last time, to give the Tatars a fright and praise the Lord God's might. Well, they did their best, those bell ringers! It's a shame I wasn't there! . . . How they rang! How they thundered! The earth's whole breast was shuddering!

"And from that ringing flowed rivers of pure silver: the harder the bell ringers worked, the swifter the rivers flowed. But the earth wouldn't take the silver, wouldn't soak it up. You couldn't get through the town walking or riding, the one-story houses were already over their heads in water, only the prince's palace held on. And in answer to this ringing, another kind of chiming started up: the heathen hosts approached, their curved sabers clanked. The prince climbed up on the very top of the palace — the water was up to his chest — he stood bareheaded, the chiming flowed silver down his curls. He looked: the hoards were at the gate. And he shouted out in a wild voice:

'Hey you, ringer-singers!'

"Only what it was he wanted to say — no one heard! And no one ever saw that town again!

"The Tatars broke down the gates — everything was smooth as a mirror. Just a few little streams snuffling.

"That's how the town drowned in its own ringing."

( )

Stenka Razin, I'm no Persian princess, but I'll give you a ring — silver — as a keepsake.

Look: a two-headed eagle, wings spread, that is: a tsarist ten-kopeck piece in a silver frame. Will it fit your hand? It will. My hand isn't lady-like. But you, Stenka, don't understand hands: the form, the nails, the "breed." You understand the palm (warmth) and the fingers (grasp). You'll understand a handshake.

Take the ring without thinking: there were ten — nine left! And in return, what? Never anything in return.

From my ring finger — to your little finger.

But I won't give it to you, as I give: you're a ruffian! A "keepsake of tsarist times" is enough for you. The tents and campfires — remain mine.

( )

"And I have a little book with me about Moscow, take it as well. Don't fret that it's small — it contains all the chiming of Moscow!"

(*Moscow, Chroniclers, Travelers, Writers and Poets on Moscow.* Universal Library pub. A book that I'm giving as a present for the fourth time. A treasure house!)

(( ))

"And when I come to Moscow — can I visit you? I didn't even ask your name and patronymic."

I, in my thoughts: What for?! (Out loud): "Give me the book, I'll write it down."*

(( ))

Later I see him off on the porch — while the eye still sees, the souls still . . .

(( ))

We leave tomorrow. We leave if we can get on a train. The threat of patrol detachments. By the way, Kaplan (out of respect for the mother-in-law) promises to let them know along the line that his people are traveling.

(( ))

N.'s morning visit (he spent the night in the train car).

"M.I., clear out — and we're off! What have you and the mother-in-law been up to here? That fellow, the one in the red Circassian hat, is beside himself! I worked on him half the night. I lied and said you were close to Lenin and Trotsky, that you'd been telling them a yarn, that you're on a secret mission, the devil knows what kind of nonsense I concocted! Otherwise he wouldn't get us out of here! Counterrevolution, he shouts, Judaiophobia; she was rocked in the same cradle with Uritsky's murderers, he screams! It was the mother-in-law who was in the cradle I tell him! (Kolka will get the mother-in-law out!) Both of them, both of them, he screams — they're birds of a feather! When I got on to Trotsky and Lenin, he settled down a little bit. And then Kaplan says to me — out of the blue: 'Get out of here today, our people will get you on the train. But I can't promise anything tomorrow.' There you have it!

*I never saw him again.

"And another charming bit of news: I woke up in the night—to a conversation. That devil was talking to another one. The peasants want to blow the train up, there's an investigation going on . . . Three villages for sure . . . What a hotbed Marina Ivanovna! A real thieves' market! I was tearing my hair out that I left you here alone with them! You don't understand anything: they will all be shot!"

I: "Hanged. I even wrote it down in my book."

He: "Not hanged. Shot. And by the Soviets. They're expecting an inspection here. Levit denounced Kaplan, and Kaplan denounced Levit. So it's a matter of who'll get whom. There's going to be such a settling of accounts here . . . I mean, this is the main grain-collecting station—do you understand?"

"Not a word. But we should definitely leave. And the mother-in-law's son?"

"He's going with us, supposedly to accompany his mother. He won't come back. Well, M.I., there's work to be done: get your things ready!"

" . . . And, for love of God, not another word! Kolka and I have already passed the mother-in-law off as a madwoman. Otherwise that'll be it for us, and all for nothing!"

(( ))

I clear out. Two baskets: one gentle, round, the other square, vicious, with iron corners and a metal top. Into the first—lard, wheat, the dolls (I put the amber on, and haven't taken it off since), into the square one—N.'s half pood and my own 10 lbs. All in all, about 2 poods. I test the weight—I'll manage!

When she realizes that I'm leaving, the mistress simpers; when I realize that I'm leaving, I grow brazen.

"It's always comrade, comrade, but people still have their own names, don't they. Maybe you'll tell me what your name is?"

"Tsiperovich, Malvina Ivanovna."

(Of the whole triplet, only Ivan has survived, but Ivan won't betray me!)

"Now fancy that, I wouldn't have thought. I'm very, very pleased to meet you."

"It's my common-law husband's name, he's an actor in all the Moscow theaters."

"Ach, and in the opera, too?"

"Yes, of course—he's a *bass*. The first after Chaliapin (thinking a bit) . . . But he can sing tenor as well."

"Ach, you don't say! So then, if Yossi and I get to Moscow . . ."

"Oh, please, be my guest—all the theaters! Unlimited quantities! He sings in the Kremlin as well."

"In the Krem . . . ?!"

"Yes, yes, at all the Kremlin receptions." (Intimately): "Because you know, people are people everywhere. Everyone wants to enjoy himself after work. All these executions and shootings . . ."

She: "Oh, well, of course! Who could blame them? Human beings can't be all sacrifice, you have to do something for yourself too . . . And tell me, does your husband earn a lot?"

I: "In money—no, in goods—yes. After all, the Kremlin has its stores. In the Uspensky cathedral—there's silk, and in the Archangel cathedral (a flash of inspiration) fur and diamonds . . ."

"A-aaahh!" (Suddenly doubtful): "But then why did you come here, comrade, dressed like that, to these uncultured provinces? And walking around on your own two feet carrying ten boxes of matches?"

I, like a burst of gunfire in her ear: "A secret mission!"

(Twitch. A gulp of air, and, recovering):

"So then, you little fox, you've put something away after all? A little something for a rainy day?"

I, condescendingly: "Come to Moscow, we'll do business. It's not possible here at the requisition base, where everyone lives for others . . ."

She: "Oh, you're absolutely right! And it's risky. You'll give me your address now, won't you, to remember you by? Yossi and I will definitely, and maybe quite soon . . ."

I, patronizingly: "Only hurry up now, these goods won't lie around for long. It's not like I have tons, but still . . ."

She, feverishly: "And you'll give me a fair price?"

I, regally: "My own price."

(Grasping my hands with her own tiny, tenacious ones):

"Perhaps you'd write down your address for me then?"

I, dictating: "Moscow, Execution Place—it's a little square where they used to execute tsars—Brute St., Trotsky Lane."

"Oh, so there's already a Trotsky Lane?"

I: "It's new, they just finished laying it down." (Embarrassed): "Only the building isn't very good: No. 13, and the apartment number—just imagine—it's also 13! It even frightens some people."

She: "Oh, Yossi and I are above such prejudices. And it's not far from the center, you say?"

"It's right in the center: three steps and you're at the Soviet."

"Oh, how lovely . . ."

The mother-in-law's arrival puts an end to our pleasantries.

The last second. We say good-bye.

"If only Yossi had known! He'll be upset! He would have seen you off personally. Just imagine, such an acquaintance!"

"We'll meet again, we'll meet again."

"I myself, Malvina Ivanovna, would be delighted to see you to the station, but we have travelers coming for dinner today, Russians, and I have to make pancakes for seven persons. Oh, you just can't imagine how tired I am of all these petty interests."

I pronounce words of thanks, respectfully, with a touch of gallantry, and shake her hand.

"Now, remember, my humble abode is always at your disposal, as are my husband and I. Only be sure to let us know, so we can meet you at the station."

She: "Oh, Yossi will send an official telegram."

( )

The mother-in-law, once we're free:

"M.I., what's this sudden love between the two of you? Don't tell me you really gave your address to that little cheat?"

"What do you think? Devil's Place, Demon Lane, go look for the wind in the field!"

(We laugh).

(( ))

The road.

We laugh, but not much. It's three versts to the station. The square basket bangs against my legs, it feels like my arms reach down to my knees. I refuse N.'s help — you can't see the man for all the sacks! A three-humped camel.

I walk — and squeak. The basket on the right squeaks too — a nasty little squeak at every step. About one pood. I just hope the handle doesn't come off! (O, what idiocy: to go for flour — with baskets! Flour, which rhymes with only one word: sack! The entire Russian intelligentsia is in these baskets!) I need to think about something else. I have to understand that all of this is a dream. After all, in dreams everything is backwards, so . . . Yes, but dreams do have their surprises: the handle could fall off . . . along with the hand. Or: instead of flour in the basket there could be . . . no, worse than sand: the complete works of Steklov! And you have no right to be indignant: *it's a dream* (Is this perhaps why I have felt so *little* indignation during the Revolution?).

"Wait, do you hear! The sack split!"

Baskets set on the ground. I run to the call. In the middle of the road, standing over the sack as over a corpse, is the matchmaker. She raises her face, red and horrible, as if it had been skinned.

"Well, don't you at least got a safety pin? So many needles I broke sewing for your aunt!"

I find the pin and hand it over: a large, reliable one, a man's pin. We stanch the craftily flowing sack as well as we can. The mother-in-law exclaims:

"I had a needle and thread, I had them ready on purpose! I felt it in my heart!" (To the sack): "You bastard, you lousy traitor! And then I started saying good-bye to that revolting hussy of yours, and I got distracted and took them out. I would have been better off poking out that hussy's eyes with my needle!"

"Tomorrow, tomorrow, Mama!" Kolka hurried her — "right now we have to get to the train!"

We hoisted the sack and went on.

((·))

. . . There's a children's book: *Everything is Possible in Dreams,* and also Calderon has *Life Is a Dream*. And a charming Englishman, not Beardsley, but someone like him, once said: "I go to sleep exclusively in order to dream." He was talking about dreams to order, about dreams where you give hints. Dream, be dreamed! Be dreamed, dream, like this: the telegraph poles — are guards, they escort me. In the basket, not flour, but gold (I stole it from *them*). I carry it to *the others*. And under the gold, at the very bottom, a plan with the position of all the Red troops. I've been walking for ten days, I'll soon reach the Don River. The telegraph poles are escorts. The telegraph poles are leading me to —

"Now then, M.I., hold on! Only a half a verst left!"

((·))

My hands really do reach down to my knees, especially the right hand. Sweat streams, tickling my temples. At the side my hair is soaked. I don't wipe it off: my hand, the metal of the basket, the repetitive blows against my leg — are all one. If they were to unravel — that would be it. When you're in pain you can't start over.

((·))

One way or the other — we arrive at the station.

((·))

The station.

The Station. Gray and undulating. The ground is like the sky in battle paintings. I take fright from afar, grab my companion's hand.

"What?!"

N. is amused: "It's people, Marina Ivanovna, waiting to get on the train."

We come closer: hills and waves of sacks, in between them sighs, scarves, backs. There are almost no men: in the Revolution, as always, the weight of everyday life falls on women: previously — in sheaves, now in sacks. (Everyday life is a sack: with holes. And you carry it anyway.)

Mistrustful heads turn in our direction.

"City folk!"

"They licked Moscow clean, now they've come to gobble up the countryside!"

"Look at all the peasants' goods they've hauled in for themselves!"

I — to N.: "Let's move away!"

He, laughing: "Now, now, M.I., this is just the beginning!"

I grow cold with recognition: of their rightness — and my wrongness.

(( ))

The platform is alive. There's no room to move — anywhere. And more keep coming: they all look alike. Not people with sacks — sacks on people. (I think to myself with hatred: there it is — bread!) And how do men still manage to recognize women? Homespun coats, rough leather jackets . . . Wrinkles, sheepskin . . . Not men and not women, but bears: *it*.

(( ))

"They came last, but they'll get on first."

"City folk get into heaven first too . . ."

"Just watch, they'll get on and we'll still be here . . ."

"Two weeks we've been sleeping outside . . ."

Ooo-ooo-ooo . . .

(( ))

Boarding.

The train. Simultaneously, as if from underground: twelve, with rifles. *Our guys!* At the last second they came to put us on the train. My heart sinks: Razin!

"What now, comrade, gone shy have you? Don't worry! We'll get on!"

It's hopeless, I don't even move. These aren't trains — they're mounds. And facing the train mounds — roaring, wailing, imploring and shouting — are platform mounds.

"They crushed a child! A chi-ild! Chi-i- . . ."

The sitting wave—rises. The horizontal—becomes a headlong and deranged vertical. They climb up. Drag in. Heave on. Shove through.

I—over everyone—to Razin: "Well, Well?"

"We'll manage, Miss! Don't worry! We'll take care of them! . . ."

"Come on now, back up, or we'll shoot!"

The crowd's responding roar, a click in the air, a blow in the back, I don't know where, what, my eyes pop, I rise.

"What is this? Who are your fine feathered friends? With *bayonets*? Robbed the peasants and now you step on a live human being?"

"Just put them off lads, and that'll be that! Let them breathe some fresh air!"

I realize that I'm on and we're moving (all of us? I can't look around). Gradual awareness: I'm standing, one of my feet is in place. And the other, "obviously" is too, only where—I don't know. I'll find it later.

The storm of voices grows.

"Nothing to think about . . . the bayonet put them on, the muzhiks will put them off. What are they doing—making fun of us? We've been waiting for this train seventeen days, like some kind of Heavenly Kingdom . . . And then they . . ."

I take comfort in one thing alone: pulling someone out of this thicket would be like pulling a cork out of a bottle with no corkscrew: unthinkable. For me to be thrown out—others would have to move. And if they move, the whole train will collapse. The precise sensation of capacity limit: no further to go, and more is impossible.

I stand, rocked slightly by the cramped, common human breath: back and forth, like a wave. Chest, sides, shoulders and knees fused, I breathe in unison. And from this extreme corporeal cohesion arises— the sensation of complete body loss. I is what moves. The body is paralyzed—it is an it. The freight car is a forced paralysis.

"City folk: O-oh-oh—Ooo ooo oo . . ."

But . . . my foot: isn't there! (Irritable.) Anxiety about my foot masks the meaning of the threats. My foot—comes first . . . Now, when I find my foot . . . And, oh joy: it's found! Something hurts—somewhere. I pay close attention. It's there, it's there, my darling! Somewhere far away, deep . . . The pain sharpens, unbearable now, I make a desperate effort . . .

A roar: "Who's sticking their boots in my face?!"

But the oak is uprooted: next to me, like a smokestack (neither stocking nor shoe is visible) is my vital, righteous, second foot.

(( ))

And — a sudden spark in the memory: something dark held aloft! It gleams.

Ah, it's a hand bidding farewell, with my ring! Usman Station, Tambov Guberniya — last regards!

Moscow, September, 1918

My Jobs

Moscow, November 11, 1918

"Marina Ivanovna, do you want a job?"

My lodger flew in, X, a communist, the gentlest and most ardent.

"You see, there are two: at the bank and at Narkomnats . . . and actually (snapping of the fingers), for my part, I would recommend that you . . ."

"But what do you have to do? I don't know how to do anything."

"Oh, everybody says that!"

"Everybody says it, I do it."

"In short, as you see fit! The first job is on Nikolskaya St., the second right here, in the first Cheka building."

I: "?!"

He, wounded: "Don't worry! No one is going to make you execute anybody. You'll only be making lists."

"Making lists of the executions?"

He, irritated: "Oh, you don't want to understand! As if I were inviting you to join the Cheka! People like you aren't needed there . . ."

I: "We're harmful."

He: "It's the Cheka *building*, the Cheka has left. You probably know it, on the corner of Povarskaya and Kudrinskaya streets, in Lev Tolstoi it was (a snap of the fingers) . . . the house of . . ."

I: "The Rostovs' house. I accept. What's the name of the institution?"

He: "Narkomnats. The People's Commissariat of Nationalities."

I: "What do you mean, nationalities, when it's supposed to be the International?"

He, almost boasting: "Oh, more than in tsarist times, I assure you! . . . So then, it's the Information Section of the Commissariat. If you agree, I'll talk to the director right away, today." (Suddenly doubtful): "Though, actually . . ."

I: "Just a moment, it isn't anything against the Whites is it? You understand . . ."

He: "No, no, it's completely mechanical. Only, I must warn you, there are no rations."

I: "No, of course not. How could there be in a respectable institution?"

He: "But there will be trips, perhaps they'll raise the pay . . . And you definitely don't want the bank job? Because in the bank . . ."

I: "But I don't know how to count."

He, thoughtfully: "And Alya, does she know how?"*

I: "Alya doesn't know how either."

He: "Yes, then the bank is hopeless . . . What did you call that building?"

I: "The Rostovs' house."

He: "Perhaps you have *War and Peace?* I would love to. . . . Though actually . . ."

I'm already flying down the staircase at breakneck speed. A dark corridor, the former dining room, another dark corridor, the former nursery, the cabinet with the lions . . . I grab the first volume of *War and Peace,* knock over the second volume nearby, glance at it, forget, sink into forgetfulness . . .

(( ))

"Marina, X left! Just after you went out! He said that he reads three newspapers a night and also a little paper and that he won't have time for *War and Peace.* And for you to call him tomorrow at the bank at 9 o'clock. And also, Marina," (a blissful face) "he gave me four pieces of sugar and — just imagine — a piece of *white* bread!"

She lays them out.

"Did he say anything else, Alechka?"

"Just a moment . . ." (she wrinkles her brow) " . . . yes, yes, yes! sa-

---

*Alya is four and a half years old.

bo-tage . . . And he also asked about Papa, have there been any letters. And he made such a face, Marina, a grimacing one! As if he wanted to get mad on purpose . . ."

《》

The 13th of November (a good day to start!). Povarskaya St., the house of Count Sollogub, "Information Section of the Commissariat of Nationalities."

Latvians, Jews, Georgians, Estonians, "Moslems," some sort of "Mara-Maras," "En-Dunyas"—and all these are men and women in short, fur-lined vests with inhuman (ethnic) noses and mouths.

And me, who has always felt unworthy of these hearths (burial vaults!). *Of clans.*

(I'm talking about houses with columns and my timidity before them.)

《》

November 14th, the second day of my job.

Strange job! You arrive, set your elbows on the table (fists against cheekbones) and rack your brains: what to do to make the time pass? When I ask the director for work, I note a certain hostility in him.

《》

I'm writing in the pink hall—pink all over.

There are marble window bays, two huge hanging chandeliers. Small things (like furniture!) have disappeared.

《》

November 15th, the third day of my job.

I'm compiling an archive of newspaper clippings. That is: I rephrase Steklov, Kerzhentsev, reports about prisoners of war, the movements of the Red Army, and so forth, in my own words. I rephrase once, I rephrase twice (I copy from the "journal of newspaper clippings" onto "cards"), then I glue these clippings onto enormous sheets. The newspapers are delicate, the type barely visible, then add captions in lilac pencil, and then the glue — it's utterly pointless and will return to ashes even before it's all burned.

There are different desks here: Estonian, Latvian, Finnish, Moldavian, Moslem, Jewish and several entirely inarticulate ones. In the morning each desk receives its share of clippings, which it then processes over the course of the day. I see all this clipping, labeling and pasting as endless, convoluted variations on one and the same, very meager, theme. As though a composer had it in him to invent only one musical phrase, and he had to fill about thirty reams of musical notation paper — so he "variates": and we variate.

I forgot to mention the Polish and Bessarabian desks. I, not without justification, am the "Russian" desk (the assistant of either the secretary, or perhaps of the director).

Each desk is — grotesque.

To my left are two dirty, doleful Jewesses, ageless, like herring. Further on: a red, fair-haired Latvian woman, also frightening, like a person turned into a sausage: "I knew khim, such a sveetie. Khe partissipated in ze plot, und now zey haf zentenced khim to be shot. Chik-chik." . . . And she giggles with excitement. Wears a red shawl. The fat, bright, pink display of her neck.

The Jewess says: "Pskov is taken!" I have the tormenting thought: "By whom?!!"*

To my right — two people (the Oriental table). One has a nose and no chin, the other has a chin and no nose. (Who is Abkhazia and who is Azerbaijan?)

Behind me sits a seventeen-year-old child — pink, healthy, curly-headed (a white Negro), easy thinking and easy loving, a real live Atenais from Anatole France's *The Gods Thirst,* the one who arranged her skirts so carefully in that fateful carriage — "fière de mourir comme une Reine de France."

Also — a type of institute class-supervisor lady ("an inveterate theatergoer"), also — a greasy, obese Armenian woman (chin resting on

---

*Only later did I understand: "taken" is of course: "by us!" If it were the Whites — then it would be: "surrendered." (M.Ts.)

chest, impossible to say what's where), a mongrel in student uniform, also an Estonian doctor, sleepy and a born drunk . . . Also (variety!) a doleful Latvian woman, all sucked dry. Also . . .

(( ))

(I'm writing at work)

A typographical error:

"If foreign governments would leave the Russian people in peaces," and so forth.

The Herald of Poverty, Nov. 27, No. 32.

I, in the margins: "Don't worry! They'll wait a bit — and they'll leave!"

In the performance of my duties I paraphrase, in my own words, a newspaper clipping on the necessity of having literate people on duty in train stations:

"Day and night, literate people should be on duty in train stations in order to explain the difference between the old order and the new order to those arriving and departing."

The difference between the old and new orders:

The old order: "A soldier came by" . . . "We made pancakes" . . . "Our grandmother died."

Soldiers still come, grandmothers die, only no one makes pancakes anymore.

(( ))

An encounter.

I'm running to the Commissariat. Supposed to be there at nine — it's already eleven: I stood on line for milk on Kudrinskaya St., for salted fish on Povarskaya St., for hemp-seed oil on the Arbat.

There's a lady in front of me: ragged, skinny, with a bag. I come up alongside her. The bag is heavy, her shoulder bowed, I feel the tension of her arm.

"Excuse me, ma'am. May I help you?"

Frightened flight:

"Oh, no . . ."

"I'd be glad to carry it, don't worry, we'll walk together."

She gives in. The bag really is hellish.

"Do you have far to go?"

"To Butyrki, I'm bringing a package."

"Has he been in long?"

"Quite a few months."

"No one to vouch?"

"All Moscow would vouch for him — that's why they won't let him out."

"Young?"

"No, middle-aged . . . Perhaps you've heard of him? The former town governor, D-sky."

()

I had the following encounter with D-sky. I was fifteen and cheeky. Asya* was thirteen and insolent. We were visiting a grown-up friend. There were lots of people. Father was there. Suddenly, the doorbell: D-sky. (And the answering ring: "Well, D-sky, hold on!")

We are introduced. He's kind, charming. I'm taken for a grown-up, and asked whether I like music. And father, remembering my antediluvian wunderkindness:

"What do you mean, why of course! She's been playing since she was five!"

D-sky, politely:

"Perhaps you'd play something?"

I, putting on a show:

"I've really forgotten everything. I'm afraid you'll be disappointed . . ."

D-sky's courtesy, the guests' persuasion, father's insistence, the friend's fright, my acquiescence.

"But first, if you don't mind, let me play four hands with my sister to work up my courage."

"Oh, of course."

I go up to Asya and whisper in my own language:

"Wi(pi)r we(pe)rde(pe)n To(po)nlei(pei)te(pe)r spi(pi) . . ."

Asya can't take it.

*My sister. (M.Ts.)

Father: "What are you up to, you little imps?"
I — to Asya: "Scales, backward!"
To my father:
"Asya's being shy."

()

We begin. My right hand is on re, the left on do (I'm playing bass).
Asya's left hand is on re, her right on do. We start toward each other (I —
from left to right, she — from right to left). At each note a thunderous
double-voiced count: One and two and three and . . . Deathly silence.
After about ten seconds, father's uncertain voice:
"Ladies, why so . . . monotonous? How about something a bit more
lively?"
Without stopping, in unison:
"This is just the beginning."

()

Finally my right and Asya's left hand meet.
We rise with gleeful faces.
Father — to D-sky: "Well, what do you think?"
And D-sky, rising in turn: "I thank you. It was very distinct."

()

I tell the story. At her request I give my name. We laugh.
"Oh, he wasn't only tolerant of jokes. All Moscow . . ."
We say good-bye on the corner of Sadovaya. Once again her shoul-
der bows under the weight of the bag.
"Your father died?"
"Before the war."
"You don't know anymore whether to be sorry or envious."
"Live. And try to keep others alive. God be with you!"
"Thank you. The same to you."

()

The Institute.
Did I ever think that after so many schools, boarding schools and

gymnasiums, I would be handed over to an Institute as well?! For I'm in an Institute, and have in fact been handed over (by X). I arrive between 11 and 12 o'clock; each time my heart stands still: the Director and I have the same habits (ministerial ones!). I'm talking about the head Director — M-r, my own personal director, Ivanov, I write with a small letter.

Once we met at the coat rack — it was all right. A Pole: courteous. And then, I'm also Polish on my grandmother's side.

But more terrifying than the director are the doormen. The former ones. They seem disdainful. In any event, they don't greet you first, and I'm shy. After the doormen, my main worry is not to mix up the rooms. (My idiocy for places.) I'm ashamed to ask, it's my second month here. Enormous idols stand in the hall — knights-in-armor. Left for their use-lessness . . . to everyone but me. I need them, just as I alone of everyone here am akin to them. I ask for protection with a glance. From beneath their visors they answer. If no one's watching, I quietly stroke a forged leg. (Three times taller than I am.)

The hall.

I enter, awkward and timid. In a mousy man's jersey — like a mouse. I'm dressed worse than everyone here, and that's not reassuring. Shoes tied with strings. There may even be some shoe laces somewhere, but . . . who needs them?

The main thing is to understand from the first second of the Revolution: all is lost! Then — everything is easy.

I steal by. The director (my own, the small one) — from his seat:

"Were you waiting in line, Comrade Efron?"

"In three lines."

"What did they have?"

"They didn't have anything, they had salt."

"Yes, well, salt sure isn't sugar!"

Heaps of clippings. Some are quite long, some only a line. I look for ones about the White Guards. The pen scratches. The stove crackles.

"Comrade Efron, we have horse meat for lunch today. I suggest you sign up."

"No money. Did you sign up?"

"Certainly not!"

"Well then, we'll drink tea. Shall I bring you some?"

(( ))

The corridors are empty and clean. The click of typewriters behind doors. Pink walls, columns and snow in the windows. My noble, pink, paradise Institute! Wandering about, I come upon the descent to the kitchen: the descent of the Virgin into hell or of Orpheus into Hades. Stone tiles, worn by human feet. Sloping, nothing to hold on to, the steps twist and turn, in one place they fly headlong. Those peasant feet certainly did their work! And to think, in indoor homemade shoes! It's as though they've been gnawed by teeth! Yes, the tooth of the only old man with any bite! The tooth of Chronos!

Natasha Rostova! Did you ever walk here? My ballroom Psyche! Why wasn't it you — later, at some point — who met Pushkin? Even the name is the same! Literary historians wouldn't have had to relearn anything. Pushkin — instead of Pierre, and Parnassus — instead of nappies. To become a fertility goddess, having been Psyche — Natasha Rostova, isn't that a sin?

It would have been like this. He would have come to call. Having heard so much about the poet and Moor, you would have turned up your pointed, bright-eyed little face — and laughing at something, already feeling a pang . . . Oh, the flounce of a pink gown against the column!

The column overflows with heavenly foam! And your lyrical foot — Aphrodite's, Natasha's, Psyche's — on the slippery peasant stones.

Actually, you were only flying down the stairs to the kitchen for bread!

(( ))

But everything comes to an end: Natasha, serfdom, and the staircase (they say eventually, even Time!). By the way, the stairs are not that long — only twenty-two steps in all. It's just that I walked down them for so long (1818–1918).

Firm. (I almost said: firmament. I was younger and there was the monarchy — and I didn't understand: why the *heavenly* firmament. The revolution and my own soul have taught me.) Potholes, pitfalls, cave-ins. Groping hands grip wet walls. Close over my head, the vault. It smells of damp and Bonivard. Methinks chains are clanking. Ah, no, it's the clang of pots and pans from the kitchen! I go toward the lantern.

(( ))

The kitchen is a crater. So red and hot it's obvious: hell. A huge, six-and-a-half meter stove spews forth fire and foam. "The seething cauldrons boil, they sharpen their knives of steel, they ready the goat for slaughter" . . . And I am the goat.

The queue for the kettle. They scoop ladlesful straight from the boiler. The tea is wood pulp, some say from bark, others from buds, I just lie — from roots. Not glass — but a burn. I pour two glasses. I wrap them in a flap of jersey. On the threshold I inhale horse flesh with a slight movement of the nostrils: I can't sit here — I have no friends.

(( ))

"Well then, comrade Efron, now we can goof off a bit!"

(I arrive with the glasses.)

"With saccharine or without?"

"Pour on the saccharine!"

"They say it affects your kidneys. But you know, I . . ."

"Yes, you know, I too . . ."

My director is an Esperantist (that is, a communist from Philology). An Esperantist from Ryazan. When he talks about Esperanto, a quiet madness glimmers in his eyes. The eyes are light and small, like the ancient saints', or like Pan in the Tretyakov Gallery. See-through. A touch of the lecher. But not the lechery of the flesh, some other kind — if it weren't for the absurdity of the association, I'd say: otherworldly. (If it's possible to love Eternity, then it's also possible to lust after her! And the lusters — philologists — are more numerous than the silent lovers!)

Dark blonde. Something in the nose and chin. The face is puffy, groggy. A drunkard, I imagine.

He writes in the new style — in anticipation of worldwide Esperanto. Has no political convictions. Here, where everyone's a communist, even this is a blessing. Doesn't distinguish Reds from Whites. Doesn't distinguish right from left. Doesn't distinguish men from women. Thus his comradery is completely sincere, and I willingly pay him in the same coin. After work he goes somewhere on Tverskaya St., where on the left side (if you're heading down toward Okhotny Row) there's an Esperanto store. They closed the store, the storefront window remained: fly-blown postcards Esperantists have sent one another from all corners of the earth. He looks and lusts. He works here because it offers a wide field for propaganda: all nations. But he's already beginning to despair.

"I'm afraid, Comrade Efron, that here there are more and more . . ." (in a whisper) "kikes, kikes and Latvians. It wasn't even worth applying: Moscow's full of these goods! I was counting on Chinese, on Indians. They say that Indians readily absorb foreign cultures."

I: "Not Hindus — American Indians."

He: "Redskins?"

I: "That's right, with feathers. They'll slit your throat — and absorb you all in one piece. If you're wearing a jacket, then jacket and all, in a tuxedo — tuxedo and all. But Hindus — just the opposite: terribly dense. Won't swallow anything foreign, neither ideology nor foodstuffs." (Becoming inspired): "Do you want a formula? The American Indian absorbs (the European), the Indian disgorges (Europe). And rightly so."

He, embarrassed: "Now, really, you're . . . I, by the way . . . I've heard more from the communists, they are *also* counting on India . . ." (Becoming inspired in his turn): "I thought — I'll up and esperanto them all!" (Subsiding): "No rations — and not one Indian. Not one Negro! Not even a Chinaman! . . . And these" (a circular glance at the empty hall) "don't want to hear of it! I tell them: Esperanto, and they say: 'the International!'" (Frightened by his own outcry.) "I've nothing against it, but first Esperanto, and then . . . The *word* first . . ."

I, falling in: "And then the *deed*. Of course. In the beginning was the word and the word was . . ."

He, in another outburst: "And that Mara-Mara! What is it? Where did they get it from? Not only haven't I heard a word from him: I haven't even heard a sound! He's just a deaf mute. Or an idiot. Doesn't get any clippings — only his salary. I don't begrudge it. To hell with him, but *why does he come?* The fool, he comes in every day. Sits here till four, the idiot. He should just come on the 20th, for payday."

I, craftily: "Poor thing, maybe he keeps hoping? I'll come in and on my desk there'll be a newspaper cutting about my Mara-Mara?"

He, irritated: "Oh, Comrade Efron, really! What cuttings? Who's going to write about that Mara-Mara? Where is it? What is it? Who needs it?"

I, thoughtfully: "It isn't in geography . . ." (Pause). "And it isn't in history . . . What if it doesn't exist at all? They just made it up — to show off. You know, all nations. And they dressed this guy up . . . But he's mute." (Confidentially): "They chose a deaf mute on purpose, so he wouldn't give himself away in Russian . . ."

He, gulping down the last bit of cold tea with a shudder:
"Who the d-d-devil knows!"

(( ))

Clatter and crash. It's the nationalities returning from their feed. Fortified with horse flesh, it's on to the cutting files (on to filet cutlets would be better, eh? By the way, before the Revolution, cross my heart, I not only couldn't tell filet from tripe — I couldn't tell groats from flour! And I don't regret it in the least).

Comrade Ivanov, anxiously: "Comrade Efron, Comrade M-r might drop in, let's get rid of our mess quickly, eh?" (He rakes it in.) "'The Red Army's Advance' . . . Steklov's articles . . . 'The Liquidation of Illiteracy'. . . . 'Down with the White Guard Scum' — that's for you. 'The Bourgeoisie Schemes' . . . You again . . . 'All to the Red Front' . . . mine . . . 'Trotsky's Address to the Troops' . . . mine . . . . 'The White Hoarders and the White Guard' . . . yours . . . 'Kolchak's Lackeys' . . . yours . . . 'The Whites' Atrocities' . . . yours . . ."

I'm drowning in whiteness. At my elbow — Mamontov, on my knees — Denikin, near my heart — Kolchak.

Greetings, my "White Guard Scum!"

I write with relish.

"What's going on, Comrade Efron, why haven't you finished? The paper, number, date, who, what — no details! I was that way at first too — filled sheets full, then M-r admonished me: 'You're using up a lot of paper.'"

"Does M-r believe in it?"

"What's to believe! You copy, you clip, you glue . . ."

"And into the Lethe — boom! Like in Pushkin."

"Yes, but M-r's a very educated person, I still haven't lost hope . . ."

"You don't say! You know, I thought so too. I ran into him not long ago at the hangings . . . ay, good Lord . . . at the coat hangers: I've got all those 'White Guard atrocities' in my head . . . A quarter past twelve! It was all right, he even looked at me rather intelligently . . . So, you have hope?"

"Somehow I'll manage to get him to the Esperanto club one of these evenings."

"An aspirant to the Esperantists?

Espère, enfant, demain! Et puis demain encore . . .
Et puis toujours demain. Croyons en l'avenir.
Espère! Et chaque fois que se lève l'aurore
Soyons là pour prier comme Dieu pour nous bénir
Peut-être . . .

Lamartine's poetry. Do you understand French?"

"No, but fancy that, it's very pleasant to listen. Oh, what an Esperantist we could make of you, Comrade Efron . . ."

"Then I'll recite some more. I wrote a composition about this in 6th grade:

'A une jeune fille qui avait raconté son rêve.'
Un baiser . . . sur le front! Un baiser — même en rêve!
Mais de mon triste front le frais baiser s'enfuit . . .
Mais de l'été jamais ne reviendra la sève,
Mais l'aurore jamais n'éteindrera la nuit —

Do you like it?" (And, not allowing him to answer) " — then I'll continue:

Un baiser sur le front! Tout mon être frisonne,
On dirait que mon sang va remonter son cours . . .
Enfant! — ne dites plus Vos rêves à personne
Et ne rêvez jamais . . . ou bien — rêvez toujours!

It's piercing, isn't it? The French teacher I wrote the composition for — he was a little in love with . . . Actually, I'm wrong: it was a French-woman, and I was a little in love with . . ."

"Comrade Efron!" (A whisper almost in my ear.) I jump. My "white negro" is standing behind me, and she's all red. There's bread in her hand.

"You didn't have lunch. Perhaps you'd like it? Only I warn you, it's made with bran . . ."

"But you yourself, I'm so embarrassed . . ."

"Do you think . . ." (an ardent face, a challenge in every sheep's curl) " . . . I bought it at Smolensky? Filimovich from the Eastern desk gave it to me — it's from his rations, he doesn't eat it himself. I ate half, half's for you. He promised more tomorrow. But I still won't kiss him!"

◯

(Illumination: Tomorrow I'll give her a ring — that slender one with the almandine. Almandine — Aladdin — Almanzor — Alhambra . . . with an almandine. She's pretty, and she needs it. And I won't know how to sell it anyway.)

◯

Don. Don. Not the river Don, a ringing gong. Two o'clock. And — a further illumination: I'll think up some emergency and I'll leave right away. I'll finish up the White Guards — and I'll leave. Quickly and without any more lyrical digressions (I myself — am just such a digression!) I shower the gray official paper with the pearls of my script and the vipers of my heart. But that counterrevolutionary *yat* keeps popping up like a church cupola. *Yat!*!! "Comrade Kerzhentsev ends his article by wishing General Denikin a good and speedy hanging: we, in turn, wish the same for Comrade Kerzhentsev . . ."

"Saccharine! Saccharine! They're signing up for saccharine!" Everyone jumps up. I must take advantage of other people's sweet cravings to satisfy my own freedom craving. Ingratiatingly and impudently I slip Ivanov my clippings. I cover them with half of the white negro's bread. (The other half is for the children.)

"Comrade Ivanov, I'm leaving now. If M-r asks, say that I'm in the kitchen getting a drink of water."

"Go on, go on."

I rake up the draft of Casanova, a purse with a pound of salt . . . and sidling, sidling . . .

"Comrade Efron!"—he catches up with me near the knights. "I won't be coming in at all tomorrow. I'd really appreciate it if you'd come—well—at least by 10:30. And then the day after tomorrow, don't come at all. You'll really help me out. All right?"

"Yes sir!"

There and then, in front of the perplexed doormen, I salute dashingly, and rush—rush through the White Guard colonnade, over the snowy flowerbed, leaving behind me nationalities and saccharine and Esperanto and Natasha Rostova—to my house, to Alya, to Casanova: homeward!

( )

From *Izvestia:*
"Sovereignty of the water—is sovereignty of the world!"
(I'm enraptured, as if it were poetry.)

( )

9/23 of January (Central Executive Committee News, "The Heir.")
Someone reads: "Kornilov's son, Georgy, a minor, was appointed a constable in Odessa."

I, through the general mocking laughter, innocently:

"Why a constable? His father didn't serve in the police!"

(But in my chest everything seethes.)

The reader: "Well, you know, they're all gendarmes there!"

(What is most touching is that at that moment neither the communist nor I even suspected the existence of the Cossack constables.)

( )

In our *Narkomnats* there's a private chapel—Sollogub's, of course. Near my pink hall. The "white negro" and I stole in there not long ago. Dark, sparkling, cellar air. We stood in the choir gallery. The "white negro" crossed herself, and I was thinking more about ancestors (ghosts). In church I feel like praying only when there's singing. But I don't feel God inside places at all.

Love — and God. How do they manage to combine them? (Love as the element of loving, the earthly Eros). I glance at my "white negro": she's praying; innocent eyes. Those very same innocent eyes, those praying lips . . .

If I were a believer and loved men, these things would fight in me like vicious dogs.

My "white negro's" father works as a doorman in one of the houses (palaces) where Lenin often comes (the Kremlin). And my "white negro," who is often at work with her father, sees Lenin all the time. "So humble, wears a cap."

My "white negro" is a White Guard, that is, not to confuse things: she loves white flour, sugar and all earthly blessings. And what's even more serious, she is passionately and profoundly devout.

"He walks by me, M.I., and I say 'Good day, Vladimir Ilich!' — while I think to myself" (a boldly cautious look around): "I'd like to shoot you right now, you so and so, with a revolver. Don't rob churches!" (Flaring up). "And you know, M.I., it would be so simple — pull a revolver out of my muff and finish him off! . . ." (Pause.) "Only I don't know how to shoot, you see . . . And they'd shoot Papa."

If my negro were to fall into the right hands, hands that know how to shoot and how to teach shooting, and, more important — that know how to destroy and know no regret —— e-ekh!

(( ))

There's an old spinster in the Commissariat — gaunt, with a ribbon, who's in love with her overgrown doctor-brothers, she gets them chocolate with children's ration cards. A finagler, a conniver, who knows languages, by the way ("that sort of family"), etc. As soon as she hears that someone's ill, she diagnoses, with unshakable certainty, as if pounding a gavel: "He's caught it," or "She's caught it," depending on whether she's talking about a person of the male or female sex.

Typhus or sciatica — it's all syphilis to her.

Spinster psychosis.

《 》

But there's another one — plump, raw, a grandmother's granddaughter, friend of my "white negro", a provincial lass. A very poignant little girl. She arrived only recently from Rybinsk. Her grandmother and brother remain at home. A twofold, inexhaustible mine of bliss.

"That's just the way our grandmother is: she can't stand little children. She won't go near an infant: they smell, she says, and they're trouble. But when they get bigger — well, all right then. She'll dress them, teach them. Me she raised from the age of six. 'Do you want to eat?' 'Yes.' 'Well, then, go to the kitchen and watch how dinner's made.' So by ten I already knew how to do absolutely everything." (Animatedly): "Not just your meat pies and cutlets — pâtés and aspics and cakes . . . The same for sewing: 'You, little one, you'll be a woman one day, a housewife, with children and a husband to sew for.' I'd want to run around, she takes my hand and sits me down on the bench: 'hem those kerchiefs,' 'embroider those towels,' and when the war started — for the wounded. Cut patterns herself, sewed herself. Then Papa got married — I'm an orphan — and little brother came along, she made his whole layette herself . . . All the diapers with embroidered initials, with satin-stitch . . . And his little blanket, clothes to take him out in, all sewn with my lace, four-fingers wide, cream-colored . ." (Blissfully): "You know, grandmother taught me to knit and satin-stitch . . . She ordered me my own embroidery hoop. We lived well! And she did everything by herself! Grandmother made things herself, I made things myself . . . I can't stand for my hands to lie idle!"

I look at her hands. Golden hands! Small, plump; slender, tapered fingers. A tiny ring with a tiny turquoise. There was a fiancé, shot by a firing squad not long ago in Kiev.

"His friend wrote to me, he's a student too — a medical student. My Kolya left the house, hadn't gone two feet — shots rang out. And a man fell right at his feet. All bloody. And Kolya's a doctor, he couldn't leave someone who's wounded. He looked around: no one in sight. So he took him, dragged him into his own house and looked after him for three days. He turned out to be a White officer. And on the fourth day they came, took them both, and shot them together . . ."

She dresses in mourning. Her face a sallow gray amid the blackness. Not enough food, not enough sleep, loneliness. Tedious, incomprehensible, unfamiliar work in the Commissariat. Her fiancé's ghost. Homelessness.

Poor Turgenevian petite bourgeoise! The epic orphan of Russian fairy tales! In no one do I feel the great orphanhood of Moscow 1919 as I do in her. Not even in myself.

She dropped by to see me recently, stood over my disarrayed trunks: a student uniform, officer's jacket, boots, riding breeches — epaulets, epaulets, epaulets . . .

"Marina Ivanovna, you should shut them. Shut them and put a lock on. Dust builds up, moths will eat them in the summer . . . He might still return . . ."

And, pensively smoothing a helpless sleeve:

"I couldn't. Just like a living person . . . I'm crying now . . ."

( )

We went to an operetta recently: she, the "white negro" and I (for the first time in my life). The tunes were nice, the verse bad. Dry and harsh is the Russian tongue on Polish lips. But . . . a sort of love, but . . . beyond herring and heavy bags, but . . . light, laughter, gesture!

Mediocrity? For me the worse — the better. "Genuine art." It would offend me right now. All my requirements would arise: "I'm not cattle!"

But this way — a fake for a fake: after the Soviet farce — a sophomoric farce.

( )

A few more words about my "bride." With eyes (marvelous, dark-brown eyes) tear-stained and puffy from crying over her fiancé, she goes on plaintively for hours, wearing out herself and everyone around her: "I just so love everything fatty and sweet . . . I used to be much plumper. . . . I can't live without butter . . . I just can't swallow frozen potatoes . . ."

O thee, sole provision
Of the Communist nation!

(A poem about salted dried fish in the Menshevik paper *Forever On-ward*.)

( )

My assistant.

Our desk has been enhanced by a new coworker (co idler would be more exact). A ripe, red-blooded Hercules from the Volga region. Perpetually and bestially hungry. At lunch he despairingly asks for extra: the silently proffered plate meekly and doggedly pleads. He eats everything.

Handsome. Eighteen years old, so ruddy-cheeked that you get hot sitting next to him: a furnace! No beard and no moustache. Timid. Afraid to move — knows he'll break something. Afraid to cough — knows he'll deafen everyone. The timidity and gentleness of a giant. I feel tenderness for him, as for a huge calf: hopeless tenderness, because I've nothing to give.

Seeing him for the first time at the desk — a huge bear from the Urals leaning over the lace of *Izvestia,* Ivanov and I grinned simultaneously. I don't know what Ivanov was thinking, but right away I knew: "I won't come in tomorrow, or the day after tomorrow, or the day after the day after tomorrow. I'm going to wash the clothes and write."

I didn't come in for six days, not three. On the seventh I showed up. The desk is neat — not one clipping: licked clean. Not a sign of Ivanov. The bear, leaning on his elbows, rules alone.

I, distraught: "But where's Ivanov? Where are the clippings?"

The bear, beaming: "I haven't seen hide nor hair of Ivanov since! I've been in charge here alone for a whole week."

I, horrified: "But the clippings?! Did you keep up the journal?"

He, blissfully: "What journal! Everything's in the basket! I gave it a try — the pen was bad, the paper crumbling, I write — can't read it myself. And I get so sleepy . . . It must mean spring's coming."

(I, mentally: "Wrong, bear, it means winter!")

He, continuing: "Well, I thought, what will be will be! I raked 'em up, the sheets, that is, and into the basket with them. In the morning when I come — it's empty. The cleaning woman must have burned them. The same thing every day. The little ones are all in one piece, I saved them for you."

He opens a drawer: a swarm of snow-white butterflies!

And I, captivated by the line and already taking off, think to myself: "A swarm of snow-white butterflies! One, two . . . four" . . .

(— no! —)

A swarm of snow-white maidens! One, two . . . four . . .
A swarm of snow-white maidens! But no — in the air
A swarm of snow-white butterflies! A charming swarm
Of little Grand Princesses . . .

and, breaking off, to my "coworker":

"We'll reconstruct all this right now . . ." (mentally: except the Grand Princesses!). "We'll sort them out chronologically."

He: "How's that?"

I: "By dates. You know, the 5th of February. The Roman II — that's February, do you see? I — is January, II — is February . . ."

He doesn't breathe or blink.

"Then, wait a minute . . . Just write a letter home. Take a pen and write: 'Dear Mama, I'm very bored and hungry here' . . . Something like that, or the other way around: 'I'm very happy and well fed here.' Because otherwise, she'll be upset. And I'm going to reconstruct Steklov's and Kerzhentsev's articles."

He, admiringly: "From your head?!"

I: "Not from my heart!"

And, in a trice: In an article of February 5th, 1919, "White Guardism and the White Elephant,"* Comrade Kerzhentsev claims . . .

We decamp to another campfire — from the Rostovs' house to the Jerusalem town house. It takes a whole ten days to sort ourselves out. We make off with the remains of the Rostov-Sollogub goods. I take a plate with a coat of arms as a souvenir. In a brick-red field — a borzoi. A

---

*Which never existed. (M.Ts.)

lyrical theft, even chivalrous: the plate isn't deep or small, by current standards — it's obviously for salted fish stew, but in my home the inkwell will stand in it.

Those poor Sollogubian Elzevirs! In open boxes! In the rain! Parchment bindings, ornate French type . . . They carry them away by the cartloads. The library commission is headed by Briusov.

They take away: sofas, chests of drawers, chandeliers. My knights remain. So do the portraits painted on the wall, it seems. Right on the spot — the divvy. The jealous dispute of the "desks."

"That's for our director!"

"No, for ours."

"We already have the Karelian birch table, and the armchair goes with it."

"That's precisely why. You have the table, we get the armchair."

"But you can't break the set!"

I, sententiously:

"Only heads can be broken!"

The "desks" are disinterested — we won't get anything anyway. Everything goes into the directors' offices. In flies my "white negro":

"Comrade Efron! If you only knew how wonderful it is at Ts-ler's! A redwood secretary, a rug, bronze sconces! Just like in the old days! Do you want to take a look?"

We run through the floors. Room Number . . . . Section such and such . . . The director's office. We enter. My "negro", triumphantly:

"Well?"

"Just add a cushion under foot and a lapdog . . ."

"A cat would be enough!"

In her eyes, a joyful demon.

"Comrade Efron! Let's catch him a cat! There's one in apartment 18. What do you say?"

I, hypocritically:

"But he'll dirty everything here."

"That's exactly what I want! Darn thugs!"

Three minutes later the cat is nabbed and shut in. "Work" is over. We fly down all six flights, forgetting everything.

"Comrade Efron! The raspberry ottoman, eh?"

"And the countess's rugs, no?"

The diabolic meowing of the avenger pursues us.

(( ))

The three vital M's.

"So, how'd you carry the potatoes back?"

"It wasn't too bad. My old man met me."

"You know, to make meal you have to mix 2/3 potatoes with 1/3 flour."

"Really? I'll have to tell my mother."

I have neither mother, nor man, nor meal.

(( ))

Frozen potatoes.

"Comrade Efron! They've brought potatoes! Frozen!"

I, of course, find out later than everyone, but bad news — always too soon.

Some of "our people" went on an expedition, promised sugar deposits and lodes of lard, traveled about for two months and brought back . . . frozen potatoes! Three poods a head. First thought: how to get them home? Second: how to eat them? The three poods are rotting.

The potatoes are in the cellar, in a deep, pitch-dark crypt. The potatoes croaked and were buried, and we, the jackals, are going to dig them up and eat them. They say they arrived healthy, but then someone suddenly "prohibited" them, and by the time the prohibition was lifted, the potatoes, having first frozen and then thawed out, had rotted. They sat at the train station for three weeks.

I run home for sacks and the sled. The sled is Alya's, a child's sled, with little bells and blue reins — my gift to her from Rostov in the Vladimir region. Spacious wickerwork like they use for baskets, the back upholstered with a handmade rug. Just hitch up two dogs — and mush! — off to the Northern Lights . . .

But it was I who served as the dog, and the Northern Lights stayed behind: her eyes! She was two years old then, and she was regal. ("Marina, give me the Kremlin!" pointing at the towers.) Oh, Alya! Oh, the sled along midday lanes! My little tiger-fur coat (Baltic leopard? Snow leopard?) that Mandelstam, having fallen in love with Moscow, stubbornly designated Boyaresque. Snow leopard! Sleigh bells!

There's a long line to the cellar. The frostbitten steps of the staircase. Cold at your back: how to lug them? My hands — I believe in these marvels, but 100 pounds *up*stairs! Up thirty leaning, pushing steps! Besides which, one of the runners is broken. Besides which, I'm not sure the sacks will hold. Besides all of which, I'm so cheery that — even if I died — no one would help.

They let us in in groups: ten at a time. Everyone's in pairs — husbands have run over from their jobs, mothers have dragged themselves over. Lively negotiations, plans: one will exchange, another will dry two poods, a third will put them through the meat grinder (100 pounds?!) — obviously, I am the only one who intends to *eat* them.

"Comrade Efron, are you going to take the supplement? A half pood for every family member. Do you have a certificate for the children?"

Someone:

"I wouldn't! There's only slime left."

Someone else:

"You can unload it!"

We forge ahead. Grunts and sighs, occasionally laughter: someone's hands have met in the darkness: men's and women's (men's and men's — isn't funny). Apropos, whence this jollying effect of Eros on the simple people? Defiance? Self-defense? Impoverished means of expression? Timidity under the guise of levity. After all, when they're afraid, children often laugh as well. "L'amour n'est ni joyeux ni tendre."

But maybe — more likely — no *amour,* just surprise: men's hands — cursing, a man's and a woman's — laughter. Surprise and impunity.

There's talk of an impending trial for our coworkers — they presented huge bills for both purchases and expenses. Lodging, supplies carts, drivers . . .

They brought a lot of everything for themselves, of course.

"Did you notice how so-and-so has fattened up?"

"And so-and-so? His cheeks are about to burst!"

They let us in. We run into a crazed string of sleds. Runners over feet. Shouts. Darkness. We go through puddles. The smell is truly putrid.

"Move aside, will you!!!"

"Comrades! Comrades! The bag broke!"

Squish. Squelch. The feet disappear up to the ankles. Someone, braking the entire team, furiously removes his footwear: his felt boots are soaked through! I stopped feeling my feet a long time ago.

"Hey! Is there ever going to be any light?!"

"Comrades! I lost my identification! In the name of all that's holy—light a match!"

It sputters. Someone on their knees, in the water, is helplessly raking aside the slime.

"You should look in your pockets!"

"Could you have left it at home?"

"How do you think you'll find it here?"

"Move along! Move along!"

"Comrades, there's another group coming this way! Watch out!!!"

And—a glade and a waterfall. A square hole in the ceiling, through which rain and light fall. It gushes, as if from a dozen pipes. We'll drown! Leaps and jumps, someone lost their sack, someone else's sled got stuck in the passageway. Lord Almighty!

The potatoes are on the floor: they take up three hallways. At the far end they're more protected, less rotten. But there's no way to get to them except over them. And so: with our feet, our boots. Like climbing over a mountain of jellyfish. You have to take them with your hands: one hundred pounds. The unthawed ones have stuck together in monstrous clusters. I don't have a knife. So, in despair (I can't feel my hands)—I grab whatever kind comes my way: squashed, frozen, thawed . . . The sack won't hold any more. My hands, numb through and through, can't tie it. Taking advantage of the darkness, I start to cry, but then and there I stop:

"To the scales! To the scales! Who's ready for the scales?!"

I hoist and haul.

Two Armenians are doing the weighing, one in a student uniform, the other in Caucasian dress. The snow-white felt cloak looks like a spotted hyena. Just like an archangel of the Communist Last Judgment! (The scales undoubtedly lie!).

"Comrade Meess! Don't hold up the public!"

Quarreling, kicking. Those in back push. I've blocked the entire passageway. Finally, the Caucasian, taking pity — or growing angry — shoves my sack aside with his foot. Poorly tied, the sack spills open. Slip. Slobber. I gather them up patiently, taking my time.

《 》

The return route with the potatoes. (I only took two poods, the third I stashed away.) First through raging hallways, then up a resistant stairway — whether it's tears or sweat on my face I can't tell.

And I know not whether it be tears or rain
That burn my face . . .

Maybe it was rain! That's not the point! The runner is very weak, it's split in the middle, it's unlikely we'll make it back. (It's not I who pulls the sled, we pull together. The sled is my comrade-in-woe, and the potatoes are the woe. We carry our own woe!

I'm scared of the plazas. The Arbat can't be avoided. I could have gone by the Prechistenka lanes, but would have gotten lost there. Neither snow, nor ice: I'm sliding on water, and in some places — on dry ground. I admire the cobblestones pensively, some are already pink . . .

"Oh how I loved all this!"

I remember Stakhovich. If he could see me now, I would indubitably become the object of his loathing. Everything, even my face, is dripping. I am no better than my own sack. The potatoes and I are now one and the same.

"Where the hellrya goin? Canya like that — right into people?! Tailless bourgeoise!"

"Of course I've no tail — only devils have tails!"

Laughter all around. The soldier, not assuaged:

"Some hat yer decked out in! And that mug could use a washing . . ?"

I, in the same tone, pointing to his leg wrappings:

"Some rags you're decked out in!"

The laughter grows. Not wanting to relinquish the dialogue, I stop, and pretend to adjust the sack.

The soldier, working himself up:

"The upper classes they call 'em! Huh! Intellygents! Can't wash our face without a servant, can we?!"

A simple woman, shrilly:

"You'll give her some soap then, will you? Who's slipped off with all the soap, tell me? What's soap going for at Sukhareva, d'ya know?"

Someone from the crowd:

"How would he know? He gets it for free! And you, Miss, you've got potatoes there?"

"Frozen. From my job."

"Of course they're frozen — they need the good ones for themselves! Give you a hand, then?"

He gives a push, the reins grow taut, I'm off. Behind me the woman's voice — to the soldier:

"So what, she wears a hat, so she's not a human being?"

The ver-r-r-dict!

(())

The day's outcome: two tubs of potatoes. We all eat: Alya, Nadya, Irina, I.

Nadya — to Irina, slyly:

"Eat, Irina, it's sweet, with sugar."

Irina, stubbornly, lowering her head: "Nnnnnoooo . . ."

(())

March 20th.

Instead of Monplenbezh, lost in thought, I write "Monplesir" (Monplaisir) — something like a small Versailles of the 18th century.

Annunciation 1919.

Prices:

1 lb. flour — 35 rubles.
1 lb. potatoes — 10 rubles.
1 lb. carrots — 7.50 rubles.
1 lb. onions — 15 rubles.
Herring — 25 rubles.

(Salary — our raises haven't gone through yet — 775 rubles a month.)

(( ))

April 25, 1919.

I quit the Commissariat. I quit because I can't put together a classification. I tried, I racked my brains—nothing. I *don't* understand. I don't understand what they want from me: "Compile, compare, sort . . . In each section—a subsection." As if they'd rehearsed it. I asked everyone: from the department director to the eleven-year-old messenger boy. "It's very simple." And the main thing is that no one believes that I don't understand. They laugh.

Finally, I sat down at the desk, dipped my pen in ink, and wrote: "Classification." Then, having thought a bit: "Section." Then, having thought a bit more: "Subsection." On the right and on the left. Then I froze.

(( ))

I've worked for 5¹/₂ months, two more weeks—and vacation (with salary). *But I can't take it.* And the last three months of clippings aren't pasted up. And they're starting to suspect my *yat*. "Come on, comrade, haven't you gotten used to the new spelling yet?" . . . The classification has to be presented by the 28th. At the very latest. I have to be fair—communists are trusting and patient. An old regime institution would have taken one look at me, and fired me immediately. Here, I myself resign.

The director, M-r, reading my letter of resignation, briefly:

"Better conditions?"

"Military rations and discounted meals for all family members."

(Faster than lightning, a brazen invention.)

"Then I couldn't possibly keep you. But be careful: those kinds of institutions can fall apart quickly."

"I'm an executive."

"On whose recommendation?"

"Two *pre*-October Party members."

"What's your position?"

"Translator."

"Translators are needed. I wish you success."

I leave. I'm already at the door — and he calls out:

"Comrade Efron, you'll be presenting the classification, of course?"

I, pleading:

"All the materials are there . . . My assistant will have no problem . . . Or just deduct it from my salary!"

(( ))

They didn't deduct it. No, hand on heart, I can say that to this day I, personally, haven't seen communists do anything bad (maybe I haven't seen any bad communists!). And it isn't them I hate, but communism (for two years now all I've heard everywhere is: "Communism is wonderful, but communists are horrid!" I'm sick and tired of it!).

But, to return to the classification. (Illumination: isn't this the entire essence of communism?!) exactly the same as with algebra when I was 15, with arithmetic when I was seven! Full eyes and an empty page. It's the same with cutting patterns — *I don't understand,* I don't understand: what's left, what's right, my temples whirl, there's a lead weight on my brow. It used to be the same with selling at the market — with hiring servants, with all of my hundred-pood earthly life: I *don't* understand, I *can't* stand it, it *doesn't* work out.

I think that if others were forced to write *Fortuna,* they would feel the same.

(( ))

I go to work at *Monplenbezh* — in the card file division.

April 26th, 1919.

I've only just returned, and I've made a momentous vow: I'm not going to work at a job. Never. Even if it kills me.

It happened this way. Smolensky Boulevard, a building in the garden. I enter. The room is like a coffin. The walls are made of index cards: not a ray of light. The air is paper (not noble, like book paper, but — ashen. Thus, the difference between a library and a card catalogue file: there you breathe the air of refuge, here — of refuse!) Frighteningly elegant ladies (coworkers). In bows and "boots." They look you over — and scorn you. I sit opposite a grill-covered window, the Russian alphabet in my hands. The cards have to be separated by letters. Everything starting with A, everything with B, then by the second letters, i.e., Abrikosov, Avdeev, then by the third letters. From 9 in the morning until 5:30 in the evening. Lunch is expensive, I won't have to eat. Previously, they gave out this and that, now they don't give out anything. I missed the Easter rations. The directress is a short-legged, ungainly, forty year old cuttlefish in a corset and in spectacles — terrifying. I smell a former inspectress and a current prison guard. With caustic frankness she's astounded at my slowness: "We average two hundred cards a day. You obviously aren't familiar with this . . ."

I cry. A stony face and tears like cobblestones. It probably looks more like a tin idol melting than a woman weeping. No one sees because no one raises their brow: they're competing for speed.

"I've done this many cards!"

"I've done this many!"

And suddenly, I don't know why, I stand up, collect my belongings, and walk up to the directress:

"I didn't sign up for lunch today, may I run home?"

A perspicacious, bespectacled look:

"Do you live far away?"

"Nearby."

"But be back here in half an hour. This sort of thing isn't done here."

"Oh, of course."

I leave — still a statue. At Smolensky market, tears — a torrent. Some woman, frightened:

"They've robbed you, have they Miss?"

And suddenly — laughter! Exultation! Sun full on my face! It's over. Nowhere. Never.

It wasn't I who left the card file: my legs carried me. From soul to legs: without going through the mind. This is what instinct is.

EPILOGUE

July 7, 1919.

Yesterday I gave a reading of *Fortuna* in the "Palace of Arts" (52 Povarskaya St., Sollogub's house, my former job). Of all the readers, I alone was well received — with applause (a measure not of me, but of the audience).

In addition to me the readers were: Lunacharsky — from the Swiss poet Karl Müller, a translation; a certain Dir Tumanny — his own poems, that is, Mayakovsky's, there are lots of Dir Tumannys — and it's all Mayakovsky!

Lunacharsky I saw for the first time. Jolly, ruddy, uniformly and proportionately protruding from a foppish jacket. The face of a middle-brow member of the intelligentsia, the impossibility of evil. A fairly round figure, but of a "light plumpness" (like Anna Karenina). No baggage at all.

He listened well, as I was told, even shushed when someone moved. But the audience wasn't bad.

I chose *Fortuna* because of the monologue at the end:

. . . So that serves you right, the triple lie
Of Liberty, Equality and Fraternity!

I have never read so distinctly.

And I, Lauzun, with a hand as white as snow
Raised my glass, the mob to flatter.
And I, Lauzun, claimed nobleman and woodcutter
Equal to each other in the sun's fair glow!

I have never breathed with such a sense of responsibility. (Responsibility! Responsibility! What delight can compare with thee? And what glory?! A nobleman's soliloquy — to a commissar's face. That's living! Only too bad that it was Lunacharsky and not — I wanted to write "Lenin," but Lenin wouldn't have understood anything — and not the whole of No. 2 Lubianka!)

I prefaced the reading with a kind of introduction: who Lauzun was, what he became and why he died.

At then end I stood alone, with a few casual acquaintances. If they hadn't come — I would have been completely alone. Here I'm as much a stranger as I am among the lodgers of the house where I've lived five years, as I am at work, as I once was in all seven of the Russian and foreign boarding schools and primary schools where I studied, as I have always been — everywhere.

（ ）

I read in the same pink hall where I had worked. The chandelier was shining (before, it had been covered up). The furniture had resurfaced. The grandmothers on the walls had recovered their sight. (The chandeliers, and the furniture, and the great-grandmothers, and the luxury items, and the utensils — down to the dishes — everything had been reclaimed from Narkomnats by the "Palace of Arts." Weep directors!)

In one of the halls — a charming marble Psyche. The guardedness of the soul and of a bather. A lot of bronze and a lot of darkness. The rooms are sated. Then, in December, they were starving: stark. This sort of house needs things. Here things are least of all materiality. A thing that is not for sale — is already a sign. And behind the sign — inevitably — is a meaning. In such a house things are meanings.

（ ）

I caressed my knights.

（ ）

July 14, 1919.

Three days later I found out from B. that the director of the "Palace of Arts," R-ov, appraised my reading of *Fortuna* — an original play, never read anywhere, the reading of which lasted 45 minutes, maybe more — at 60 rub.

I decided to refuse them — publicly — in the following words: "Take these 60 rub. for yourself — for 3 lbs. of potatoes (maybe you'll still be able to find some at 20 rub.!) — or for three pounds of raspberries — or for 6 boxes of matches; and I, with my *own* 60 rub., will go light a candle at the Iverskaya Virgin for the end of the regime that thus values labor."

Moscow, 1918–19

Attic Life

From Moscow Notes, 1919–20

I'm writing in my attic—I think it's the 10th of November—since everyone started living by the new calendar I don't know the dates any more.

I know nothing of S. since the month of March, the last time I saw him was January 18, 1918, how and where—someday I'll say, right now I don't have the strength.

I live with Alya and Irina (Alya is six, Irina is two years and seven months) on Boris and Gleb Lane across from two trees, in an attic room which used to be Seriozha's. There's no flour, no bread, under the desk there's about twelve pounds of potatoes, the leftovers of a bushel "loaned" by our neighbors—that's the entire pantry! The anarchist Charles took away Seriozha's "élève de Breguet" antique gold watch—I've gone to see him a hundred times. At first he promised to return the watch, then he said that he'd found a buyer for it but had lost the key, then that he'd found a key for it at Sukhareva but had lost the buyer, then that fearing a search he'd given it to someone else to keep, then that it had been stolen from the person he gave it to for safekeeping but that he was a rich man and wouldn't bicker over such trifles, then, turning nasty, he started to scream that he couldn't be expected to answer for other people's things. The upshot: no watch, no money. (That sort of watch goes for 12,000 now, i.e., fifty lbs. of flour.) The same thing happened with the baby scales. (Charles again.)

I live on donated meals (children's). Not long ago the wife of the shoemaker Gransky—a thin, dark-eyed woman with a pretty, long-suffering face—the mother of five children—sent me a lunch ticket and a little "doughnut" for Alya through her oldest daughter (one of her girls had left for camp). Mrs. G-man, our neighbor on the floor below, sends the children soup from time to time and today forcibly "loaned" me a third thousand. She herself has three children. Small, gentle, worn down by life: by the nanny, by the children, by a powerful husband, by the routine — immutable as the movement of the spheres — of lunches and dinners. (In our home — a meal is always a comet!) She helps me secretly, hiding it from her husband, a Jew and a lucky man, whom I — in whose home everything but the soul has frozen and nothing save books has escaped destruction — naturally cannot help but irritate.

Occasionally, when they remember my existence — and I'm not blaming them, for we've known each other a short time — the actress Z-tseva and her husband help me, she, because she loves poetry, and her husband because he loves his wife. They brought potatoes, and several times the husband has torn down beams from the attic and sawed them up.

There's also R.S. T-kin, the brother of Mrs. Ts-lin, whose literary evenings I used to attend. He gives matches, bread. Kind, sympathetic.

And that's it.

Balmont would be glad to, but he himself is destitute. (If you drop by, he always gives you food and drink.) His words — "I keep feeling pangs of conscience, I feel I should help" — are already help. People don't know how immensely I value words! (They're better than money, for I can pay with the same coin!)

My day: I get up — the upper window is barely gray — cold — puddles — sawdust — buckets — pitchers — rags — children's dresses and shirts everywhere. I split wood. Start the fire. In icy water I wash the potatoes, which I boil in the samovar. (For a long time I made soup in it, but once it got so clogged up with millet that for months I had to take the cover off and spoon water from the top — it's an antique samovar, with an ornate spigot that wouldn't unscrew, wouldn't yield to knitting needles or nails. Finally, someone — somehow — blew it out.) I stoke the samovar with hot coals I take right from the stove. I live and sleep in one and the same frightfully shrunken, brown flannel dress, sewn in Alexandrov in the spring of 1917 when I wasn't there. It's all covered with burn holes from falling coals and cigarettes. The sleeves, once gathered with elastic, are rolled up and fastened with a safety pin.

Cleaning is next. "Alya, take out the basin!" A few words about the basin — it warrants them. This is the main protagonist in our life. The samovar stands in the basin because when the potatoes are boiling it splashes everything around. All the garbage is thrown into the basin. The basin is carried out during the day, and at night I rinse it out in the backyard. Without the basin — it would be impossible to live. Coals — sawdust — puddles . . . And the stubborn desire to keep the floor clean! I go for water to the G-mans by the back stairs: I'm afraid to run into the husband. I return happy: a whole bucketful of water and a tin can! (Both the bucket and the can belong to others, mine have all been stolen.) Then the wash, dishwashing: the dishpan and the primitive pitcher with no handles, "the playschool one," in short: "Alya, get the playschool ready for the washing!" Then the cleaning of the copper mess kit and the milk can for Prechistenka St. (an enriched meal from the patronage of that same Mrs. G-man) — a little basket containing the purse with the lunch tickets — a muff — fingerless mittens — the key to the back entrance around my neck — and I'm off. My watch doesn't work. I don't know what time it is. So, having mustered the courage, I ask a passerby: "Excuse me, could you please tell me approximately what time it is?" If it's two o'clock — I feel heartened. (Come to think of it, what is the present tense? Feel heartening? Doesn't sound right.)

The route: to the kindergarten (Molchanovka St. 34) to drop off the dishes — along Starokoniushenny Lane to Prechistenka St. (for the enriched meal), from there to the Prague cafeteria (with the shoemakers' tickets), from Prague (the Soviet one) to the old Generalov store — to see if by chance there's bread on sale — from there back to the kindergarten to pick up the lunch — from there — along the back stairs, with pitchers, bowls and cans hanging from me — not a finger free! and fright in the bargain: has the purse with the lunch tickets fallen out of the basket?! Along the back stairs — homeward. Straight to the stove. The coals are still smoldering. I blow on them. Warm them up. All meals go into one pot: a soup that's more like kasha. We eat. (If Alya has been with me, the first order of business is to untie Irina from the chair. I started tying her up after the time she ate half a head of cabbage from the cabinet when Alya and I were out.) I feed Irina and put her down for a nap. She sleeps on a blue armchair. There's a bed, but it won't go through the door. I boil coffee. I drink. Smoke. Write. Alya writes me a letter or reads. About two hours of quiet. Then Irina wakes up. We heat up the remains of the mush. With Alya's help I fish out the potatoes stuck at the bottom of the samovar. We—either Alya or I—put Irina to bed. Then Alya goes to bed.

At 10 o'clock the day is over. Sometimes I chop and saw wood for tomorrow. At 11 or 12 I am also in bed. Happy with the lamp right next to my pillow, the silence, a notebook, a cigarette, and sometimes—bread.

I write badly, in a hurry. I didn't write down either the *ascensions* to the attic—there's no staircase (we burned it)—pulling myself up on a rope—for firewood, nor the *constant* burns from coals, which (impatience? embitteredness?) I grab with my bare hands, nor the running about to secondhand stores (has it been sold?) and cooperatives (are they selling anything?).

I didn't write down the most important thing: the gaiety, the keenness of thought, the bursts of joy at the slightest success, the passionate directedness of my entire being—all the walls are covered with lines of poems and NB! for notebooks. I didn't write down the trips at night to the terrible icy depths—to Alya's former playroom—for some book, which I suddenly have to have, I didn't write down Alya's and my abiding, guarded hope: wasn't that a knock at the door? Yes, someone must be knocking! (The bell hasn't worked since the beginning of the Revolution; instead of a bell—there's a hammer. We live at the top and through seven doors we hear everything: every scrape of someone else's saw, every stroke of someone else's axe, every slam of someone else's door, every sound in the yard, everything, except knocking at our door!) And—suddenly—someone's knocking!—either Alya, throwing on her blue coat, made for her when she was two years old, or I, not throwing on anything—head downstairs, groping, galloping, first past the staircase with no banister (we burned it), then down those stairs—to the chain on the front door. (Actually, you can get in without our help, but not everyone knows it.)

I didn't record my eternal, one and the same—in the same words!—prayer before sleep.

But the life of the soul—Alya's and mine—grows out of my verse—my plays—her notebooks.

I wanted to record *only the day*.

◖◗

Alya and I.

Alya: "Marina! I didn't know how many people there were with such wonderful names! For example: Dzhunkovsky."

I: "He's the former governor-general of Moscow(?), Alechka."

Alya: "Aha! I know — the governor. That's in *Don Quixote* — the governor!"

(Poor Dzh-sky!)

◖◗

I tell a story:

"You see, there was an ancient old woman, not at all silly. A dried flower — a rose! Fiery eyes, a proudly set head, she used to be a cruel beauty. And it's all still there — only it's ju-ust about to disintegrate . . . A rose-colored dress, splendid and terrible, because she's seventy years old, a rose evening cap, delicate slippers. Under her sharp heel a taut, tightly stuffed satin pillow — also rose-colored — a heavy, dense, squeaky satin . . . And so, at the stroke of midnight — her granddaughter's fiancé appears. He's a little late. He's elegant, gallant, handsome — a camisole, a sword . . ."

Alya, interrupting, "Oh Marina! — Death or Casanova!"

(She knows the latter from my plays, *Adventure* and *The Phoenix*.)

◖◗

"Alechka, what do you think the last word should be in *Grandmother*?* Her last word — rather, breath! — after which she dies?"

"Of course — Love!"

"True, true, only I thought perhaps: *Amour.*"

I explain the difference between a concept and its incarnation: "Love — is a concept, *Amour* — the incarnation. A concept — is general, round, the incarnation — is sharp — upward! everything toward one point. Do you understand?"

"Oh, Marina, I understand!"

*A play that I didn't finish, and lost.

"Then give me an example."

"I'm afraid it won't be right. They're both too airy."

"It doesn't matter, go ahead. If it's not right, I'll tell you."

"Music is a concept, a voice the incarnation." (Pause) "And also: glory is a concept, a heroic deed — the incarnation. But Marina, how strange! A heroic deed is a concept, but a hero is the incarnation."

《 》

"Alya! What a wonderful thing — dreams!"

"Yes, Marina, and also: a dress ball!"

"Alya! My mother always wanted to die suddenly: to be walking along the street and suddenly, from a building under construction — a brick would fall on her head! And that would be it."

Alya, slightly amused: "No, Marina, I don't really like that idea, a brick . . . Now — if the whole building fell down!!!"

《 》

Alya, before going to sleep:

"Marina! I wish you the best of everything on earth. Maybe: of everything left on earth . . ."

《 》

If I get through this winter I'll really be *fort comme la mort* — or just *morte* — without *fort* — with an *e muet* on the end.

《 》

Grocery stores now resemble the windows of beauty salons: all the cheeses — aspics — cakes — not a whit more alive than wax dolls.

That same, slight terror.

《 》

Oh, "Wahrheit und Dichtung"! And I stop, for in this cry there is as much rapture as dissatisfaction. Goethe wanted to convey the history of his life and his development simultaneously, but they didn't blend for him. Whole places seem pasted in: "hier gedenke ich mit Ehrfurcht eines gewissen X-Y-Z" — and so on for dozens of pages in a row. If he had woven these "treffliche Gelehrte" into his life, forced them to come into the room, move about, speak, there wouldn't have been such a diagrammatic feeling (calculation) in places: a person gets it into his head to thank everyone who contributed to his development — and so he lists them. It isn't boring — everything is significant, but Goethe himself somehow disappears, you can't see his black eyes anymore . . .

But then — Lord! — the walks, as a boy, through Frankfurt — the friendship with the little Frenchman — the incident with the artist and the mouse — the theater — the relationship with his father — Gretchen ("Nicht küssen, ist 's was so gemeines, aber lieben, wenn's möglich ist!") their nocturnal meetings in the cellar — Goethe in Leipzig — the dance lessons — Sesenheim — Frederika — the moon . . .

Oh, when I read that scene with the disguise, my heart trembled because — it was Frederika and not me!

The coziness of that almost peasant house — the pastor — playing at forfeits — reading aloud . . .

Because of all this I couldn't manage to get out of bed at all today: just didn't feel like living!

(( ))

How I would have raised Alya in the 18th century! Buckles on her shoes! Clasps on the family Bible! And what a dancing instructor!

(( ))

Nowadays, probably because of the axe and the saw, there are far fewer *enfants d'amour.* For that matter, only the intelligentsia saws and hacks. (The muzhiks don't count! Nothing affects them!) And the intelligentsia has never been noted for either *enfants* or *amour.*

(( ))

Not long ago at Smolensky Market: a buxom peasant lass — wearing a fabulous shawl crisscrossed, her gait from the hips — and a little withered spinster — a spiteful old hag! A wrinkled finger stuck into the girl's high bosom. An ingratiating whisper: "What's that you've got there? A piglet?"

And the girl, pulling her shawl ever tighter around her, haughtily: "Three hundred and eighty."

❨❩

Now today, for instance, I ate all day long, though I could have written all day long. I really don't want to die of starvation in 1919, but even less do I want to make a pig of myself.

❨❩

By nature I can't abide surpluses. I'll either eat something or give it away.

Just so it wouldn't seem so terrifying, one could imagine things this way: a loaf of bread doesn't cost 200 rubles, but 2 kopecks, as it used to, but I don't have those 2 kopecks — and never will.

And the Tsar is in Tsarskoe Selo as always — only I'll never go to Tsarskoe Selo, and he — will never come to Moscow.

❨❩

Good Lord! How many Nozdrevs there are in Russia these days (who hasn't defamed whom and how, who hasn't bartered what for what!) — Korobochkas ("and how much are dead souls going for in the city now?" "and how much are female mannequins going for at the market now?": me, for instance) — Manilovs ("The Temple of Friendship" — "The House of the Happy Mother") — Chichikovs (a born speculator!). But there's no Gogol. It would be better the other way around.

❨❩

Just as rare are those — what's his name? the one with the Armenian surname, idze or adze, from Part II, so irreal that I can't even remember his name!

❨❩

Alongside our ignoble life — there is another: ceremonial, incorruptible, immutable: the life of the church. The same words, the same movements — everything as it was centuries ago. Outside time, that is, outside the treachery of change.

We don't remember this often enough.

❨❩

"No longer laughing."
(The inscription on my cross.)

◉

I've taken the year 1919 in somewhat exaggerated terms — the way people will understand it a hundred years from now: not a fleck of flour, not a speck of salt (clinker and clutter enough and to spare!), not a speck, not a mote, not a shred of soap! — I clean the flue myself, my boots are two sizes too big — this is the way some novelist, using imagination to the detriment of taste, will describe the year 1919.

◉

My room. — I'll leave it some day surely. (?) Or, upon opening my eyes, I'll never ever see anything other than the high window in the ceiling — the basin on the floor — clothes on all the chairs — the axe — the iron (I sharpen the axe on the iron) — and the G-mans' saw.

◉

People, when they do visit, only irritate me: "You can't live like this. This is horrible. You need to sell everything and move."

Sell! Easy to say! I liked all my things too much when I bought them — and therefore no one buys them.

The year 1919 has taught me nothing about practical matters: neither thrift nor abstinence.

I take — eat — and give away bread as easily as if it cost 2 kopecks (now it's 200 rubles). And I have always drunk coffee and tea without sugar.

◉

Is there presently in Russia — Rozanov is dead — a genuine thinker and observer who could write a genuine book about hunger? About a person who wants to eat — a person who wants to smoke — a person who's cold — about a person who has but does not give, about a person who has nothing and gives; about the formerly generous — turned stingy, about the formerly miserly — turned generous, and, finally, about me: a poet and a woman, alone, alone, alone — like a lone oak — a lone wolf — like God — amid the many plagues of Moscow in the year 1919.

I would write it — if it weren't for the romantic flourish in me — my nearsightedness — all of my idiosyncrasies — which at times prevent me from seeing things as they are.

(( ))

Oh, if I were rich!

Dear 1919, it is you who has taught me this cry! Before, when everyone had plenty, I still managed to give; and now, when no one has anything, I can't give anything, except my soul — a smile — sometimes a bit of kindling (out of frivolity) — and that's too little.

Oh, what a field of action exists for me now, for my insatiableness for love. Everyone bites at this bait — even the most complex — even I! At the moment, I for one definitely love only those who give to me — who promise and don't give — it doesn't matter! — just as long as they sincerely (and maybe *not* sincerely — who cares!) want to give for a minute.

By whim of hand and heart, this sentence, and therefore the whole meaning, could have turned out differently and it would also have been true:

Before, when everyone had everything, I still managed to give. Now, when I have nothing, I still manage to give.

All right?

(( ))

I give, like everything I do, from a sort of spiritual adventurism — for the smile — mine and the other's.

(( ))

What do I like about adventurism? The word.

(( ))

Balmont — in a woman's crisscrossed Scottish shawl — under the covers — frightful cold, steam rising like a stake — a plate of potatoes fried in coffee grinds nearby:

"Oh, this will be a shameful page in Moscow's history! I'm not talking about myself as a poet, but as a toiler. I've translated Shelley, Calderon, Edgar Poe . . . Haven't I been sitting with dictionaries since I was 19 instead of going out and having a good time and falling in love?! And I'm starving—in the literal sense. Only death from starvation awaits! Idiots think hunger—is the body. No, hunger—is the soul, the whole weight of it falls directly on the soul. I'm oppressed, I'm suffering, I can't write!"

I ask for a smoke. He gives me his pipe, and orders me not to distract myself while I smoke.

"This pipe requires a great deal of concentration, so I advise you not to talk, since there are no matches in the house."

I smoke, that is, I draw with all my might—the pipe seems stopped up—1/10 of a drag comes through with every draw—for fear it will go out I not only don't talk, I don't think—and—after a minute, relieved:

"Thank you—I've had enough!"

Moscow, Winter 1919–20

On Love
From a Diary

The complete concurrence of souls requires the concurrence of the breath, for what is the breath, if not the rhythm of the soul?

And thus, for people to understand one another, they must walk or lie side by side.

( )

The nobility of the heart — of the organ. Unremitting caution. It is always first to sound the alarm. I could say: it is not love that makes my heart pound, but my pounding heart — that makes love.

( )

The heart: it is a musical, rather than a physical organ.

( )

The heart: sounding line, plummet, log, dynamometer, Reaumur — everything, but the timepiece of love.

( )

"You love two people, therefore you don't love anyone!" Forgive me, but if in addition to N., I also love Heinrich Heine, you wouldn't say that I don't love the first person. Therefore, to love a living and a dead person simultaneously — is all right. But imagine that Heinrich Heine came to life and could walk into the room any minute. I am the same, Heinrich Heine is the same, the only difference is that *he could walk into the room.*

Thus: love for two individuals, either of whom could enter the room at any minute isn't love. In order for my simultaneous love for two individuals to be love, one of these individuals has to have been born a hundred years before me or not born at all (a portrait, a poem). A condition that cannot always be met!

And still, Isolde loving someone else in addition to Tristan is unthinkable, and the cry—"O, l'Amour! l'Amour!"—of Sarah (Marguerite Gautier) with regard to someone other than her young friend is ridiculous.

(( ))

I would propose another formula: a woman who doesn't forget about Heinrich Heine the moment her beloved enters, loves only Heinrich Heine.

(( ))

"Beloved" is theatrical, "lover" is frank, "friend" is vague. We are not a loving country!

(( ))

Old men and old women. A shaved, slender old man is always a little bit antique, always a little bit the marquis. And his attention is more flattering to me, stirs me more than the love of any twenty-year-old. To exaggerate: there's the feeling that an entire century loves me. There's nostalgia for his twenties, and joy for one's own, and the opportunity of being generous—and the utter inopportuneness of it. Béranger has a little song:

. . . Your glance is keen
But you're twelve
And I'm twice eighteen.

Sixteen and sixty is not monstrous, and most important—it's not at all ridiculous. At any rate, it's less ridiculous than most so-called "equal" marriages. The possibility of a genuine pathos.

But an old woman in love with a young man is, at best—touching. The exception: actresses. And old actress—is the mummy of a rose.

《 》

. . . "And they had a game they played. He sings to her, 'Marusya, Marusya, close your eyes,' and her name really was Marusya — and she would lie down on the bed and cover herself with a sheet — like she were a corpse. He says to her: 'Marusya! Don't go and die on me all the way! Marusya! Don't die on me for real!' He cried tears every time. They worked at the same factory, she was fifteen, he was sixteen . . ."

(Nanny's story.)

《 》

"What a husband I had, my dears!!! Just looked human. Didn't eat anything, just drank. Drunk up my pillow, went and spent my blanket on the girls. Everything bored him, girls: work was boring, and drinking tea with me was boring. A handsome devil: curly hair, straight eyebrows, dark blue eyes . . . Gone five years now!"

(Nanny — to her girlfriends.)

《 》

The first sight of love is that very shortest distance between two points, that divine straight line, of which there's no second.

《 》

From a letter:
"If you were to enter the room now and say: 'I am leaving for a long time, forever' — or: 'I don't think I love you any more' — I would not, I believe, feel anything new: each time you leave, each hour that you are not here — you are not here forever and you do not love me."

《 》

In my feelings, as in a child's, there are no degrees.

《 》

A woman's first victory over a man is the man's tale of his love for another. But her final victory is the tale of the other woman about her love for him and his love for her. What was secret has become manifest, your love becomes mine. And until that happens, you can't sleep peace-fully.

Everything that is untold is unbroken. Thus, an unrepented murder, for instance — *endures.* The same goes for love.

You don't want people to know that you love a certain person? Then say: "I adore him!" But some people know what this means.

A story.
"When I was eighteen, a banker, a Jew, was madly in love with me. I was married, he was too. He was fat, but amazingly sweet. We were almost never alone, but when we happened to be, he would say only one word to me: 'Live, live!' And he never kissed my hands. Once he arranged an evening specially for me, he brought in wonderful dancers — I just loved to dance at the time! He himself couldn't dance because he was too fat. Usually he played cards at such gatherings. That evening he didn't play."

(The teller is thirty-six years old, charming.)

"Just live!" I dropped my hands.
On my hands I dropped a burning brow . . .
Thus the young Tempest listens to God
Somewhere in the field, at some dark hour.

And on the high crest of my breath, sudden,
Mighty, hands descend — as though from heaven.
And someone's lips descend on my lips.
Thus God — listens to the young Tempest.

(*Nachhall,* echo.)

The parlor is the field, yesterday's Smolny student — the Tempest, the fat banker — God. What survived? That one word, which the banker said to the student and God said to everything on the first day: "Live!"

"Be" — is the only word of love, human and divine. The rest: parlor, field, banker, school girl, are details.

What survived? Everything.

(( ))

It's better to lose someone *with your entire self* than to hold on to him with just a fraction of yourself.

Where does the commander go after victory, the poet after the poem — to a woman. Passion is man's last chance to express himself, just as the sky is the tempest's only chance of *being*.

A person is a tempest, passion is the sky, which dissolves it.

(( ))

O, poets, poets! The only true lovers of women!

(( ))

The desire to go deep: to the depths of the night, the depths of love. Love: a gap in time.

(( ))

In "one's own name" is love through life, "in your name" — through death.

(( ))

"An old lady . . . What am I going to do with an old lady?!" The delightful — in its frankness — formula of the masculine.

(( ))

"Why do old ladies dress up? It's pointless! I would order identical 'uniforms' for all of them, and since they're all rich, I would create a fund from which I'd dress — dress quite well, mind you! — all the young, beautiful women."

"Don't keep me from writing poems about you!"

"Keep me from writing poems about myself!"
In between is the entire gamut of the poet's love.

( )

A third person is always a diversion. At the beginning of love — from wealth, at the end of love — from poverty.

( )

The story of several encounters. A tightrope walk of feelings.

( )

A Junker's tale: . . . "I declare my love to her, and of course I start singing . . ."

( )

Sensual love and motherhood almost exclude each other. Genuine motherhood is manly.

( )

How many motherly kisses fall on unchildlike heads — and how many unmotherly ones — on children's heads!

( )

Passionate motherly love — misdirected.
There, where I should *think* (because of others) about an action, compose it, it is always incomplete — begun and not finished — unexplained — it isn't mine. I remembered A precisely and don't remember B — and right away, instead of B — my holy hieroglyphs!

( )

A conversation:
I, about a novel I would like to write: "You see, in the son I love the father, in the father — the son . . . If God grants me a century, I'll definitely write it!"
He, calmly: "If God grants you a century, you'll definitely do it."

◖◗

On the Song of Songs:

The Song of Songs affects me like an elephant: it's both frightening and ridiculous.

◖◗

The Song of Songs was written in a country where grapes are the size of cobblestones.

◖◗

The Song of Songs: the flora and fauna of all five parts of the world in one single woman. (Including undiscovered America.)

◖◗

The best thing in the Song of Songs is Akhmatova's poem:

And a red maple leaf was placed
In the Bible at the Song of Songs

"I could never love a dancer," he says; "I would always feel like a bird was fluttering in my arms."

◖◗

A widow who remarries. For a long time I sought the formula for this legitimation, which repulses me. And suddenly — in a French book, obviously a woman's (the author of *Amitié amoureuse* —) *my* formula:

"Le remariage est un adultère posthume."

— I breathed a sigh of relief!

Previously, everything that I loved was called — I, now it's — You. But it's the same thing.

There are lots of wives, few mistresses. A true wife results from a shortage (of love), a true mistress from an excess. I love neither wives nor mistresses — but "amoureuses." Like a musician — less music! And like a lover — less love!

◖◗

(NB! "Lover" both here and further on in the general, medieval sense of *"amant."* Avoiding the vernacular, I return to the word its original meaning. A lover: he who loves, he through whom love is manifested, the conductor of the element of Love. Perhaps in one bed, but perhaps — from thousands of versts away. Love not as a "bond," but as an element.)

(( ))

"There are two kinds of jealousy. One" (an attacking gesture) " — from the self; the other" (a blow to the chest) " — into the self. What is base about thrusting a knife into oneself?"

(Balmont)

(( ))

I should be drinking you from a mug, but I'm drinking you in drops, which make me cough.

(( ))

How slowly those people make friends with you! They advance millimeters where I advance — miles!

(( ))

A nighttime conversation.

Pavel Antokolsky: "The Lord had Judas. But who is the Devil's Judas?"

(( ))

I: "It would be a woman, of course. The Devil would fall in love with her, and she would want to return him to God — and she would."

Antokolsky: "And then she would shoot herself. But I maintain that it would be a man."

I: "A man? How could a man betray the Devil? He doesn't have any access to the Devil, the Devil doesn't need him, what does the Devil need from men? The Devil is a man himself. The Devil is manliness itself. The Devil can only be tempted by love, that is, by a woman."

Antokolsky: "And then a man would turn up who would attribute the honor of this victory to himself."

I: "And do you know how it would happen? The woman would fall in love with the Devil, and a man would fall in love with her. He would come to her and say: 'You love him, don't you feel sorry for him? After all, he's in a bad way, return him to God.' And she would return him."

Antokolsky: "And fall out of love with him."

I: "No, *she* won't fall out of love. *He* will stop loving her, because now he has God, and he doesn't need her any more. She wouldn't stop loving, but would run to the other one."

Antokolsky: "And gazing into his eyes, she'd see that they are the very same eyes, and that she herself has been conquered—by the Devil."

I: "But there was a moment when the Devil was conquered—the moment when he returned to God."

Antokolsky: "And he was betrayed—by a man."

I: "But I'm talking about a love drama!"

Antokolsky: "And I'm talking about the name that will be inscribed on the tablets."

(( ))

I: "Woman is possessed. Woman goes along the path of inhalation" (I breathe deeply). "Like that. And Heine missed it with his *horizontales Handwerk!* It's actually on the vertical!"

Antokolsky: "And man wants it to be like that." (The thrust of an arm. A jump.)

I: "Men don't do that, tigers do. By the way, if instead of 'man' the word were 'tiger,' I might love men. What an absurd word—*muzhchina!* It's so much better in German, *Mann,* and in French: *Homme. Man, homo* . . . No, all the other languages are better . . .

"But to go on. Thus, woman follows the path of breath . . . Woman is breath. Man is gesture. (The breath is always first, you don't breathe while you're jumping.) Men are never the first to desire. If a man desires, then a woman already desires."

Antokolsky: "And what will we do with tragic love? When a woman —really—doesn't desire?"

I: "That means that it wasn't she who desired, but another woman nearby. He mistook the door."

( )

I, timidly: "Antokolsky, can what we're doing now be called thought?"

Antokolsky, even more timidly: "It's a cosmic affair: like sitting on the clouds and ruling the world."

( )

I: "Two attitudes toward the world: a lover's and a mother's."

Antokolsky: "We have two also: a lover's and a son's. But there's no such thing as a father's. What is fatherhood?"

I: "Fatherhood doesn't exist. There is motherhood: Mary — Mother — a large M."

Antokolsky: "But fatherhood is a big O, that is, nought, zero."

I, conciliatorily: "But we don't have daughterliness."

We talk about love.

Antokolsky: "To love the Madonna is insurance against creditors. (The creditors are women.)"

We talk about Joan of Arc, and Antokolsky suddenly bursts out:

"But the king doesn't need his kingdom at all, he wants what is more than a kingdom — Joan herself. And you . . . And she doesn't need him: 'No, you should be King! Go to your kingdom!' — the way they say: 'Go to school!'"

( )

A saturated solution. Water *can't* dissolve more. Such is the law. You are a solution saturated with me.

I am not a bottomless vat.

( )

I must learn to approach a person's loving present the same as his loving past, that is — with the complete aloofness and passion of creativity.

The rival is always — either God (you pray!) — or a fool (you can't even despise).

《 》

Betrayal already points to love. You can't betray an acquaintance.

《 》

1918
The trial of Admiral Shchastny. The verdict is pronounced. The convicted man is led away. And, on leaving, half turning, into the crowd: "Will you come?"
A woman's: "Yes!"

《 》

I'm not a romantic heroine, I'll never merge with a lover, always — with love.

《 》

"Life can be divided into three periods: the intimation of love, the action of love, and the memory of love."
I: "And the middle lasts from the age of 5 to 75 — right?"

《 》

A letter:
Dear Friend! When I, in desperation from the destitution of days, suffocated by the everyday grind of my life and other people's stupidity, finally enter your house, all my being has the right to you. A person's right to bread may be disputed (the grandfather didn't work — so the grandson won't eat!) — but one can't dispute a person's right to air. My air — with people — is elation. Whence my hurt feelings.

You are hot, you're irritated, you're "worn out," someone calls, you approach (pick up the phone) lazily: "Oh, so it's you?" And the complaints about the heat, about your exhaustion, the admiration of your own laziness — "admire me, I'm so good!"

You're not interested in me, my soul, three days — an infinity (not for me — without you, for me — with myself), I must have dreamed a thousand and one dreams in three nights, but I dream them during the day as well!

(( ))

You say: "How can I love you? I don't even love myself." Love for me is included in your love for yourself. That which you call love, I call a favorable disposition of the soul (body). As soon as the least little thing goes wrong for you (problems at home, the heat, the Bolsheviks) — I no longer exist for you.

Home is all "problems," the heat — comes every summer, and the Bolsheviks are only beginning!

Dear friend, I don't want it that way, I don't breathe that way. I just want a humble, murderously simple thing: that a person be glad when I walk into the room.

(( ))

At this point, my friend, I fell asleep with pencil in hand. I had horrible dreams — I flew off high New York buildings. I woke up: the light is burning. The cat on my chest is arching like a camel. (When she was two, Alya would say: camhill.)

(( ))

To love — is to see a person as God intended him and his parents failed to make him.

To not love — is to see a person as his parents made him.

To fall out of love: is to see, instead of him, a table, a chair.

(( ))

Family . . . Yes, it's boring, yes, insufficient, yes, the heart doesn't pound. Wouldn't it be better to have a friend, a lover? But, on quarreling with my brother, I still have the right to say: "You must help me, because you're my brother . . . (son, father . . .)." And you can't say that to a lover — not for anything — you'd sooner cut out your tongue.

The right of intonation nesting in blood.

(( ))

Kinship by blood is coarse and strong, kinship by choice — is fine.
And what is fine can tear.

(( ))

My soul is hideously jealous: it wouldn't be able to abide me if I were
beautiful.

To speak of outward appearances in *my* case — doesn't make sense:
it's so obviously and entirely not the point!

"How do you like her looks?"

"But does she *want* her looks to be liked? I simply don't grant the
right — to such a value judgment!"

I am me: my hair is me, and my masculine hand with square fingers
is me, and my hook nose is me. And, more precisely: neither my hair,
nor my hand, nor my nose are me. I am me: invisible.

Honor the shell, made happy by God's breath.

And go: to love — other bodies!

(( ))

(If I were to publish these notes, they would inevitably say: *par
dépit*).

A letter about Lauzun:*

You want me to give you a short summary of my last love. I say
"love," because I don't know, I don't bother to know . . . (Perhaps: anything at all — but not love! But — any and everything!)

Thus: first of all — divinely handsome, secondly — a divine voice.
Both of these divinities — an acquired taste. But people with such tastes
are many: all men who don't love women, and all women who don't
love men.

He is receptive, both mentally and epidermally, this is his main, un-
doubtable essence. From chills to exaltation — a single step. He easily
becomes chilled. There is no other interlocutor and partner like him in
this world. He knows what you didn't say, and maybe wouldn't have
said . . . if he didn't already know it! Honoring only his own laziness,
without wanting to, he forces you to be whatever is convenient to him.
("The way he wants" doesn't apply — he wants nothing.)

*The hero of my play, *Fortuna*.

Kind? No. Affectionate? Yes.

For kindness is a primary feeling, and he lives exclusively by the secondary, the reflected. So, instead of goodness — affection, instead of love — disposition, instead of hate — retreat, instead of exaltation — admiration, instead of participation — sympathy. Instead of the *presence* of passion — *the absence* of impassivity (instead of the partiality of presence — the impassivity of absence).

But he is quite strong in everything secondary: pearls, the first violin.

"And in love?"

I don't know anything about this. My sharp ear tells me that the very word "love" somehow — grates on him. He is afraid of words in general, as he is generally afraid of everything — obvious. Ghosts don't like for others to incarnate them. They reserve that luxury for themselves.

"Love me however you like, but manifest it in a way that's convenient to me. And it's convenient to me that I know *nothing*."

Ill will? None at all. The delight and danger of him is his very profound innocence. You could die, and he wouldn't ask about you for months. And then, upset: "Oh, what a shame! If only I'd known, but I was so busy . . . I didn't know that one could die so quickly."

Knowing the universal, he of course doesn't know the everyday, and death on such and such a day, at such and such an hour is of course, everyday life. And the plague is everyday life.

But in place of everything he doesn't have, there is one thing: imagination. This is his heart, and soul, and mind, and gift. The root is clear: receptivity. Sensing what you see in him, he becomes that.

So: dandy, demon, spoiled child, archangel with a horn — he is everything that you like, only a thousand times more so. A toy that avenges itself. *Objet de luxe et d'art* — and woe to you if this *objet de luxe et d'art* becomes your daily bread!

"Innocence, innocence, innocence!"

Innocence in vanity, innocence in egotism, innocence in forgetfulness, innocence in helplessness . . .

There is, however, one vulnerable spot in this most innocent and invulnerable of criminals: a mad — only he'll never lose his mind! — love for his nanny. His entire humanity was used up once and for all with this.

The upshot — a nonentity as a human, and perfection as a being.

( )

Of all the temptations he offers me, I would single out the three most important: the temptation of weakness, the temptation of impassivity — and the temptation of what is Other.

Moscow, 1918–19

The Death of Stakhovich
From a Diary

Alya and I are at Antokolsky's.* It's Sunday. It's thawing. We've just come from the Church of Christ the Savior, where we heard the counterrevolutionary whisperings of pilgrims and of those — in little hats — in fur coats with "puffs" — thin and kind — not just women — not quite ladies, with whom one feels so right at cemeteries.

"They've ruined Russia" . . . "It's all in the Scriptures" . . . "Antichrist" . . .

The church is huge and dark. Up above there's a headspinning God. Little islands of candles.

(( ))

Antokolsky reads me his poetry — "Prologue to My Life," which I would call "The Justification of Everything." But since I can't do that, since at the moment I am Russian, I hold my tongue with a silence that is sharper and weightier than words. We say good-bye. Alya puts on her hood. The student V. appears in the door with a stony face.

"I've brought terrible news: Aleksei Aleksandrovich Stakhovich hanged himself yesterday."

(( ))

There was a double mist of incense and breath in the church (near Strastnoi Boulevard, I don't remember the name). I took off my mitten each time I crossed myself. The wax dripped, but my tears didn't.

I see hands — made of something else, not flesh — which have pre-

*A poet and student of the Vakhtangov studio.

served only the form of the living — an entrancing form! The same hands with which he grafted roses in the Crimea, and — when the roses were gone — made a noose of curtain ties. The head in the heavy magnificence of death. The eyelids like curtains: they're lowered, the end. If there is any suffering — then it's at the temples. The rest is at rest.

When I stand over the coffin, whether of someone close or distant, I invariably ask the question: "Who is next?" Will I stand over another's face this way? Whose? This thought resides in me like temptation. I know that the dead person knows. Not a question, but an interrogation. And the never-endingness of this answer . . .

One more thing: whoever the dead person is to me, rather: however little I may have been to him when he was alive, I know that at this particular hour (the hour of he who is done with hours), I am closer to him than anyone. Perhaps it's because, more than others, I am *on the edge,* I will (would) follow him more easily than all the others. That wall doesn't exist: living — dead, was — is. There is a double-edged trust: he knows that despite my body — I am; I know that he is — despite the coffin! A friendly compact, contract, conspiracy. He is simply a little older. And with every departing, a part of me, of my longing, of my soul, departs for *over there,* for the *beyond.* Overtaking me — it heads home. It's almost like: "Please give my regards to."

But, resurrecting with him, I also die with him. I can't cry over a coffin, because I am being buried, too! I pay for my hold on other worlds with a certain loss of my earthly presence. (Payment for transportation? After all, the shades paid Charon, didn't they? I send my shade ahead of me — and pay *here!*)

And one other thing: why are friends and relatives so unjealous of the coffin? They yield so easily — even those last inches. His seconds on this earth are running out and every inch is precious! I never exceed my rights, I leave the emptiness around the coffin unfilled — if not the family, then no one! — but with such bitterness, with such hurt for he who lies there. (The coffin: intersection of all human lonelinesses, the last and most extreme loneliness. Of all the hours — this is the hour when one should love close up. Actually stand *right over the soul.*)

Lord, if he were mine (that is, if I had the right!) how I would stand, and gaze, and kiss, how — when everyone is gone — I would talk with him — talk to him about such simple things — maybe about the weather — after all, he existed just recently! He still hasn't had time to *not exist!* How I would tell him the *earth* for the last time.

I know that his soul is nearby! No one ever heard anything with the ears.

( )

The church is crowded, I don't know anyone. I remember Stanislavsky's gray head and my thought: "He must be cold without his hat" — and a rush of tenderness for that gray head.

From the church they carried him to Kamergersky Lane. The crowd was enormous. All strangers. I walked, feeling half dead, dying with every step — from all the strangers around me, from him — alone — up ahead. The crowd was enormous. Automobiles had to turn off the road. I was a little proud of this (for him).

At Zubovskaya Square the crowd began to thin out. In the gradualness of this thinning it emerged that only young people were following him — the students of the II Studio — his *Green Ring*. Their singing was lovely.

By the time the streets became completely alien and I could no longer feel my body or my soul, V. L. M[chede]lov* came up to me. I was overjoyed to see him and immediately transferred a portion of my tenderness for Stakhovich to him. I felt — I ordered myself to feel — that he felt the same way I did, I instilled this in him, instilled with all my powers of autosuggestion — and if I have ever in my life experienced a feeling of fellowship, it was precisely at that hour, in the snows of Devichye Pole, following Stakhovich's coffin.

"I didn't tell you at the time. Do you remember? Last year you wrote me a letter with a few lines about him: something to do with white bones, white flour. I read it to him. It made an extraordinary impression. He followed me around for three days asking me to copy those lines down for him . . ."

I listen silently.

"Everyone really loved him, everyone came to see him during his ill-

*A director of the II Studio, now also deceased.

ness. Just a day before his death one of the students brought him a horse-meat cutlet. He stuck in his fork and said with a laugh: 'Maybe I'm eating my own horse' . . . He used to own horse farms you know. He loved horses with a passion."

"But how is it that all of these students, all these young men, all these young women? How is it they didn't manage . . ."

"To guess?"

"Didn't defend him from death?! After all, they have youth — love — power — in their hands!"

"Ah, Marina Ivanovna! Pity isn't love. Especially for an old man. Stakhovich hated pity. 'I'm a useless old man,' he'd say."

We move over to the sidewalk to smoke. My fingers can barely hold the cigarette. There was a thaw, now there's a blizzard.

"He didn't leave any note?"

"No, but on the day of his death when he was still in the theater, he came up to me and asked: 'Well, have you got a job?' 'No.' 'That's too bad. That's too bad.' And he squeezed my hands."

"Who's the small man who was crying so hard in church?"

"His valet. He used to work as a busboy in the cafeteria. The day before his death Stakhovich paid the man his salary a month in advance and gave him a bonus. He paid all his debts before his death."

We arrive at the cemetery. The divine whiteness of Devichy Monastery, the calming vault of the arch. (About this cemetery, one of my companions, a Jew, said in 1921: "It's worth dying to be buried here," and, after a pause: "maybe even worth being christened.") We walk to the grave. The students want to lower the coffin themselves, but the coffin, made in the Moscow Art Theater, is too wide (I think to myself with a chuckle: it's lordly!) and it won't fit. The grave diggers widen the hole. A nun, hurrying and stumbling, approaches the priest: "Father, can't we go faster? There's another body at the gates."

The snow drifts haven't been cleared, so I'm standing on Sapunov's grave, a little tormented by the fact that this, well, this is very un-Stakhovichian. I remember a lady in mourning dress. Large blue eyes, glassy with tears. As the coffin is lowered, she follows its trajectory with small, frequent crosses.

Later I find out — she's an actress whose mother and sister were killed in Kiev not long ago.

(( ))

The civil memorial service for Stakhovich (the Art Theater).

First comes Beethoven's funeral march.

Stakhovich and Beethoven. This is something to think about.

The first thing I feel — is the incongruity, the second — discomfort, as if from an indiscretion. What's wrong? Too grandiose . . . Too obvious. So?

Stakhovich — is the XVIII century, Beethoven — is outside (any century). What links these two names? Death. The accident of death. Because, for this one, Stakhovich, death is always an accident. Even if willful. Not a completion, but a break. Not an author's dash, but the censor's scissors cutting the poem. Stakhovich's death, brought on by the year 1919 and old age, doesn't correspond to Stakhovich's essence — the XVIII century and youth. Knowing how to die does not yet mean loving immortality. To know how to die means to be able to overcome dying — that is, once again: it's *to know how to live.* Moreover — and this time I'll say it in French (the language of formulas):

Pas de savoir-vivre sans savoir-mourir.

Savoir-mourir — what a Russian noun — is the opposite of *savoir-vivre.* I'm pleased to be the one to introduce it for the first time with the following formula:

Il n'y a pas que le savoir-vivre, il y a le savoir-mourir.

(( ))

But what about Beethoven and Stakhovich?

Ah! I think I understand. Stakhovich — is more XVIII century than Beethoven, who was born in it, just as Beethoven's funeral march is more death than Stakhovich, who lies in the coffin. The meaning of Stakhovich (of the XVIII century!) — is Life. And on the day of death, as on that of love: *"Point de lendemain!" All* of Stakhovich departs. Beethoven is that paradise which Stakhovich is meant to enter. There's a sort of double rudeness in Beethoven's funeral march, in relation to

Stakhovich: *acte de décès* (they don't perform it for the living) and *acte d'abdication* (he's through performing!)

Is it clear what I want to say?

Oh, Stakhovich himself would have understood me better than anyone!

(( ))

Stanislavsky's speech:

"My friend had three loves in his life: his family, the theater, and horses. Family life — is a secret, I'm not a connoisseur of horses . . . I'm going to talk about the theater."

He tells a story about how the handsome adjutant Stakhovich first appeared backstage at the Hunting Club,* in the grand princes' entourage. "The grand princes, as befit them, didn't stay long. The adjutant stayed on." — And the gradual — unpublicized — participation of the dashing guardsman in the productions — as an *arbiter elegantarum*. ("We'll have to ask Stakhovich," "that's not Stakhovich's way," "how would Stakhovich do it?") The trip to study the gentry and peasant life at Stakhovich's estate near Moscow. — "We were treated like tsars." — Stakhovich's gentleness. "If someone in the group got sick, who stayed with the patient in the stifling Moscow heat? The dashing, worldly guardsman was instantly transformed into the most attentive nanny." The story of how Stakhovich, breaking away from a court ball, flew over to the Art Theater for five minutes in order to bark like a dog into a gramophone horn for a production of *The Cherry Orchard*.

(( ))

The wrong people are saying things the wrong way. Stanislavsky — too simply (I would even say — simple-mindedly), reducing all of Stakhovich to the quotidian: first the court-military quotidian, then the theatrical, and what's worst of all — the Art Theater quotidian: that is, to the embodiment of the everyday — missing the element of rebellion that pushed the courtier to the stage, naively confusing the hold that the bold word "Khudozhestvenniki" had over Stakhovich with attraction

---

*The first location of the Art Theater. (M.Ts.)

to the Art Theater as such, forgetting both the background and tone of that stifling epoch, forgetting *whence* and remembering only — *where*.

Rossi (in an article that someone else reads) boils the complex lyrico-cynical-stoical-epicurean essence of Stakhovich down to nests of Russian gentry and presents a feuilleton rather than a poem. Yuzhin — as a public figure accustomed to burying the same kind of people — for some incomprehensible reason recalls the sins of the nobility and places his emphasis on "the social usefulness of the Stakhoviches" (a lie! they are completely useless, like racehorses. Except for those people, like myself, who place their *bets* on them).

Everyone applies Stakhovich to something: to the theater, or to society, or to the nobility . . . No one stands apart: Stakhovich as a phenomenon.

Best of them all — upset, bold, not a single superfluous word — is the actor's studio student Sudakov. One sentence is completely mine:

"And the best lesson in *bon ton, maintien, tenue,* that Stakhovich gave us was on the 11th of March 1919." (February 27–March 11, the day of his death.)

(()

I listen, listen, listen. My head sinks lower and lower, I understand the fatal mistake of this winter, every word is a knife, the knife goes deeper and deeper, I don't allow myself to feel it fully — oh, it doesn't matter — after all, I *too* will die!

And I'll talk about one more thing that no one else mentions, but everyone knows (?): Stakhovich and Love, about the lovefulness of this *causeur,* about his meaninglessness outside of love.

And I'll talk about one more thing that no one knows: if I had gone to see Stakhovich at Christmas 1918, as I wanted to, he wouldn't have died.

And I would have come alive.

(()

They wouldn't let me read any poems to him at the memorial. Kameneva and someone else were there. Nemirovich-Danchenko simmered and hesitated: on the one hand — "a performance," on the other — the cameras.

You didn't greet the rabble with bread and salt,
And in the black kingdom of 'labor's blisters'
Your hands crossed, exquisite to a fault,
In noble boredom.

"Now, if we could just drop this bit . . ."
"You can't, it's the most important part." But I didn't insist: Stakhovich wasn't in the room.

I copied this poem out for his lovely sister — the only person who needed it. Performing for me is always an overcoming; given my distaste for spectacle and society, this is natural. Not timidity: a certain uncertain alienation: stranger hear.*

. . . In the black kingdom of "labor's blisters."

I'm not talking about blisters caused by work, but about the imposed blisters of equality that have blistered our eyes and ring incessantly in our ears. That's why I put it in quotation marks.

MY ENCOUNTER WITH STAKHOVICH

The only one. A year ago. We were introduced by V. L. Mchedelov, whom I've known for a long time, but became friendly with only last winter. I always liked in him, a man of the theater, that penchant for other worlds: in the man of the spectacle — the passion for the unseen. I forgave him the theater.† I saw his production of *A Studio Diary* (an excerpt from Leskov, *The Story of Lieutenant Ergunov* and *White Nights*) three or four times I liked it so much! I remember a tear in the eye of the sleeping lieutenant in *Lieutenant Ergunov*. A large, sleepy one. It ran and froze. It burned and cooled off. He resembled a man wounded in battle. Resembled the whole White Army. Perhaps that's why I went to see it.

And the room — a slum! — a den where a Persian girl flatters the lieutenant! Eyes in the corners, knots in the corners. Those worn-out shoes,

---

*In English in the text. Tsvetaeva apparently meant "I'm a stranger here" [translator].

†The following on the theater, I pass over, since it's already been published. (M.Ts.)

rubble, rubbish. It was a room whose center was — a shoe. That shoe in the middle of the floor; the royal — in its dispassionateness — gesture of a foot flying up to the ceiling! The absence of common sense in that room! The absence of a room in that room! My Boris and Gleb St. life, live as the day! My furnishings. My housecleaning. All my seven rooms in one. The skeleton of my everyday life. My home.

I remember the Persian girl (a little devil): whisperings. Whispering — babbling — muttering. *Around and about* words. Mumbling chanting, clinking, clanking. Amulets — bracelets. Under the bracelets — the lieutenant's epaulets. Babbling — and beads, nightingale rumblings — and hands. Hands, streams.

(( ))

Then he took me to see Stakhovich's *Green Ring*. I won't judge the play. The voice — was that of a great enchanter. The only instance when I don't believe my ears. (The theater.) You don't always have time to translate the sentence from the voice into meaning — to make sense of it, to understand what has been pronounced: you swim with the voice. The voice — and feeling in response, exist outside the intervals of words. Theater doesn't need words, they aren't important — the actor slides over the words. (Further proof that Heine was right.) A meaningless a-a-a-a, o-o-o-o can turn a whole crowd to ashes, can bring on fits. Just as — if the voice is unsound — there's no helping either Shakespeare or Racine. (The voice here is meant not only as the throat, but as reason.) How this vocal reason can exist in the range of idiocy which the singer often represents — is another question, which could take us far away. Maybe — a good teacher, perhaps — simply the meddling of the gods. (No less than poets and women, the gods are tempted by unworthy vessels.) In short, to finish with the voice:

I — am a miracle: neither good nor evil.

And so, to finish with the play — I really don't know, I was listening to Stakhovich.

(( ))

Stakhovich: velvet and grandeur. No corners. The vocal and plastic line is unbroken. I'm talking about what the five senses perceive. Spiritually — a bit haughty. It isn't at all important that this fits the play. It's as clear as a mirror that he's playing himself. "My dear children" he says not to his partners — but to all of us, to the whole audience, the whole generation. "My dear children" should be read as: "I'm tired, I know everything that you'll say, all the dreams that you have yet to dream I already saw a millennium ago. And nonetheless, despite my exhaustion, I'll hear you out: both the confessions and rebukes. Tolerance — isn't it the lesser of Petronius's virtues? Moreover, like all aging people, I am an insomniac. Won't your prattling serve me as that very petal-strewn stream in which, finally, the eyelids of my happier confrère closed shut?"

(( ))

Was this what the author wanted? It's unlikely. In this way, with the magic of essence and voice, a very local image (of the Russian gentleman), extremely class-based (very much of the gentry) and very temporal (fin du siècle of the last century) was transformed into something atemporal and universal — eternal.

The image of the past gazing into the future.

(( ))

After the play V. L. M-lov took me to meet him — somewhere down below. I remember green and steam: furniture and tea. Stakhovich rose to greet us. Very tall (I belong to one of those tribes that sees its gods as giants!) — a lithe uprightness; the color of the suit, eyes, hair — something between steel and ashes. I remember the eyelids, the heavy breed that rarely open wide. Eyelids that are naturally haughty. An aquiline nose. An impeccable oval.

M-lov's accompanying flattering words; I, forcing myself to look directly:

"I'm enchanted, but you already know that. It's enough for you to listen to yourself. I hate the theater, but I adore enchantments. Today I'm very happy. That's all."

They both laugh. I laugh too. And, to disperse, no — to cloud — the directness of what was said and heard — as if sweeping it away with a tail! — I light a cigarette. Then — Stakhovich will forgive me for recall-

ing one of the more charming slips of the tongue I've heard in my life! —
came his frightened exclamation:

"But why burn your hair?! You have so little anyway!"

I, righteously indignant:

"Little? Hair?"

"I meant to say — it's so short."

We laugh again. Laughter, in the first moments, is the best connection. Laughter and a slight (someone else's) blunder. I sit down at the
table. While he pours the tea I admire his hand.

"I love your poetry. When we were in Kislovodsk, Kachalov received
a poem from you, unsigned . . ."

I, seething:

?!!

Stakhovich, putting out the flame a bit with his hand, says with a
smile: "A vain precaution, I assure you, for everyone recognized you immediately. Cupolas, bells . . . Magnificent poem. Both architectural,
and musical, and philological — marvelous. I immediately learned it by
heart and recited it at many soirees. Always with a success . . . (a slight
bow), which I attribute entirely to you."

I listen, astounded. I — sent poems to Kachalov?! Kachalov, who has
been spoiled rotten by shop ladies? I sent Kachalov — and unsigned?!
Unsigned?! Me?!!!

"I love poets' readings. Won't you read that poem for me?"

"But . . ."

And suddenly — hopelessness: Stakhovich loves this poem. Stakhovich is 60 years old, and he has overcome disgust for "contemporaneity."
Stakhovich insists on praising this poem. And it turns out that the
poem — isn't mine! The whole building collapses. And under the ruins
— there's Stakhovich!

So, revealing nothing, swallowing both the anonymity and someone
else's poems, as well as Kachalov — heroically:

"But I read so badly . . . Like all poets . . . I couldn't bring myself . . ."
(NB: I read well — like all poets — and I can always bring myself.)

"Such a Charlotte Corday? I would never have suspected you of
timidity!"

And I, relieved (Wordplay! Something at which I can't be beat):

"I thank you for the honor, but am I indeed in the presence of Marat?"

He laughs. We laugh. He asks again. I decline. I divert. What can I tell him? I don't know that poem. A tragic absurdity: here, where everything is "yes" — to begin with a refusal! Then, a sudden brainstorm:

"Perhaps you'd recite it for me yourself?"

He, embarrassed:

"I . . . I have forgotten it a bit, I'm afraid."

(I didn't write it, and he doesn't remember it ! "Go to the right — you lose the horse, to the left . . .")

And — making a precipitous and irreversible turn:

"If I were Vera Redlikh* I would turn the whole play upside down!"

"What do you mean?"

"You are on stage — the text is forgotten, the fiancé is forgotten . . ."

"Are you so forgetful?"

"No, it's you — who are unforgettable!"

Stakhovich to M-lov:

"O-o-o! I had no idea that poets were such a tribe of flatterers. That part usually fell on the poor heads of courtiers."

"Every poet — is a court poet: of *his own* king. Poets always have a weakness for greatness."

"As do kings — for flattery."

"Which I adore, since I do it not from hypocrisy, but for the pleasure of charming — the person I flatter. To flatter — is to be captivated. I know no other flattery. And you?"

(( ))

Then we parted — apparently captivated by one another. (About myself I can say for certain.) Then I wrote a letter to V. L. M-lov, which had nothing to do with the addressee except for the address. (From the date to the signature — it was about Stakhovich and for Stakhovich.) Then it was all forgotten.

(( ))

---

*An actress who in the play was in love with a high school student. (M.Ts.)

Two months ago I heard about his illness from Volodya Alekseev.*
He was sick, he was depressed. But we had only met once, just for an
hour! And — since he's ill — family, friends . . . You can't get close, and I
don't know how to push my way through. (They won't just up and part
for me.) The vision of someone else's home, someone else's everyday
life. The relatives, who will inspect me, since they've never seen me before . . . The well-dressed aspiring actresses — and me in these boots.

Also: for me, to visit (always, and especially now, in the Revolution),
for me to visit — means to bring something. What could I bring him?
My empty hands (never aristocratic, and now — not even human!), my
empty hands and overflowing heart? But the latter — because of the former (my embarrassment!) — he won't see. I'll torture myself for nothing
and waste his time.

But every time Volodya comes, I say plaintively: "Take me to see
Stakhovich!" For me, the attainability of the desired (whether things or
souls) is in reverse relation to its desirability: the more desired — the
more unattainable. In advance. As a matter of course. And I don't even
try to want. Stakhovich is living on Strastnoi Blvd., therefore — Strastnoi is not Strastnoi and even Stakhovich — is not Stakhovich. ("He'd be
surprised . . . He'd be angry . . ." He, Petronius!!)

In short, I didn't go.

(( ))

One more remark, at the funeral, from M-lov: "Why didn't you ever
visit him? He would have been so glad. He loved poetry, conversation,
loved to tell stories himself, only no one wanted to listen . . . And there
was a lot to listen to! He had an unusual life. So many encounters, travels . . . In his youth — the war . . . And such different circles: the court,
the military, the theater . . . And he liked you so much that time . . ."

(( ))

March 16, 1919.
I'm walking along the street. It's thawing a bit. Suddenly I have
the thought: "Moscow's first spring without Stakhovich . . ." (Not:

*An actor of Studio II, later a volunteer in the White Army, who went missing in
action in 1920. (M.Ts.)

"Stakhovich's first spring without Moscow" — that was exactly how the thought came to me.)

( )

March 19.
Every time I see a gray head on the street my heart clenches.

( )

I also forgot to say: Stakhovich had a marvelous voice once. He sang with some famous Italian.
The voice! The cruelest fascination for me!

( )

Yes, the waltz was lovely, languid.
Yes, it was a wonderful waltz.

He often sang that song, wonderfully. He'd finish — and invariably:

If I were young,
How I would love you!

"Aleksei Aleksandrovich! Aleksei Aleksandrovich! That's not in the ballad! You're making up your own song!"
"Yes it is, yes it is! And if it isn't — *se non è vero è ben trovato!*
And no one understood!

(Recounted by a student actress.)

Moscow, February–March 1919

On Gratitude
From a Diary, 1919

When five-year-old Mozart, running from the harpsichord, fell flat on the slippery parquet of the palace, and seven-year-old Marie-Antoinette was the only one who flew to him and helped him up, he said, "Celle-là — je l'épouserai," and when Marie-Thérèse asked him why — "Par reconnaissance."

And later, as Queen of France, how many others she helped up from the parquet, which was always slippery — for gamblers — for the ambitious — for those who burned the candle at both ends — and did anyone shout to her — *par reconnaissance* — "Vive la Reine!" — as she rode in her carriage to the block?

◖◗

Reconnaissance — recognition. To recognize — despite all the masks and wrinkles — right away, the true face once beheld.

(Gratitude)

◖◗

I am never grateful to people for deeds — *only* for essences! The bread given to me could turn out to be an accident; a dream dreamed about me is always essence.

◖◗

I take as I give: blindly, as indifferent to the giving hand as to my own, receiving.

◖◗

A person gives me bread. What is the first thing to do? Return the gift. Repay the gift so as not to give thanks. Gratitude: a giving of the self for some good, that is: bought love.

(( ))

I respect people too much to insult them with bought love.

(( ))

Insulting to me, therefore insulting to others as well.

(( ))

Goodwill directed at me has never predetermined anything. The individuality of a gift (its directedness *at me*), in my understanding of a gift, does not exist. I am not grateful for myself or for my neighbor, I am merely grateful.

(( ))

You can't buy me. That's the essence of it. You can buy me only with essence (that is — buy my essence!). With bread you can buy: hypocrisy, pseudo-enthusiasm, courtesy — you can buy all my froth, though it may be only scum.

To buy — is to pay off. You can't pay me off.

(( ))

I can be bought — but only by all the heaven inside of you! By that heaven in which there may not even be room for me.

(( ))

I am impersonally grateful, that is, only when I myself can take something, regardless of the other's goodwill, and without his knowledge.

(( ))

A relationship is not a value judgment. I am tired of repeating this. From your giving me bread, I have perhaps become kinder, but you have not become more sublime.

◖◗

A deed is not a relationship, a relationship is not a value judgment, a value judgment (on the part of a critic, regarding Blok, for example) is not the essence (Blok).

Essence is intent, audible only to the ear.

◖◗

A piece of bread from a despicable person. A bit of luck. Nothing more.

◖◗

I eat your bread and I abuse you. Yes. Only selfishness is grateful. Only selfishness measures the whole (essence) by the pieces it is given. Only childish blindness, looking at the hand, affirms, "He gave me sugar, he is good." Sugar is good, yes. But to judge the essence of a person by sugar and tips received from him is forgivable only in children and servants. Instinct can be forgiven. Yes, but that's not right either: we often observe that dogs prefer the master who gives them nothing to the cook who feeds them.

To identify the source of a good with the good (the cook with the meat, uncle with sugar, a guest with tips) is an indication of the complete underdevelopment of soul and mind. A creature that has gone no further than its five senses.

The dog that loves because it is looked at is above the cat that loves because it is petted, and the cat, loving because it is petted, is above the child who loves because it is fed. It's all a matter of degree.

Thus, from the simplest love because of sugar — to love because of caresses — to love upon sight — to unseeing love (at a distance)* — to love, in spite (of nonlove), from a little love *because of* — to the great love *outside* (of me) — from receiving love (by another's will) to love that takes (regardless of that will, unbeknownst, against that will!) — to *love itself.*

◖◗

*All of me — comes from this.

The less we value superficial goods, the more easily we give and take them, and the less grateful we are for them.

(())

(Practically speaking: I allow only silent gratitude for bread (a donation). In obvious gratitude — there is something that shames the giver, a sort of reproach.)

(())

To find joy in the bread — that is the best gratitude! Gratitude that ends when the last bite has been swallowed.

(())

Can it really be that this detail, this trifle, this implication (for me) — to give — must inevitably grow into some sort of mountain, all due to the words: *to me?*

After all, I know how it's given — blindly! And could I actually stand being thanked for bread? (I can't stand being thanked for poetry — so there you have it!) Bread — is it really me?! Verse (the accidental gift of song) — is it really me?

I am unique under this heaven. Walk away and give thanks.

(())

I don't want to think basely of people. When I give bread to a person, I give to a hungry person, that is, to the stomach, not to him. His soul doesn't have anything to do with it. I can give to anyone — and it isn't me who gives: anyone would. Bread gives itself away. And I don't want to believe that anyone, in giving to my stomach, would demand something in return from my soul.

(())

But it isn't the stomach that gives — it's the soul! No — the hand. These gifts are not personal. It would be strange to prefer one stomach to another, and if a preference is to be made — then the hungrier one. Today mine (yours) is the hungrier. I am not responsible for this.

(( ))

Thus, having established the giver (the hand) and the receiver (the stomach), it is strange to expect one piece of meat to be grateful to another piece of meat.

(( ))

Souls are grateful, but souls are grateful exclusively for souls. Thank you — for being. Everything else, whether from me to another person or vice versa, is an insult.

(( ))

To give — this is not our sphere of activity! Not our personality! Not passion! Not choice! It is something that belongs to everyone (bread): therefore (I don't have any) it has been taken from me, and returns (through you) to me (through me to you).

To give bread to a poor man is a reinstatement of rights.

If we give to whom *we* want, we would be the most thorough scoundrels. We give to the one *who wants*. His hunger (will!) elicits our gesture (bread). Given and forgotten. Taken and forgotten. No strings, no kinship. Having given, I refuse to acknowledge. Having taken, I refuse to acknowledge.

Without consequences.

(( ))

"So why should I give you anything?"
"So as not to be a bastard."

(( ))

I remember when I was in high school — in the church courtyard — a beggar. "Give a little something, for the sake of Christ!" I walk by. "Please give, for the sake of Christ!" I keep on walking. Running up to me, he said, "If not for God's sake — then for the Devil's if you like!"

Why did I give to him? He was indignant.

(( ))

Bread. A gesture. Give. Take. There won't be any of this *there*. Therefore, everything arising from giving and taking is a lie. Bread itself is a lie. Nothing built on bread will survive (what is mixed with yeast — won't rise).

The leaven of our bread-senses will inevitably fall in the cold of immortality. It's not worth kneading it.

( )

To take is shameful, no, to give is shameful. If the taker takes, it means he doesn't have anything: since the giver gives, he clearly has. And so this is a confrontation of have and have not.

One should give on one's knees, the way beggars beg.

( )

Fortunately, only beggars are awarded with the shame of donation. (The delicacy of their gift!) The rich limit themselves to a brief delay in paying a doctor's fee.

( )

Gratitude: from admiration to being bowled over.

I can admire only the hand that gives away its last; therefore I could never be grateful to the rich.

And if I could be, then only for their timidity, their guiltiness, which immediately makes them innocent.

( )

When a poor man gives, he says, "Forgive me for giving so little."

The embarrassment of the poor — "I can't do any more." When a rich man gives, he doesn't say anything. The embarrassment of the rich — "I don't want to give more."

( )

To give is so much easier than to receive — and so much easier than *to be.*

( )

The rich buy off. Oh, the rich are terribly afraid — if not of the Revolution, then of the Last Judgment. I know a mother who buys milk for another child (a sick child) only to ensure that her own (healthy) child won't die. A rich mother, saving another's child from death (actual death), buys off her own from a possible death. ("To entreat Fate!")

I look into the source of the act — its intent. The rich mother's milk will flow with tar at the Last Judgment.

( )

Charity: Polycrates' ring.

( )

The beggar's gift (the life's blood, the last gift!) is impersonal. "God gives." The rich man's gift (surplus, almost refuse) has a name, patronymic, surname, position, calling, family, day, hour, date. And — a memory. The right hand gives, but both hands remember.

( )

The beggar, giving from hand to hand, forgets. The rich man, sending the gift out with a servant, remembers. If you think about it carefully, it's understandable: some self-justifying evidence for the Last Judgment.

— Problematic evidence.

Moscow, July 1919

Excerpts from the Book *Earthly Signs*

The mysterious tedium of great works of art — even of their names: the *Venus de Milo,* the *Sistine Madonna,* the Coliseum, the *Divine Comedy.* (Music is the exception. The *Ninth Symphony* — now that always raises the spirits!)

(( ))

It's as though the tedium of all their readers, admirers, patrons, interpreters, fell on them like a ton of bricks.

And the mysterious attraction of world-famous names: Helen, Roland, Caesar (including the creators of the above-mentioned creations, if their names have reached us).

(( ))

This applies to the sound of their names, to my aural perception. Regarding essences — the following:

I definitely prefer the Creator to the Creation. Let's take the Joconda and Leonardo. The Joconda is an absolute, Leonardo, who gave us the Joconda — is a great question mark. But perhaps Joconda is in fact the answer to Leonardo? Yes, but not an exhaustive one. Beyond the limits of the creation (of what is manifested!) there is still an entire abyss — the Creator: all the creative Chaos, the whole sky, the whole depths, all the tomorrows, all the stars — everything broken off here by earthly death.

Thus the absolute (the creation) transforms itself for me into relativity: landmarks on the way to the Creator.

"But that's the destruction of art!"

"Yes. Art is not the goal: it's a bridge, not the goal."

(( ))

The work of art answers, a living fate asks (the longing of he who was born, to be embodied in art!). The work of art, as something complete, commands; a living fate, as something incomplete, requests. If you want *the absolute,* go to the de Milo — Venus, to the Sistine — Madonna, to Leonardo's Smile; if you want to give the absolute (to answer!), go to plain — Aphrodite, plain — Mary, a plain — Smile: skirting interpretation — to the original source, that is, do what the creators of these creations, known or unknown, have done.

( )

You won't detract from Goethe, or Leonardo, or Dante that way. Your muteness before them — is your tribute to them. How can you respond to an exhaustive answer? You keep your mouth shut.

But if you were born in the world to give answers, don't freeze in blissful nonbeing, that's not the way Goethe, Leonardo and Dante created, and in creating, that's not what they wanted. To be overturned — yes, but to know how to get up again as well: falling down to break away, losing the way — to resurrect.

Genuflect — and walk on by: into the unborn, uncreated and yearning world.

( )

In this *repelling* force lies the primary strength of great works of art. The absolute repels — to the creation of other absolutes! In this lies their efficacy and eternal life.

( )

But between the Joconda (the absolute interpretation of a Smile) and myself (consciousness of this absoluteness) there is not only my muteness — there are also the billions of interpreters of this interpretation, all the books written on Joconda, the entire five-century-long experience of eyes and heads striving to grasp her.

There's nothing for me to do here.

Absolute, complete, perfect, interpreted, endlessly admired.

The only thing one can do faced with the Joconda — is to *stop being.*

《 》

"But Joconda's smile asks a question!" To this I would answer: "Her smile's question — is its own answer." The inevitability of the question is in fact the absolute of the answer. The essence of the smile — is a question. The question is given in continuousness, therefore what is given is the essence of a smile, its answer, its absolute.

It's pointless for scholars, artists, poets and tsars to interpret the Smile (Joconda). What has been given is Mystery, mystery as essence and essence as mystery. The gift is Mystery in itself.

《 》

To love — is to see a person as God intended him and his parents failed to make him.

To not love — is to see instead of him: a table, a chair.

《 》

A daughter whose father has been killed — is an orphan. A wife whose husband has been killed is a widow. But a mother whose son has been killed?

《 》

I always cross myself when I cross a river. Without even thinking. I wonder whether there is such a folk superstition. If not, then — there once was.

《 》

Kinship by blood is coarse and strong, kinship by choice — is fine. And what is fine can tear.

《 》

"I won't leave you!" Only God can say this — or a man with milk in Moscow, winter 1918.

《 》

The Theater and I:

I am one of those viewers who tears Judas to pieces when the mystery play is over.

The whole secret is to have been able to see things a hundred years ago as they are today, and today to see them as they were a hundred years ago.

(The destruction . . . I wanted to write: of space. No, of time. But you can't conceive of "time" other than as: distance. And "distance" — immediately gives you versts, mileposts. Therefore: versts are spatial years, just as a year — is a temporal verst.

One way or the other, you have to transpose years and versts.

( )

A verst: leading away! How much better this is than "outgoing" (I won't say anything about "entering": I came in — and I stayed!)

( )

Love — as a conspiracy:

Zur rechten Zeit,
Am rechten Ort,
Der rechte Mann —
Das rechte Wort.

And the main thing — *Wort! Zeit, Ort, Mann* — I yield.

( )

When I leave a city, it always seems to me that the city ends, ceases to be. Thus about Freiburg, for example, where I was a girl. Someone is talking: "In 1912, when I was traveling through Freiburg . . . " My first thought: "Really?" (That is, does Freiburg really continue to exist?) This isn't self-importance; I know that I am nothing in the life of cities. This isn't: *without me?* but: *on its own?!* (That is: it really exists, outside of my vision, I didn't invent it all?)

When I leave a person, it always seems to me that he ends, ceases to be. Thus about Z, for example. Someone is talking: "In 1917, when I ran into Z" . . . My first thought: "Really?" (That is: Z really continues to exist?) This isn't self-importance; I know that in the lives of people I am nothing . . .

(( ))

"Ends, ceases to be." Here one should distinguish two situations. The first:

People and cities that have been strongly inhabited (enlivened? exploited?) by me disappear irrevocably: as if they'd plunged into the abyss. Not sonorous Kitezhes — but sunken Herculaneums.

Cities and people who have only served as fleeting playthings for me — freeze: in the same place, with the same face. Stereoscope.

When I hear about the former, I'm surprised: Is it really *still standing?* When I hear about the latter, I'm surprised: is he really *growing?*

I repeat, this isn't self-importance; this is a profound, innocent, sometimes joyous amazement. I listen, I ask questions, I participate, sympathize . . . and, secretly: "It's not really Freiburg. Not the same Freiburg. A mask of Freiburg. A deception. An impersonation."

(( ))

You have to lock many things with a key in the Revolution: everything except your trunks! And, locking up, throw the key. . . . but there's no sea deep enough!

No, locking up, silently and bravely present the key — to God.

I pronounce God like a drowning man: with a sigh. A murky feeling: God shouldn't be bothered (know) when you can do it yourself. And the "can do it yourself" grows every day . . .

Mandelstam has a wonderful (adolescent) poem about this:

. . . Lord Almighty! — I said by mistake,
Without thinking to say it at all . . .

and, further:

God's name, like a great bird,
Flew out of my chest . . .

Inadvertently. But I would never dare to call myself a believer, and this — a prayer.

(( ))

What in life have I not promulgated at the expense of what! Photography at the expense of the portrait, serfdom at the expense of the law in general, cabbage at the expense of the rose, Martha at the expense of Mary, Old Believers at the expense of Peter . . . The very opposite of myself — at my own expense!

And not from a sense of sport (I don't have one!), not for argument's sake (I suffer!) — from pure justice: the underdog is always right.

And another thing: from the complete incapacity for co-mmiseration (co-thought, co-love) with hypocrites who in secret indisputably prefer: photography to the portrait, serfdom to just the law, the cabbage to the rose, Martha to Mary, and long-beards to Peter!

(( ))

But there is another mystery: when a thing has been hurt it begins to be right. It gathers all its strength — and rights itself, gathers all its rights to exist — and stands.

(NB! The effectiveness of persecuted ideas and people!)

After all, there is no completely definitive lie, every lie does have at least one ray directed — at the truth. And the whole truth goes along this ray. Guilt detected and punished becomes misfortune; responsibility falls on the judges' heads. The criminal, convicted here, is pure before God. But there is another mystery, and the most frightening one, perhaps: the infectiousness of punished ailments, the heredity of guilt. The criminal whom we forcibly rid of a disease gives the disease to us. Every judge and executioner — is an heir.

In this there is also a certain blood will. Earthly blood must flow. The criminal doesn't exist, the nearest relative is the executioner (or the judge, it doesn't matter!) Blood the criminal has not yet spilt cries out to the executioner: spill me! The moment of the execution — is a moment of union. The first splattered drop of the criminal's blood is an initiation into ownership — and obligation.

There are marriages more mysterious than that of husband and wife.

(( ))

(The mysterious correspondence: altar, execution block; ax, cross; the people, the chorus; the judge, the priest; the executioner and the victim — all betrothed: instead of an unseen God — an unseen Devil. A Devil's wedding the other way around, with the same immutability of the unspoken vow.

(( ))

Not a single truth (from the kingdom Over There) can help but become a lie in the kingdom of Here. Not a single lie (from the kingdom Here) can help but become the truth in the kingdom Over There.

Truth — is a turncoat.

(( ))

In the Commissariat:

I, innocently: "Is it difficult — to be an instructor?"

My comrades at the Commissariat, an Estonian woman, a communist: "Oh, it's not hard at all! You just stand up on the trash can — and you scream, scream, scream . . ."

(( ))

The bourgeoisie was forbidden to use horsepower for removing snow from the streets. So the bourgeoisie, without a second thought, hired itself a camel, and the camel hauled the snow. And the soldiers laughed in sympathy: "Good for them! They got around that decree!"

(I saw it with my own eyes on the Arbat.)

(( ))

O thee, sole dish
Of the Communist nation!

(A poem about dried fish in the newspaper *Always Onward!*)

(( ))

Theater people hate the way I read my poems: "You ruin them!" They don't understand, these peddlers of stanzas and emotions, that the job of the poet and the actor is different. The poet's job: having opened

—to hide. The voice for him is armor, a mask. Unsheltered by the voice—he is naked. The poet always covers his tracks. The poet's voice —like water—puts out the fire (the line). The poet *cannot* declaim: it's shameful and insulting. The poet—is solitary, the stage boards for him—are a pillory. To present your poems with the voice (the most perfect of conductors!), to use *Psyche* for *success?!* The great negotiation of writing them down and publishing them is enough for me!

"I am not the impresario of my own shame!"

An actor is something else. An actor—is secondary. As much as the poet—is *être,* so is the actor—*paraître.* The actor is a vampire, the actor is ivy, the actor is a polyp. Say what you like: I will never believe that Ivan Ivanovich (and they are all—Ivan Ivanoviches!) can summon the will to feel himself Hamlet each evening. The poet is imprisoned by Psyche; the actor wants to imprison Psyche. Finally, the poet—is a goal unto himself, rests in himself (in Psyche). If you put him on an island— will he stop *being?* But what a pitiful spectacle: an island—and an actor!

An actor—is for others, unthinkable without others, an actor—is because of others. The last applause—is the last beat of his heart.

The actor's job—lasts merely an hour. He must hurry. And primarily, he must use: his own, another's—it doesn't matter! Shakespeare's verse, his own powerful thigh—everything goes into the pot! And you propose that I, a poet, drink my fill of this dubious swill? (I'm not talking about myself nor for myself: for Psyche!)

No, gentlemen of the stage, our domains—are different. We want— an island without beasts, you—beasts without the island. And it's no accident that in former times you were buried beyond the churchyard gates!

(( ))

(An exception for: singers enslaved by the element of voice, who dissolve into it, for actresses, that is: for women: that is for those who naturally play themselves, and for all those who, on reading me, *have understood* and *arrived.*)

(( ))

All of this, and undoubtedly this and nothing else, was already said by the Jew for whom I would give away and betray all Russians, specifically: Heinrich Heine — in the following restrained note:

"The theater is not salutary for the poet, and the Poet is not salutary for the Theater."

(( ))

The mastery of conversation is in being able to hide from your partner his poverty. Genius — is to force him, *at this very* moment, *to be* Croesus.

(( ))

Moscow now looks on trams with distrust, like some resurrected Lazarus. (And, instantly forgetting both Moscow and the tram: but Lazarus's distrust of the world — is more frightening!)

(( ))

Lazarus: eyes glazed forever. Lazarus — glassy eyes — *Glas* . . . And also *glas des morts* . . . (Could it really be from this?)

(( ))

"Resurrect him because we're bored without him!" — is the same as saying: "Wake him up, because we can't sleep without him . . ." Is that really a reason? Oh, what a dead, carnal, monstrous miracle! What a violation of Lazarus and what a violation — the most horrible one — of oneself!

Lazarus, returning *from over there:* a dead man to the living, and Orpheus, descending *down there* : a live being — to the dead . . . a gaping ditch and the Elysian fields. Ah, I see! Lazarus could only bring back decay *from there:* the spirit resurrecting into Life doesn't "resurrect" itself in life. Orpheus departed life — into Life. At no one's command: through his own desire.

(Perhaps it's just a burial custom? There — you have the urn, here — the mausoleum. In Hades Orpheus was approached by a ghost made of ashes revived. Mary and Martha — by a corpse.)

(◖)

How sorry I feel for Christ! How I pity him for his forced miracles! Christ, who came to move mountains — with a word! "Prove it, then we'll believe!" — "We believe, but confirm it for us!" There is a strange echo between the miracle at Cana (at Mary's request) and Thomas's probing finger. If Mary had been more sharp sighted, after the changing of the water into wine she would have seen another transformation: of the wine — into blood . . .

I am certain that John did not ask Christ for miracles.

(◖)

In the Commissariat: (the 3 M's).

"Well, how did you get the potatoes home?"

"It was all right, my old man met me."

"You know, you mix potatoes and meal, 2/3 potatoes, 1/3 meal."

"Really? I'll have to tell my mother."

I have neither: mother, nor man, nor meal.

(◖)

"Prague Cafeteria" on the corner of Nikolo-Peskovsky and the Arbat. I remember that during the war there was a bust of Bonaparte. The February Revolution replaced it with Kerensky. Ah, about Kerensky! I have a souvenir: a little turquoise cardboard book with gold trim; you open it wide: on the left there's a broken mirror, on the right — Kerensky. Kerensky, night and day staring into the smithereens of his hopes. I got this reliquary from nanny Nadya, in exchange for a real mirror, a whole one, without the Dictator.

To go back to the cafeteria: October replaced Kerensky with Trotsky. Trotsky's terrifying mug gazes at chomping children. And with Marx, who, preoccupied with Trotsky, isn't looking at the children. The famous and questionable soup, by the way, children splash into the bowl of the St. Bernard, *Mars,* who keeps guard at the doors from 12 to 2. Occasionally some ends up in the bowls of beggar women as well: Mars isn't jealous.

(◖)

It's vulgar to be hungry when someone else is full. Propriety is stronger in me than hunger — even than the hunger of my children.

"Well, how are things going, do you have everything?"

"Yes, thank God, so far so good."

Who does one have to be in order to disappoint, embarrass and destroy a person with a negative answer?

"Just a mother."

(( ))

(Now, in 1923, I would put the question differently:

Who did one have to be, in 1919, in Moscow, knowing me, seeing my children — to ask such a question?!

Just "an acquaintance.")

(A second note:

It's not lack of propriety — but sensitivity to intonation! The question dictates the answer. To "I have nothing" the best you would get would be: "Oh, that's a shame!"

He who gives doesn't ask.)

(( ))

My cruel-hearted friends! If, instead of offering me cookies with tea, you would simply give me a piece of bread for tomorrow morning . . .

But I myself am to blame, I laugh too much when I'm with other people.

Besides, when you leave the room, I steal the bread from you.

(( ))

My little thefts in the Commissariat: two marvelous checkered notebooks (yellow, shiny), a whole box of quill pens, bottles of English red inks. I'm writing with them now.

(( ))

The crooked path leads to the well; the straight and narrow, right to hell.

(( ))

Lost in thought, instead of "Monplenbezh," I write: "Mon plaisir." (Mon plaisir — something like a little Versailles in the XVIII century.)

(( ))

My "I don't want to" is always: "I cannot." There's no arbitrariness in me. "I cannot" — and meek eyes.

(( ))

My "I can't" is a certain natural limit, not only my own "I can't" — but anyone's. In "I want" there is no limit, which is why there is none in "I don't want."

(( ))

I don't want — is arbitrary, I can't — is necessity. "Whatever my right leg feels like . . . , whatever my left leg can manage." There's none of this.

I can't is more sacred than I don't want. I can't contains all the overcome I don't wants, all the corrected attempts to want — it's the upshot.

(( ))

My "I can't" — is inability least of all. Moreover: it's my most important ability. It means that there's something in me that despite all my wantings (forcing of myself) nonetheless doesn't want, that in spite of my will which wants, directed against myself, doesn't want for my entire self; that is, there is (apart from my will!) — an "in me," a "mine," a "myself" — there is a "me" that exists.

(( ))

I don't want to serve in the Red Army. I can't serve in the Red Army. The first presupposes: "I could, but I don't want to!" The second: "I would like to, but I can't." What is more important: the inability to carry out a murder, or to not want to carry out murders? In inability — lies our whole nature, in not wanting — our conscious will. If what you value most in essence is will — "I don't want" is the strongest, of course. If what you value is the entire essence — of course it's : I cannot.

(( ))

The roots of I cannot are deeper than can be accounted for. I cannot grows from the same place as our I cans: all our gifts, all revelations, all our *Leistungen:* the hands, moving mountains: the eyes, lighting up the stars. From the depths of blood or the depths of the spirit.

(( ))

I am talking about a genuine I cannot, about a fatal I cannot, about an I cannot because of which you allow yourself to be torn to bits, about a *meek* I cannot.

(( ))

I insist: I cannot, and not I do not want to create heroes!

(( ))

Let my I don't want be — I cannot: let it be the greatest and last I don't want of an entire being. We will want the most monstrous things. Feet, stomp! Hands, grab! So that at the last minute: the feet are rooted to the ground, the ax — falls from the hands: I cannot!

(( ))

Let's start from wanting! Let's want everything! "I cannot" without trying all the "I wants" — is a pitiful inability, and, of course, will end with: I can.

(( ))

"But if I not only cannot (betray, for instance), what if I also don't want *to be able* (to betray)?"

But on genuine lips I don't want is in fact I cannot (not my will alone, but my entire essence doesn't want!); but on genuine lips I cannot is in fact I don't want (not my unconscious essence alone, but my will doesn't want as well!).

I cannot want this and I don't want to be able to.

— The Formula. —

(( ))

I cannot: 1) hold a worm in my hands, 2) not come to the defense (whether right or wrong, here or a hundred versts away, nowadays or 100 years in the future—it doesn't matter), 3) come to—my own defense, 4) love jointly.

(( ))

As soon as I start telling someone what I feel, the reply comes instantly: "But that's all rationalization!"

Feelings for most people are bareheaded furies, something that happens inside them, that comes tumbling down on their heads. Rather like an avalanche of stones that immediately turns them to mush!

in other words:

The precision of my feeling makes people take them as rationalizations.

(( ))

I am not in love with myself, I'm in love with this work: listening. If another person would let me listen to him as I let myself (gave himself to me as I myself give myself), I would listen to the other person in the same way.

With other people I am left with only one option: to guess.

(( ))

"Know thyself!"

I did this. And it makes it no easier to know others. On the contrary, as soon as I begin judging another person by myself, there's just one misunderstanding after another.

(( ))

I don't think, I listen. Then I seek the exact incarnation in words. It turns out to be the icy armor of formula, under which—there is only heart.

(( ))

I don't eavesdrop, I listen attentively. Just like a doctor does: the chest.

And so often: you tap—and there's no echo!

(( ))

There are people of a particular epoch and there are epochs incarnated in people. (Not Bonaparte is the XIX century; the XIX century — is Bonaparte!)

(( ))

On being and nonbeing in the beloved:
I never want to lay my head on the chest, always in the chest! Never — fall down before! Always fall into (the abyss.)

(( ))

"A living person" will never allow himself to be loved as the "dead" will. The living himself wants to be (to live, to love). It reminds me of childhood's eternal cry: "Myself! Myself!" And invariably — the leg goes in the sleeve, the hand in the boot.

It's the same way with love.

(( ))

I want to be destroyed in you, that is, I want to be you. But you are no longer in yourself; you are already entirely in me. I get lost in my own breast (in you). I cannot lose myself in your breast, because you aren't in there. But maybe I am there? (Reciprocal love. The souls have exchanged homes). No, I'm not there either. There's nothing there. I myself am not anywhere. There is my breast — and you. I love you with yourself.

Seizure? Yes. But better than barter.

(( ))

Well, and what about mutual love? (Barter.) Simultaneous and crisscrossing seizure (release). Two losses: X's soul in its own breast, where Z resides, and Z's soul — in its own breast, where X resides.

But since I'm living in you, I am not lost! But since you live in me, you are not lost! This is being in the beloved, this "I in you and you in me," this is still *I* and *you,* it's not a matter of two becoming one. Two became one — is nonbeing. I was talking about nonbeing in the beloved.

《 》

Two—are one, that is: nonbeing in the beloved is possible only for one person. In order to not be in the other, it's necessary that the other *be*.

《 》

A stipulation: Everything said here relates, of course, to our perception of the other's soul, to our secret life with another's soul.

On the condition that neither of the two knows that the other doesn't exist, believes that the other does exist, doesn't know that the other in him has been destroyed—on the condition of not knowing the mutual nonbeing in one another, of course, it's possible.

《 》

Our seizure of the other—is only in us.

"For me, you don't exist in yourself, you are all in me." That's what the poet thinks of his Psyche, and this doesn't deter her from marrying and loving another, but her marriage, in turn, doesn't deter and cannot deter the poet.

I'll say even more: the strength of the seizure directly corresponds to its mystery, its depth—to its outward refutability. When nothing is mine—everything is mine! This leads us straight to death: the physical death of the beloved. Only please do not confuse this with jealousy! The "don't be" of jealousy—is from poverty and fear. ("Now that he's in the grave, there are no longer any rivals!") For seizure there are no rivals nor is there a grave: the "don't be" of seizure—this is the last refusal, which gives the ultimate power.

《 》

Poets! Give your beauties away in marriage, the further the better. So that not a single one of your sighs (poems) reaches them, or returns—as a sigh! Refuse even to dream of them.

The day of their marriage—is your first step to victory, the day of their interment—is your apotheosis.

(Beatrice. Dante.)

(( ))

Love for me — is the one who loves. And another thing: he who loves in response I always experience as a third person. There is my breast — and you. What is there for another person to do here (what action)?

A response in love — is a dead end for me. I am not looking for sighs, but for exits.

(( ))

There's a boy who sleeps in our kitchen, the son of the woman who brings us milk.

"I never thought I'd have to sleep on springs!" That "on springs" makes my heart clench.

There you have it: hatred for the common people!

(( ))

Yesterday, on Okhotny, one man to another:

"Don't you go oohing and ahhing! That's just the kind of year it is: the 19th!"

(( ))

"So then — do you visit Moscow?"
                          (Like a sick person.)

(( ))

Death is frightening only to the body. The soul can't conceive of it. Therefore, in suicide, the body — is the only hero.

(( ))

Suicide: *lâcheté** of the soul, transforming itself into heroism of the body. The same thing as if Don Quixote, in a fit of cowardice, sent Sancho Panza to battle — and he obeyed.

(( ))

Heroism of the soul — is to live, heroism of the body — is to die.

*The previous section, on words that don't exist in Russian, is omitted. "Lâcheté," for example, is a mixture of cowardice and baseness, not just cowardice. (M.Ts.)

◖◗

In the Orthodox church (temple) I feel the body moving into the earth, in Catholic churches, the soul flying up to the sky.

◖◗

Poetry and prose:

In prose too much seems superfluous to me, in poetry (genuine) everything is necessary. Given my attraction to asceticism of the prosaic word, I could end up with a skeleton.

In poetry — there's a certain innate measure of flesh: less is impossible.

◖◗

Two favorite things in the world: song — and formula.

(That is, a note of 1921, one of the elements — and victory over it!)

◖◗

I don't stand behind a single one of my earthly signs, that is: in the words "earthly signs" I yield the "earthly" (materiality), but not the sign (meaning).

I don't stand behind any one of my earthly signs individually, just as I do not stand behind any individual poem or hour — what's important is the totality.

I don't even stand behind the totality of my earthly signs, I stand only behind their right to exist and behind the truth — of my own existence.

◖◗

The brilliant advice of S. (the son of an artist). At some point during the winter I complained (laughing, of course!) that I had absolutely no time to write. "I work till five, then there is the fire to light, then the wash, then bathing, then putting the children to bed."

"Write at night!"

In this there was: disdain for my body, trust of my spirit, a high mercilessness, which honored both S. and me.

The highest tribute of an artist — to an artist.

◖◗

The influence of Konenkov's Stenka Razin on minds. A soldier, passing by the Cathedral of the Savior, to another soldier:

"Now, if they'd just paint this guy here!"

( )

On a desolate fence somewhere aslant the Cathedral of Christ the Savior there's a timid inscription: "I correct handwriting."

For some reason — in its hopelessness! — it reminds me of my sale (in order to leave for the south).

( )

The epigraph to my sale:

Katenka the tomboy
Went and broke her favorite toy.
Her dogs have lost their noses
Her sheep have lost their toeses.
And very, very soon,
The tea set's bound to lose its spoon,
And nothing will be left.

And there isn't anything!

Broken, for instance, are: the sewing machine, the rocking chair, the sofa, two armchairs, Alya's two children's chairs, the vanity. The marble wash basin is missing a side, the primus stove doesn't burn, the thermos doesn't keep things hot, of the lightning lamp — only the lightning remains, the gramophone is missing a screw, the bookcases won't stand up, the tea sets are missing cups, the cups are missing handles, the handles have no feet.

And neither of the piano pedals works! And the barrel organ made of redwood — well, it never worked! (The first second it seemed to be about to utter two bars of "Schlittschuhläufer" — and then it fell silent, that is, it groaned *so horribly,* that *we* all fell silent!) And the three squirrel cages — have no squirrels and no doors! (The smell remains.) And the baby bath with the twisted faucet and crumpled side! And the big zinc bath, grown green like a stagnant pool, unreliable as a coffin! And the Napoleonic engravings: faceted glass hanging on the honor of paper frames, threatening death every second! And the meat grinder, the roller skates, the ice skates!

For the most part, they were broken by Alya's nannies and Seriozha's Junkers. The one and the other out of youth, hotheadedness: heat of the heart and hands. The nannies were sick of watching the child, and they turned the gramophone, the Junkers were sick of voting on the charter resolution — and they turned the machine.

But it was neither the Junkers nor the nannies, just as now — it's not the Bolsheviks and not the "tenants." I say: it's fate. When a thing is insulted by a flighty attitude toward it, it seeks revenge: it falls apart.

That's the story of my "everyday life."

Raftsmen. A word from my childhood! The Oka River, late autumn, clipped lawns, the last flowers lying in the ruts of the road — all pink, Mama and Papa in the Urals (finding marble for the museum); dried apples, the governess says that the rats ate her legs off at night — the raftsmen will come and kill us . . .

The 30th coupon of the consumer goods ration card is good for a coffin, and Mariushka, Sonechka Gollidei's old servant, recently asked her mistress for permission to hoist one up into the attic storage room: "or else — you never know what might happen."

But a cruel trial awaited the poor old lady: there were no pink ones (for girls) and she, who has lived in irreproachable spinsterhood for 80 years, will have to lie down to her final rest in a man's blue coffin.

Carousel:

I rode on a carousel for the first time when I was 11, in Lausanne; the second time three days ago, on Sparrow Hills, on White Monday with six-year-old Alya. Between those two carousels — lies a whole lifetime.

Carousel! Magic! Carousel! Bliss! The first heaven of seven! Over-loaded with stars, laden with ringing bells, the first poor, common folk's, children's heaven on earth!

Only some seven inches off the ground — but the foot doesn't touch. There's *no turning back!* This feeling of no return, of being fated to fly, of entry into the circle —

The planetariness of the Carousel! The spheric music of its humming pillar! Not the earth on its axis, but the sky — on its own axis! The source of the sound is hidden. Once you sit down — you can't see anything. You tumble into the carousel as into a tornado.

Heraldic lions and apocalyptic steeds, are you not the ghosts of the beasts with which Bacchus flooded his ship?

The rites of the Khlysts — the round robin of planets — the colossi of Memnon at a sunsetless sunrise . . . Carousel!

( )

I adore the common folk: in the fields, at fairs, under church ban-ners, everywhere in the open and in mirth — and not visually, not for the women's red skirts, no — I love them lovingly, with all great faith in hu-man kindness. Here I truly have a feeling of fellowship.

We go together, in harmony.

( )

I adore wealthy people. Wealth — is a halo. Besides which, you never expect anything good from them, as from tsars, therefore a plain, rea-sonable word from their lips — is a revelation, simple human feeling — is heroism. Wealth raises everything to the 1000th degree (*the resonance of zero!*). You thought it was just a moneybags, no — a human being.

Moreover, wealth conveys self-knowledge and calm ("everything that I do — is good!") — as a gift; therefore with wealthy people I'm on my own level. With others I feel too "downtrodden."

Moreover, I swear and insist that wealthy people are kind (since it doesn't cost them anything) and beautiful (since they dress well).

If you can't be human, or handsome, or highborn, you should be wealthy.

(( ))

The mysterious disappearance of the photographer on Tverskaya St. who long and stubbornly took pictures (for free) of important Soviet cadres.

(( ))

Not long ago, in Kuntsevo, I unexpectedly crossed myself when I saw an oak tree. Obviously, the source of prayer isn't fear, but delight.

(( ))

At Smolensky market bread is now 60 rubles a pound, and they only sell you 2 lbs. at a time. Those who manage to be clever and buy more — are beaten.

(( ))

I am an inexhaustible source of heresy. Not *knowing* a single one, I profess all of them. Perhaps I even create them.

(( ))

One should write only those books from whose absence one suffers. In short: the ones you want on your own desk.

(( ))

The most valuable thing in poems and in life — is what didn't work out.

(( ))

The common people will never get lost in the city. An animal and savage's sense of place.

(( ))

At present everything is running out, because nothing is repaired: things as well as people, and people, as well as love.

(( ))

(Repairs are made: to things — by artisans, to people — by doctors, but what repairs love? Rubles, I think: presents, trips, premieres. Listening to Scriabin together. Visiting Vesuvius together.

After all, there are so few Tristans and Isoldes!)

(())

Tristan and Isolde: love in itself. Outside the incubator of envy, jealousy: the eye. Outside the resonator of reproofs, approvals: rumors. Outside the eye and reputation. No one saw them and no one had heard of them. They lived in the forest. The he-wolf and the she-wolf. Tristan and Isolde. They had nothing. There was nothing on them. There was nothing under them. There was nothing over them. Behind them — nothing, in front of them — Nothingness. Neither tomorrow, nor yesterday, nor the year, nor the hour. Time stood still. The world was called the forest. The forest was called the bush, the bush was called the leaf, the leaf was called you. You were called *I*. Nonbeing in emptiness. The background — as absence, and absence — as the background.

And — they loved.

(())

All my complaints about 1919 (there's no sugar, no bread, no firewood, no money) — are exclusively out of politeness: so that I, who have nothing, won't offend those who have everything.

And all the complaints, in my presence, about 1919 — of others ("Russia has perished," "What have they done to the Russian language," etc.) — are exclusively out of politeness: so that they, from whom nothing was taken away, don't offend me, from whom — everything was taken.

(())

Dread of space and dread of the crowd. At the foundation of both is the fear of loss. Of loss of oneself through the absence of people (space) and their presence (the crowd). Is it possible to suffer from both at the same time?

I think that dread of the crowd can be overcome only through self-affirmation, in 1919, for instance, by shouting out loud: "Down with the Bolsheviks!"

So that you're noticed — and torn apart.

( )

(NB! Dread of the crowd — is dread of death by suffocation. When they tear you apart — they don't suffocate you.)

( )

High measure. To measure with a high measure. That's what God does too. From on high to measure and with a high measure. Something like a very large sieve: little nastinesses as well as little virtues — fall through. Where to? Dans le néant. High-handedness is the complete absence of pettiness. For this reason — it's a very advantageous quality . . . for others.

( )

About a communist:

Yesterday, at a woman friend's house:

"After all, you don't shave," said the communist, "so why do you need powder?"

The communist is one of the old ones; he's dying of hunger. Such a marvelous, singing voice.

( )

Someone in the room: "There's an unbelievable program at the Hermitage!"

The communist, singingly: "And what is her Mitage?"

( )

Ah, the power of blood! I remember that my mother to the end of her life wrote: Thor, Rath, Theodor — out of German patriotism for the old days, although she was Russian, and not at all old, since she died when she was 36.

Me with my letter *yat*!

《 》

Yesterday when I was visiting friends (a birthday cake, songs, candle stubs, a story about how the Reds are fighting) — and suddenly, looking at the music:

Beethoven — Busslied

Puccini — such and such

Marie-Antoinette — "Si tu connais dans ton village . . ."

Marie-Antoinette! You wrote music to the poems of Florian, and they imprisoned you in a fortress and cut off your head. And other happy souls will sing your music — forever!

Never, never — neither in a sly eye mask, in the copses of Versailles, arm in arm with the charming mauvais sujet d'Artois, nor as the Queen of France, nor as the Queen of the Ball, nor as a milkmaid at the Trianon, nor as a martyr in the Temple — nor, finally, on the gallows cart — did you ever pierce my heart so deeply as:

Marie-Antoinette: "Si tu connais dans ton village . . ."

(Paroles de Florian)

《 》

Louis XVI should have married Marie-Louise ("fraîche comme une rose" and an idiot); Napoleon should have married — Marie-Antoinette (simply, the Rose!).

The adventurist, winning the Adventure — and the last crystal of Breed and Blood.

And Marie-Antoinette, as an aristocrat, therefore: irreproachable in her every *thought,* wouldn't have abandoned him like a dog, there on the cliff.

Moscow, 1919

On Germany
Excerpts from a Diary, 1919

My passion, my homeland, cradle of my soul! Fortress of the spirit, which is usually thought of as a prison for bodies!

The little town of Loschwitz near Dresden, I'm sixteen years old, living in a pastor's family—I smoke, have short hair, eight-inch heels (*Luftkurort,* Dr. Laman's system—the whole town is in sandals!)—I walk to a rendezvous with a statue of a centaur in the woods, I can't tell beets from carrots (in a pastor's family!)—you can't count all the antagonisms!

And what—did I antagonize them? No, they loved me, no, they put up with me, no, they *let me be.* Did anyone there ever criticize me? Was there even a sideways glance? Even the thought of one?

This is the country of freedom. I insist. The country of the highest accounting of quality with quality, quantity with quality, personality with personality, impersonality with personality. A country where the law (of community life) not only takes the exception into account: it reveres it. Because a poet slumbers in every clerk. Because in every tailor a violinist awakens. Because in every beer-hall lion a real lion will awaken at the call of the homeland.

I remember in early childhood, on the Riviera, the eighteen-year-old German, Röver, who was dying from tuberculosis. Until age eighteen he had been in Berlin, first in school, then in an office. Stuffy, sweaty, boring.

I remember how, in the evenings, drawn by his German music and my Russian mother—mother played the piano with unfeminine accomplishment—to the accompaniment of his sacred Bach, in the darkening Italian room, where the windows were like doors—he taught Asya and me the immortality of the soul.

A piece of paper held over a kerosene lamp: the paper shrivels up, turns to ash, the hand holding it lets go and—"Die Seele fliegt!"

The piece of paper flew up! It flew to the ceiling, which, of course, would part in order to let the soul pass to the sky!

( )

I had an album. It's awkward for a thirty-year-old woman, mother of two children, to start an album, so mother went and started albums for Asya and me — our own. The entire consumptive Genoan shore wrote in them. And there, amid Uland, Tennyson and Nekrasov is the following truth, strange from the pen of a German:

"Tout passe, tout casse, tout lasse . . ." — with an extremely German note, written in meticulous letters almost two inches high: "Excepté la satisfaction d'avoir fait son devoir."

( )

The German Reinhardt Röver, a model clerk and a no less model dying man (thermometer, Thiokol, departure home at sunset) — the German Reinhardt Röver died in the nineteenth year of his life, in Nervi, during Carnival.

( )

He was transferred to a private apartment (you mustn't die in the boarding house), to the top room of a tall, gloomy house. Asya and I brought him the first violets, mother — all the music of her unusual being.

"Wenn Sie einen ansehen, gnädige Frau, klingt's so recht wie Musik!"

And then one time Asya and I fly in — violets, confetti, a mouth full of news. The door is open.

"Herr Röver!"

And the frightened hiss of the sitter:

"Zitto, zitto, e morto il Signore!"

An open mouth through which the soul flew out, the bustling wings of tresses over the ashes.

We approached, placed the flowers, kissed him ("Just don't kiss! In every cubic millimeter of air there are billions of miasms" — that was what everyone taught us, not taking into account that at eight years of age you don't know what cubes are, or millimeters, or billions, or miasms — nothing except kisses and air!)

We kissed him, stood awhile, left. On the staircase — spiral and echoing — we got scared: Röver's chasing us!

For three days in a row from the window of his death room they hung out: the mattress, the pillow, the sheets — in expectation of the new inhabitants. His belongings (Mahlkasten, thermometer, several changes of underclothes, a bedside volume of Lenau) were sent home, to the office.

And nothing remained of the German Reinhardt Röver — "excepté la satisfaction d'avoir fait son devoir."

(( ))

My Röver is a mere gasp away from the world's Novalis. "Die Seele fliegt" — Novalis didn't say anymore than this, after all. No one has ever said more. Here one has Plato, and the Count August von Platen, all and sundry are here, and *there's no "except for."*

So, from children's amusements and album inscriptions, two words: soul and duty.

The soul is duty. The duty of the soul — is flight. Duty is the soul of flight (I fly, because I must). In a word, one way or the other: die Seele fliegt!

"Ausflug." Just listen carefully: flight *out of* . . . (a city, room, body, the genitive case). The habitual Sunday flight ins Grüne, the hourly — ins Blaue. Aether, heilige Luft!

I may be saying something wild, but for me, Germany is Greece continued, ancient, youthful. The Germans inherited it. And, not knowing Greek, I won't accept that nectar, that ambrosia from anyone's hands, from anyone's lips other than German ones.

(( ))

About boys. I remember, in Germany — I was still an adolescent — in the little village of Weisser Hirsch, near Dresden, where father sent Asya and me to learn housekeeping at the pastor's — a fifteen-year-old, un-

pleasantly impertinent and unpleasantly timid pink boy was once looking at my books. He saw Heinrich Mann's *Zwischen den Rassen,* with an
epigraph penned in my hand:

> Blonde enfant qui deviendra femme,
> Pauvre ange qui perdra son ciel.
> (Lamartine)

"Ist's wirklich Ihre Meinung?"
And my reply:
"Ja, wenn's durch einen, wie Sie geschieht!"

(( ))

And another boy, also pink and blonde, but utterly timid and pleasantly timid — a little *commis,* the touching thirteen-year-old Christian —
led Asya triumphantly by the hand, like his bride. He probably — certainly! — didn't think about it, but the gesture, developed by dozens of
generations (of shop assistants) was in his *hand*.

And another — dark-haired and light-eyed Hellmuth, whom we and
the other boys (Asya and I were "grownup," "rich," and "free," and they
were Schulbuben who were herded into bed at 9 p.m.) taught to smoke
at night and treated to cakes, and who wrote such a jolly note in Asya's
album when we left: "Die Erde is rund und wir sind jung — wir werden
uns wiedersehen!"

And the lycée boy Volodya — so different — but who measured the
height of our heels with just as much excitement — here in the sanctum
of Dr. Laman, where people are even born in sandals!

Hellmuth, Christian, lycéen Volodya! — who among you survived
1914–1917!

(( ))

Oh, the strength of blood! I remember that to the end of her life
mother wrote: Thor, Rath, Theodor — out of German patriotism for
the old days, although she was Russian, and not at all old, since she died
at the age of 34.

Me, with my letter *yat!*

⟨ ⟩

From mother I inherited Music, Romanticism and Germany. Simply put — Music. My entire being.

⟨ ⟩

I definitely feel music as Germany (just as amorousness — is France, longing — is Russia). There is this country — music; its inhabitants — are Germans.

⟨ ⟩

Razin's Persian girl and Undine. Both were loved, both were abandoned. Death by water. Razin's dream (in my poems) and the dream of the Knight (in Lamotte-Fouqué and Zhukovsky).

Both Razin and the Knight were supposed to perish because of their beloved — only the Persian girl comes with all the cunning of the Unloving and Persia — "for the slipper," and Undine with all the devotedness of the Loving and Germany — for a kiss.

⟨ ⟩

Treue — how it sounds!

And from their fidélité the French managed to make only Fidèle (Fidelka).

⟨ ⟩

Heine has a prophecy about our revolution: " . . . und ich sage euch, es wird einmal ein Winter kommen, wo der ganze Schnee im Norden Blut sein wird . . ."

In general, Heine on Russia is interesting. On the democraticness of the nation. On Peter — the statist revolutionary (betrothed of the Revolution).

Heine! What a book I would write. And — *without* archives, outside the luxury of personal penetration, simply — in private with six volumes of the awful German edition of the late '80s. (Illustrated poems! And since Heine often writes about women — there's nothing but sausages!)

Heine will always cover any event in my life, and not because I . . . (event, life) am weak: he — is strong!

(( ))

To bump into one another and — with no apology, to part. What crudeness in this gesture! I recall Heine, who, on arriving in Paris, deliberately tried to make people bump into him — just to hear the apology.

(( ))

In Heine, Germany and Romany reign together. I know only one other such person — another regime, another theme of the soul, another scale — but equal to Heine in his dual homeland: Romain Rolland.

But Romain Rolland, rumor has it, is a Gallo-German, Heine — as everyone knows — is a Jew. And so the miracle explains itself. I would like an inexplicable (genuine) miracle: a Frenchman through and through and he loves (senses) Germany like a German, a German through and through and he loves (senses) France like a Frenchman. I'm not talking about stylizations — they are easy, boring — about punctured dead ends and borders of birth and blood moved apart. About organic (ethnic) creation, not related to zoology. In a word, for a Gaul to create a new Song of the Nibelugen, and for a German — a new Song of Roland.

This cannot "*can be*," this must be.

(( ))

Die blinde Mathilde — memoirs of childhood.

In Freiburg, there was a woman who came to the boarding house every Sunday — *die blinde Mathilde*. She wore a blue satin dress — was about forty-five — half-closed blue eyes — a yellow face. Each girl in turn was supposed to write letters for her and glue on stamps, at her own expense. When the letters were finished, she would sit down at the piano and sing in gratitude.

For German girls: "Ich kenn ein Kätzlein wunderschön."

For Asya and me: "Der rothe Sarafan."

(( ))

Now a question: to whom did blinde Mathilde write so much? Whoever answers that question will write a novel.

《 》

How I loved — loved with longing, to distraction! — the Black Forest. The golden valleys, the resonant, threateningly cozy forest — not to mention the villages with tavern signs: "Zum Adler," "Zum Löwen." (If I had a tavern I would call it: "Zum Kukuck.")

《 》

I will never forget the voice with which the proprietor of the small Gasthaus "Zum Engel" in the little Black Forest, pointing to the only portrait of the emperor Napoleon in the hall, exclaimed:
"Das war ein Kerl!"
And after a pause that indicated complete satisfaction:
"Der hat's der Welt auf die Wand gemahlt, was wollen heisst!"

《 》

After Eckermann I can read only *Mémorial de Sainte-Hélène* by Las Cases — and if I ever envied someone in life — it is only Eckermann and Las Cases.

《 》

Strange. Here you have the epitome of happiness, there the epitome of unhappiness, and from both books an identical sadness — as though Goethe had also been *exiled* to Weimar!

《 》

O, for Goethe (1829), Napoleon was already a legend!
O, for Napoleon (1815), Napoleon was already a legend!

《 》

Goethe, moved by Napoleon's inside-out uniform.

《 》

In Goethe what bothers me is "Farbenlehre," in Napoleon—all his campaigns.

(()

Not long ago I was walking along Kuznetsky and suddenly, on a sign: "Farbenlehre." I froze.

I went closer: "Fabergé."

(()

There are many souls in me. But my primary soul—is German. There are many rivers in me, but my primary river—is the Rhine. The sight of Gothic letters immediately places me on the tower: on the very highest pinnacle! (Not letters, but teeth. *Zacken*—what grandeur!) I dissolve in the German anthem.

Lieb Vaterland, magst ruhig sein.

Just listen closely to this *magst*—it's like a lion—to a lion cub! Why, that's the Rhine itself saying: Vater Rhine! How could you not be at peace?!

(()

When I'm asked: who is your favorite poet, I sputter, because I immediately toss out a dozen German names. In order to answer right away, I need ten mouths, for a chorus, simultaneously. Poets' order of precedence in the heart is far crueler than the court's. Each wants to be the first, because there *is* a first, each wants to be the only one, because there *isn't* a second. Heine is jealous of Platen's place in my heart, Platen of Hölderlin's, Hölderlin of Goethe's; only Goethe isn't jealous of anyone: God!

(()

"What do you love in Germany?"

"Goethe and the Rhine."

"Well, and do you love contemporary Germany?"

"Passionately."

"You mean, despite . . ."

"Not only despite—*not seeing*."

"Are you blind?"

"Sighted."

"Are you deaf?"

"Absolute pitch."

"What do you see?"

"Goethe's brow over the millennia."

"What do you hear?"

"The roar of the Rhine over the millennia."

"But you're talking about the past!"

"About the future!"

(⟨)⟩

Goethe and the Rhine have not yet *happened*. I can't say it any more exactly.

(⟨)⟩

For me, France is light, Russia — is heavy. Germany — is just right. Germany — is the tree, oak, *heilige Eiche* (Goethe! Zeus!). Germany — is the exact membrane of my spirit, Germany — is my flesh: her rivers (*Ströme!*) — are my hands, her groves (Heine!) — are my hair, she is all mine, and I am all — hers!

(⟨)⟩

Edelstein. In Germany I would love the diamond. (*Edelstein, Edeltrucht, Edelmann, Edelwein, Edelmuth, Edelblut.*)

(⟨)⟩

And also: *Leichtblut.* Light blood. Not light-mindedness, but light-bloodedness. And also: *Uebermuth:* superstrength, excess, over-the-top. *Leichtblut* and *Uebermuth* — how that describes me, outside the suspect "light-mindedness," outside the cumbersome "excess of life energy."

Leichtblut and *Uebermuth* — and aren't they the *same* gods? (The only ones.)

And, most important, this doesn't exclude anything, neither sacrifice, nor death — only: a light sacrifice, flying death!

《 》

And *Gottesjüngling*! Doesn't all of Thebes arise in a chorus of its favorites!

And *Urkraft*—isn't this all of awakening Chaos! This prefix: *Ur!* *Urquelle, Urkunde, Urzeit, Urnacht.*

Urahne, Ahne, Mutter und Kind
In dumpfer Stube besammen sind.

This is eternity moaning! Like a wolf in a stovepipe. Every such *Urahne*—is a Parcae.

《 》

Drache and *Rache*—and it's all "Nibelungenlied"!

《 》

"Germany—is a country of eccentrics"—"Land der Sonderlinge." That's what I would call the book I would write about it (in German). *Sonderlich. Wunderlich. Sonder* and *Wunder* are related. More than that: outside of *Sonder* there is no *Wunder,* outside of *Wunder*—there is no *Sunder.*

O, I have seen them: *Naturmenschen* with coiffures of red Indians, pastors obsessed with Dionysis, pastors' wives obsessed with chiromancy, venerable old ladies who communicate with their dead "friend" (husband) every evening after supper—and other old ladies—*Märchenfrau,* tale tellers by vocation and craft, craftswomen of the fairy tale. The fairy tale as a craft, and as a craft *that feeds.* — Just appreciate the country.

O, I have seen them! I know them! Go tell others how commonsensical and boring Germans are! This is a country of madmen who've lost their minds over the heights of reason—the spirit.

《 》

"Germans—are bourgeois" . . . No, Germans—are citizens: *Bürger.* From *Burg:* fortress. Germans are—serfs of the Spirit.

Philistine, citizen, bourgeois, *citoyen*—for Germans themselves there's no distinction—*Bürger.* In order to distinguish the concept of the petty bourgeois—they add the prefix *klein: klein-bürgerlich.*

Is it possible that there's no separate word for a nation's primary trait? Think about it.

My eternal "schwärmen." In Germany this is quite in the order of things; in Germany I am entirely in the order of things, a white crow among white crows. In Germany I'm ordinary, *anyone.*

(( ))

In Germany only he who oppresses others is oppressed, i.e., he who spreads out beyond the limit indicated to him, whether spatial or temporal. Thus, for instance, by playing my flute in my room later than 10 o'clock, I am extending beyond the temporal limit established by the community, and in this way am oppressing my neighbor; in the most precise sense I hinder (curtail) his sleep. Know how to play silently!

For me, who is passionately indifferent to outward appearances, Germany feels spacious.

(( ))

What attracts me in Germany is the orderliness (i.e., the simplification) of external life — which doesn't and never did exist in Russia. They have beaten everyday life into submission — so as to be utterly subject to it.

In der Beschränkung zeigt sich erst der Meister,
Und das Gesetz nur kann uns Freiheit geben.

Not a single German lives in this life, but his body is efficient. You take the efficiency of German bodies for the slavery of German souls! There is no soul more free, no soul more rebellious, no soul more haughty! They are brothers to Russians, but they are wiser (older?) than us. The struggle with the marketplace of everyday life has been transferred entirely to the heights of the spirit. They don't need anything here. Hence their obedience. The limitation of the self *here* for limitless sovereignty *there*. They don't have any barricades, but they have philosophical systems that blow up the world, and poems that create it anew.

The mad poet Hölderlin rehearses on a mute harpsichord for thirty years in a row. Novalis the visionary sits behind the bars of a bank to the end of his days. Neither Hölderlin nor Novalis is oppressed by his prison. They don't notice them. They are free.

Germany — a vise for bodies and the Elysian fields — for souls. Given my boundlessness, I need a vise.

(( ))

"Well, and what about the war?"

"And with the war — it's this way: it isn't Alexander Blok and Rainer Maria Rilke fighting, but a machine gun with a machine gun. It's not Alexander Scriabin and Richard Wagner, but a dreadnought and a dreadnought. If Blok were killed — I would mourn Blok (the best of Russia), if Rilke were killed — I would mourn Rilke (the best of Germany), and no victory, neither ours nor theirs, would comfort me."

I feel *nothing* in national wars, in civic ones — *everything*.

(( ))

"Well, and what about German atrocities?"

"But I was talking about qualitative Germany, not about quantitative. Quality generated by quantity — there's an atrocity. Alone, man isn't a beast (there's no reason to be and no one to be beastly with). Bestiality begins with Cain and Abel, Romulus and Remus, that is, with the number two. From this fateful figure of the first community to reach double digits and further — there's a catastrophic growth of bestiality, multiplied by the thousands with each individual. (Remember childhood and school.)"

In short: if "pour aimer il faut être deux," then all the more so — pour tuer. (Adam could just love the sun; for murder, Cain needed Abel.)

One is enough for love, for murder you need two.

When people, crowding together, are deprived of their face, they become first a herd, then a gang.

Just wait, the hour will come when you will mourn heroic Germany just as you now mourn heroic, ruined France. Now — it's the cathedral at Rheims, tomorrow — at Cologne: *heights hinder the century!* It's not the hatred of Teutons for Gauls, Gauls for Teutons, it's the hatred of the square — for the spire, of flatness — for sharpness, of the horizontal for the vertical.

The cathedral of Rheims is a bigger wound for me than for you: in it my Joan *happened!* Mourning it, I mourn more than you: not Joan, not France — the century of bonfires, replaced by the century of cement!

(( ))

"The Germans gave us the Bolsheviks." "Germans gave us a Lenin sealed in a railway car . . ."

I am not a connoisseur of diplomatic gifts, but, even if it's true — with hand on heart — if we were in their place and had thought of it — wouldn't we have done the same?

The train car carrying Lenin — wasn't it that very same Trojan horse?

Politics — is nasty stuff a priori, and you can't expect anything else from it. With ethics — into politics!

And whether nastiness is German or Russian — I can't tell the difference. And no one can. Just as the International — is evil, so Evil — is international.

Vous avez pris l'Alsace et la Lorraine
Mais notre coeur, vous ne l'aurez jamais
Vous avez cru germaniser la plaine,
Mais malgré vous nous resterons français.

I grew up with this. (An ancient French governess.) And it is as sacred in me as "Wacht am Rhine." And there's no contradiction. The great agreement of heights.

(( ))

A passion for every country as if it were the only one — that is my International. Not the third, but the eternal.

Moscow, 1919

From A Diary

Two o'clock at night. I'm returning from friends where I go every evening. I can still hear the last, admiringly worried exclamations: "How bold! Alone — at such an hour! When there's robbery all around. And all that jewelry!" (They are the ones who beg me to sit a while longer, don't invite me to spend the night, and don't offer to walk me home — and I'm the one who's bold! You might as well call the dog bold when people kick him out of the house into a pack of wolves.)

And so, just after two. The moon shines right in my face. I catch its light in the silver shield of my ring as if in a mirror. The delicate little voice of a fountain, a garrulous, un-Russian plaint — like the younger harem wife complaining to the senior wife. The way the Persian princess complained — through braids and veils (beads and veils, tears and veils), in vain, to no one in particular — on Razin's boat. The fountain: a Pushkinian urn on Dog's Square — Pushkinian because Pushkin read his Godunov in the house across the street. Almost the fountain of Bakhchisarai!

I lift my face — to the moon; my ear — to the water: the twofold flow.

The twofold flowing
Of moon and water . . .

Flowing . . . lodging . . . lilac . . . longing . . . (What a lame word! Empty. No match for "headlong.")

On the corner of Dog's Square and Boris and Gleb Street I fan two sleeping policemen with my dress. They open their eyes drowsily. No more alive than the posts they're sleeping on. I have the idle thought: "Why don't they rob me!" Nine silver rings (the tenth is a wedding ring), an officer's wrist watch, a huge forged chain with a lorgnette, an officer's satchel over my shoulder, an antique brooch with lions, two

huge bracelets (one from a burial tomb, the other Chinese), a box of cigarettes (250! a gift) — and also a German book. But the policemen, not
hearing my advice, go on sleeping. I passed the Mileshin bakery, a Baba
Yaga-like hut, a fence, there are my two poplars, across from the house.
Home. I've already put one foot over the iron frame of the gate (at night
the entry is from the courtyard) when from beneath the overhang of the
stoop:

"Who's goes there?"

A young guy about eighteen years old, in uniform, a jaunty forelock
peeking out from under his cap. Light brown hair. Freckles.

"Any weapons?"

"What kind of weapons do women have?"

"What is that there?"

"Please, take a look."

I take out of my purse and hand him, one after another: my new, favorite cigarette case with lions (yellow, English: Dieu et mon droit), a
coin purse, matches.

"And there's also a comb, a key . . . If you have any doubts, we can go
see the yardkeeper; I've lived here for four years."

"Any documents?"

At this point, remembering the parting words of my cautious
friends, I conscientiously and meaninglessly parry:

"And do you have any documents?"

"Right here!"

The steel of a revolver, white in the moonlight. ("So it's white, and
for some reason I always thought it was black, I *saw* it as black. A revolver — is death. Blackness.")

At the same instant, the chain from the lorgnette flies over my head,
strangling me and catching on my hat. Only then do I realize what's going on.

"Put down that revolver and take it off with both hands, you're strangling me."

"Don't scream."

"You can hear how I'm speaking."

He lowers it, and, no longer strangling me, swiftly and deftly removes the doubled chain. The action with the chain is the last one. I

hear "Comrades!" behind my back as my other foot steps through the gate.

(I forgot to say that the whole time we were talking (a minute plus) there were people walking back and forth on the other side of the street.)

The soldier left me: all my rings, the lion brooch, the purse itself, both bracelets, my watch, book, comb, key.

He took: the coin purse with an invalid check for 1000 rubles, the new, wonderful cigarette case (there you have it, *droit* without *Dieu!*), the chain and lorgnette, the cigarettes.

All in all, if not a fair price — a fraternal one.

The next day at six o'clock in the evening, on Malaya Molchanovka St., he was killed! (They attacked some passerby in the light of evening, the guy allowed himself to be robbed and, letting them go, turned around and shot him in the back.) He turned out to be one of three sons of the church custodian of the nearby Rzhevskaya church released from hard labor after the Revolution.

They offered to let me go pick out my things. I refused with a shudder. How could I — one of the living (that is — happy, that is — wealthy), go and take from him, the dead, his last loot?! I quake at the very thought of it. One way or the other, I was his last (maybe next to the last!) joy, which he took to the grave with him. You don't rob the dead.

THE EXECUTION OF THE TSAR

Alya and I are returning from some food ordeals along the cheerless, cheerless, cheerless lengths of deserted boulevards. There's a shop window with a pitiful little watchmaker's display. Among the cheap trifles is a huge silver ring with a coat of arms.

Then some plaza or another. We are standing, waiting for the tram. It's raining. There's a brash, boyish, cocklike crowing:

"The execution of Nikolai Romanov! The execution of Nikolai Romanov! Nikolai Romanov is shot by the worker Beloborodov!"

I look at the other people waiting for the tram, who are also hearing this. Workers, bedraggled intelligentsia, soldiers, women with children. Nothing. If only someone! If only something! They buy the newspaper, glance at it quickly, again avert their eyes — where? Nowhere at all. But maybe they're putting a spell on the tram so it will come.

Then I say to Alya in a stifled voice, even and loud (whoever has spoken that way knows what I mean):

"Alya, they've killed the Russian Tsar, Nicholas II. Pray for his soul to rest in peace!"

And Alya's meticulous triple cross with a deep bow. (My accompanying thought: "Too bad she's not a boy. She would have taken off her hat.")

ASSASSINATION ATTEMPT ON LENIN

A knock at the door. I race down, open it. There's a stranger in a papakha. White eyes stare out of the coffee sun tan. (Later I looked more carefully: blue.) He's out of breath.

"Are you Marina Ivanovna Tsvetaeva?"

"I am."

"Lenin's been killed."

"Oh!!!"

"I've come from the Don."

Lenin's been killed and Seriozha's alive! I rush to embrace him.

Evening of the same day. My lodger-communist S., running into the kitchen:

"So, are you happy?"

I dim my eyes — not from timidity, of course: I'm afraid of offending him with too obvious a joy. (Lenin has been killed, the White Guard has arrived, all the communists are hanged, S. first among them) . . . I already feel the victor's magnanimity.

"And are you — very upset?"

"Me?" (His shoulders twitch.) "We Marxists don't recognize personalities in history; it isn't really that important whether it's Lenin or someone else. It's you people, representatives of bourgeois culture . . ." (a new shudder) " . . . with your Napoleons and Caesars . . ." (a satanic grin) " . . . but for ussss, you know . . . Today it's Lenin, tomorrow . . ."

Offended on Lenin's behalf (!!!), I say nothing. There's an uncertain pause. And then, in a hurry:

"Marina Ivanovna, I was given some sugar, three-quarters of a pound, I don't need it, I use saccharine, perhaps you'd take it for Alya?"

( )

(This very same X gave me a carved wood folk figure of the Tsar for Easter 1918.)

SCABIES

In Moscow at present there's an epidemic of scabies. All Moscow is itching. It starts between the fingers, then it's the whole body, a mite under the skin, where it stops — there's a sore. It itches only in the evenings.

At work places there are signs: "Hand shakes are canceled." ("Kisses are canceled"—would be better!)

Not long ago, when I was visiting some people, a relative of the hostess, also a guest, insistently and with a sort of restrained anxiety questioned the hostess on how and what it is, how it starts and what it ends with, and does it end at all.

And her unexpected exclamation, as it dawned on her:

"Abrasha, you probably have a scabies yourself!"

("A scabies" in her understanding is obviously the mite itself. Fleas, flies, cockroaches, bedbugs, scabies.)

Pretending to joke, no one shakes hands with departing guests. In order to avoid handshakes, the host even kisses people. The guest is unpleasant — a bourgeois. Sufficiently disgusting without scabies. The guest is a coward and sympathizes with those who refrain. Scabies — is revolting. So, taking everything into account, including the complete meaninglessness of the gesture and the sacrifice — in complete despair and a cold sweat—I not only extend my hand but I hold his an unusually long time.

This hand shake is truly pregnant with consequences: for you, the scabrous one, the certainty of my good will and thus (taking scabies into account!) a doubly sleepless night; for me, the unscabrous—the scabies and thus (taking into account your certainty!) a doubly sleepless night as well.

I don't know how he slept. As for me, I didn't scratch, and don't itch.

FRÄULEIN

The hungry crush of Okhotny Row. They're selling carrots and raspberry jellies on cardboard saucers, revolting. The undefeated hustle; the hopeless loiter. Suddenly—a familiar nape: something rare, light brown. I catch up, look closely: milky eyes, a sorrowful, reddish beak. It's Fräulein. My German teacher from my last gymnasium.

"Guten Tag, Fräulein!" A frightened glance. "Don't you recognize me? Tsvetaeva. From the Briukhonenko Gymnasium."

And she, preoccupied:

"Tsvetaeva? Where will I seat you?" And stopping: "Now where am I going to seat you?"

"Come on, lady, get moving!"

( )

Her German brains couldn't take it!

A NIGHT IN A COMMUNE

I'm visiting friends. They ask me to recite my poems. Since there's a communist in the room, I recite "The White Guard."

White Guard—your path is high . . .

After the White Guard—there's another White Guard, after the second White—a third, the entire "Don," then "Purebred Steeds" and "To the Tsar on Easter." In a word, when I come to my senses — its 12 midnight and the gates to my house are definitely locked.

I can't spend the night here — it's a "respectable house" with servants, relatives. There's only one thing to do: go to Dog's Square and sleep under the sounds of Pushkin's fountain. Which I announce. Laughing, I rise and head for the door with a firm step. Reaching the threshold, I hear a singing:

"Marinushka!"

"Yes?"

"Are you serious about sleeping on the street?"

"Completely."

"But it's . . ."

"Yes, very, but . . ."

"Then come to our place, to the commune."

"But it might not be convenient for you."

"Why? I have my own room."

"Then — thank you."

I'm beaming, for, despite all my inner adventurism, rather, thanks to all my inner adventurism, I'm perfectly willing to do without external adventurism! (NB! From an overnight on a communist street to an overnight in a communist house — the former is the real adventure!)

We head off. The commune isn't far away: it's in a marvelous stone house that recalls England (I've never been there). We enter. A carpeted staircase. Velvet silence. The silence of the night. Callused hands along the banisters' velvet. We pass through an empty (no food, no people) dining room, through several more rooms — and we've arrived. It looks like a hotel room and a half: the room, turning a corner, forms a hook. A ghostly brocade curtain, behind which there is an invisible window definitely made of whole glass — if it hasn't been broken by October. Furniture trifles like little tables, book shelves, flower stands. A low carved wooden bed, very deep, very wide. For long loungings, for late risings. A bed — for idleness, for tenderness, for fat, for everything that I hate.

"Here's where you'll sleep, Marinushka."

"And you?"

"I'll sleep on the sofa in the study."

(The study, clearly, is the hook.)

"No, I'll sleep on the sofa! I love sleeping on sofas! At home I always slept on the sofa! Even on the dog's sofa, when I'd come back from boarding school! And when the dog realized that I'd fallen asleep, it would crawl up and lie on my head in the most brazen manner . . . Honestly!"

"But you're not in boarding school, Marinushka!"

"Don't remind me where I am, my friend!"

We sit down. We smoke. We talk. He gives me his dinner: a piece of bread, three boiled beets and a glass of tea with a lump of sugar.

"And you?"

"I already ate."

"Where? No, no, together!"

We talk about poems, about Germany, which we both love passionately, he asks about my life.

"Are you having a very hard time of it?"

Embarrassed, I smooth the edges.

And he:

"Marinushka, Marinushka . . . Well, I'll be getting some flour soon, I'll bring it to you . . . How terrible this all is!"

I:

"But I assure you . . ."

He, thinking aloud:

"Maybe I can get some wheat . . ."

(And sounding quite helpless):

"And there's no chance you could leave for the south?"

(This from a high placed functionary!)

I look at his face: lovely, thin; straight in the eyes: dark brown, in horn-rimmed glasses. And such a consciousness of his innocence, his blamelessness, such a gasp of pity and gratitude, that . . . but the tears are already flowing, and he, frightened:

"At least you haven't had bad news from the south, have you?"

(())

I sleep on the bed, of course — neither the dog nor my assurances helped. Before falling asleep we chat a bit.

"N.! Would you want to be in Vienna now? This is a hotel — it's 1912, you look out the window and see a lively, schoolboy, nighttime Vienna . . . and *Wiener Blut* . . ."

And he, with a drawn out sigh:

"Oh, I don't know anything Marinushka!"

《 》

I awake with the sun. I jump into my enormous red dress (the color of a cardinal — a fire!). I write a note to N. I cautiously open the door and — O horrors! — there's a huge double bed and people sleeping in it. I retreat. Then, in a burst of decisiveness, I head for the opposite door with large, quiet steps. I push the handle down . . .

"What's going on here?"

There's a man sitting on the bed — with a disheveled head, an unbuttoned collar, looking at me.

And I, politely:

"It's me. I happened to spend the night here and I'm going home."

"But comrade! . . ."

"For God's sake, please forgive me. I didn't think that. . . . I think that . . . I'm obviously not in the right place . . ."

And, not awaiting a reply, I disappear.

《 》

(NB! Actually, it *was* the right one!)

《 》

Later I heard from N.: the sleeper took me for a red ghost. The specter of the Revolution, disappearing together with the first rays of the sun!

He couldn't stop laughing as he told me.

《 》

Only now, five years later, do I fully appreciate the situation. Having ended up in a commune, the only thing I managed to do was to stumble into someone else's bedroom: the only thing of the communists' that isn't very communistic—notwithstanding all the appeals of Mme Kollontai and Co.

"Plus royaliste que le roi!"

(A note in the spring of 1923.)

CHRIST'S WARRIOR

Early morning. Alya and I are walking past the church of Boris and Gleb. A service is going on. We drop in, following some black old lady up the steps of the white porch. The church is full, the early hour and the quiet create a conspiratorial aura. A few seconds later I hear distinctly with my own ears:

"And so, brothers, if this terrible news is confirmed, as soon as I learn of it, the bell-ringer will ring the bell and the envoys will make the rounds of all the houses, informing you all of this unspeakable evil. Be prepared, brothers! The enemy is vigilant and you must be vigilant! At the first sound of the bell, at any hour of day or night—everyone, everyone to the church! We will stand up, brothers, we'll defend our shrine! Take your young children with you; let the men leave their arms at home. We'll lift our bare hands on high with a sign of prayer, we'll see whether they dare to raise swords against a crowd of unarmed people.

"And if this does come to pass—well, then, we'll all lie down, we'll lie down on the steps of our church with a feeling of fulfilling our duty, defending the Lord our God to the last drop of blood, and our Master Jesus Christ, the patron of this church and our poor unfortunate motherland.

"The alarm bell will be frequent, staccato, with clear breaks . . . I'm explaining this to you, brothers, so that you don't confuse it with the fire bell in your sleep. As soon as you hear an unusual ringing at an untimely hour, know that you're being called, called by the Lord!

"And so, dear brothers . . ."

And my hurried response: "God grant! God grant! God grant!"

MOSCOW, 1918–19

A Hero of Labor

Notes on Valery Briusov

PART ONE

The Poet

I

And with a secret thrill I look the enemy in the face.
— *Balmont*

From the age of 16 to 17 I loved Briusov's poems with a brief, passionate love. I contrived to love what was most un-Briusovian in Briusov, that which he so lacked to his very depths, to his core — song, the element of song. More than his poems I loved — and this love lives to the present — his *Fiery Angel,* at the time both in concept and execution, now only in concept, in concept and in memory — in its unfulfillment. However, I remember that even then, at age 16, the word "interesting" struck me on one of the emotionally charged pages, a mercantile and calculating word, unimaginable either in Renata's century, or in the story of the Angel, or in the overall pathos of the work. A master — and such a blunder. Yes, mastery isn't everything. You must have an ear. Briusov didn't have one.

Briusov's antimusicality, despite the external (local) musicality of a whole series of poems — is an antimusicality of essence, a drought, a dearth of river. I remember the words of the profound and unusual poetess Adelaida Gertsyk, recently deceased, about Max Voloshin and myself, then 17 years old: "In you there's more river than riverbank, in him — more riverbank than river." Briusov was all embankment, a granite one. A municipal embankment granite that escorts and restrains (within the confines of the city) — that was the relationship between Briusov and the living river of his contemporaries' poetry. Out of town the embankment loses power. Thus, he prevented neither Mayakovsky of the outskirts, nor rye-field Esenin, nor the hero of his last and cruelest jealousy—Pasternak, who is unprecedented like the first day of creation. Everything that was city, office, guild, if it didn't dry up from him, took on his features. Listening to Goethe's forever reverberating words: "In der Beschränkung zeigt sich erst der Meister"—words directed at overcoming immeasurableness in oneself (the cradle of all creativity, which, like a cradle, is meant to be overcome)—it should be said that in this sense Briusov had nothing to overcome: he was born limited. Boundlessness is overcome by boundaries, but no one is able to overcome *boundaries* within himself. Briusov would have been a master in Goethe's sense only if he had overcome his own inborn boundaries, if he'd been able to dislodge them, and perhaps—had broken himself. In response to Moses' staff, Briusov remained silent. He remained *invulnerable* (the French is untranslatable in its full sense), outside the lyrical stream. But, I insist, his material was granite, not cardboard.

《 》

(Goethe's words—ward off *demons:* perhaps Briusov's most extreme, secret, hopeless passion.)

《 》

Briusov was a Roman. That's the only way to explain him fairly. Behind him obviously stands the Capitol and not Olympus. His gods never meddled in Trojan battles—recall Aphrodite wounded! Thetis pleading! Zeus gloomy with the knowledge of Achilles' inescapable death. Briusov's gods towered on high and sat in state, they are gods that have done away with the celestial and settled on earth once and for all. But, I maintain, their material was marble, not plaster.

《 》

I don't want any lies about Briusov, I don't want any posthumous Briusov-kicking. Briusov was not a *quantité négligeable,* even less so a *qualité.* Entirely Russian by birth, he presents an enigma. There is no one else like him in Russian lyric poetry: a completely buttoned-up poet. Tiutchev? But that was in life: in the drafts, in the interlinear translations of the lyre. Briusov is buttoned up (or perhaps nailed shut?) in his very creativity, encased in bronze with no chance of a breakthrough. What kind of Russian is this? And what kind of poet? He's Russian — true; he's a poet — also true: within the limits of human will, he's a poet. A poet of the limit. There are houses, the first ones you see when you approach a big city: they're multieyed, (multiwindowed), but they are somehow blind, life in them is unimaginable. They're official, executive, (and now, to put it lyrically) — executed. I see Briusov's work as one of those houses. And his highest achievement: a granite hallway that leads to a dead end.

Briusov: a poet of entries without exits.

That this not sound unfounded, reader, check for yourself: have you even once felt like prolonging one of Briusov's poems? (Goethe's "Verweile doch! Du bist so schön.") Have you even once had the feeling that something has broken off (he led me here and abandoned me!); did a country ever once emerge at the heart's unaccountable halt — a country beyond his lines, to which the poems are only an approach: in the farthest distance — at the farthest point — gates lie wide open? Did Briusov ever rend your soul, as Music does? ("Is that all? Already?") Did the soul, as after music, ever beg Briusov, "Already over? More!" Did you ever once leave an encounter — dissatisfied?

No, Briusov is perfectly satisfactory, he gives exactly what he promises and no more, and you leave his books as you would a profitable deal (it's telling: with other poets — the book has left, and you follow after, with Briusov: you've left, and the book — stays put). If something is missing — it's dissatisfaction.

(( ))

"The End" is invisibly written under each of Briusov's poems. For the sake of completeness Briusov should have filled it in graphically as well (typographically).

(( ))

Briusov's creations are greater than the creator. At first glance — this is flattering, on second — sad. The creator contains all tomorrow's creations, the whole Future, the whole inescapability of the possible: the unrealized, but not unrealizable, the unaccounted for — which in its unaccountedness is unconquerable: tomorrow.

Write it all down, use every ounce of strength you've got and write it all out to the very end; but if I, reading, feel this end, then — that's the end of you.

And — it's a strange miracle: the greater the creation (Faust), the less it is in comparison with the creator (Goethe). How do we know Goethe? Through Faust. Who told us that Goethe is greater than Faust? Faust himself — by his perfection.

Let's take an analogy:

"How great is God, to have created such a sun!" And, forgetting about the sun, the child thinks about God. The creation, through its very perfection, leads us to the creator. What is the sun, if not a lead to God? What is Faust, if not a lead to Goethe? What is Goethe, if not a lead to divinity? Perfection is not the end. Perfection happens here, ac-complishment — There. Goethe's period — is only the beginning! The first sign of the perfection of the creation (of the absolute) is the feeling of comparison it awakens in us. Height is only high because it is higher — than what? — than the previous "higher," and this is already consumed by the next. The mountain is higher than the brow, the cloud higher than the mountain, God is higher than the cloud — and then there's the inherently limitless height of the idea of God. For the word perfection (a condition) I would substitute perfectibility (a continuum). The breakthrough to divinity is as incomparably greater than Goethe, as Goethe — is greater than Faust; that's what makes both Goethe and Faust immortal: the insignificance of them, the great ones, in compari-son to what is incomparably higher. The only chance we have of perceiving the heights — is through a continual movement along the vertical of points that measures them. On earth the only chance of great-ness — is to convey a feeling of the height above your own head.

"But Goethe's dead and Faust lives on!" But, reader, don't you have the feeling that somewhere — in a duchy incomparably more spacious than Weimar — Part Three is taking place?

(())

A promise: tomorrow will be better! Tomorrow will be bigger! To-morrow will be higher! The promise on which all poetry — and some-thing higher than poetry — stands: the promise of a miracle above you, and for that reason of your miracle above others: nowhere in Briusov's lines does this promise exist.

> Perhaps all life is but a means
> For brightly singing verse,
> And since your carefree childhood,
> You have been searching for the words.

Words instead of meanings, rhymes instead of feelings. As if words were born of words, rhymes of rhymes, and poems of poems!

A mission implemented fifteen years later by Briusov's "Poetry Institute."

(( ))

The most perfect creation — ask an artist — is only an intention: what I wanted to do — and couldn't. The more perfect something is for us, the more imperfect for the artist. Beneath each of Briusov's lines lies: this was all I could manage. And more than that is actually impossible.

How little he wanted, if he was able to do so much!

To know your own capabilities — is to know your own inabilities. (Capability without inability — is all-powerfulness. Pushkin didn't know his abilities. Briusov — knew his own inabilities. Pushkin wrote haphazardly (the roughest of rough drafts — there was an element of miracle), Briusov wrote — for sure (statute, Institute).

(( ))

By the will of miracle — we have all of Pushkin. By the miracle of will — all of Briusov.

I can do no less (Pushkin. All-powerfulness).

I can do no more (Briusov. Abilities).

Since I couldn't do it today, I'll be able to tomorrow (Pushkin. Miracle).

Since I couldn't do it today, I'll never be able to do it (Briusov. Will).

But today — he always could.

(( ))

The *Egyptian Nights* that Briusov finished. Whether the attempt on Pushkin was carried out with adequate or inadequate means—what tempted him? A passion for the limit, for the signifying and graphic dash. Alien by his very nature to mystery, he didn't honor and didn't sense it in the unfinishedness of the creation. Pushkin didn't finish it—so I'll finish it (off).

The gesture of a barbarian. For, in some circumstances, completion is a no lesser, if not a greater act of vandalism, than destruction.

《 》

To be honest, all of Briusov's exercises with poetry—are futile attempts. He didn't have the wherewithal to become a poet (the wherewithal—is birth), and he became one. An overcoming of the impossible. *Kraftsprobe.* And the choice of his own antithesis: poetry (why not science? or mathematics? or archaeology?)—was simply the only outlet for his intensity: wrestling with the self.

And, to be more precise: Briusov wasn't wrestling with rhyme, but with his own lack of propensity for it. Poetry as an arena for self-combat.

《 》

After all that's been said, was Briusov a poet? Yes, but not by God's grace. A versifier, a composer of verses, and what's far more important, a creator of the creator in himself. Not a character from the Gospels, not one who buried his talent in the earth—but a man who by his own will forced it out of the ground. Who created something from nothing.

Onward, dreams, my faithful oxen!

Oh, this cry, which more closely resembles a gasp, is no accident; it's not there for the rhyme. If ever Briusov was truthful—to his core, then it was precisely in this gasp. With all his sinews, strength, like an ox—what is this, a poet's labor? No, his dreams! Inspiration + oxlike labor, that's the poet, oxlike labor + oxlike labor, that's Briusov: an ox, dragging a load. This ox is not devoid of greatness.

Who, but Briusov, could have compared dreams—to oxen? Let us recall Balmont, Vyacheslav, Blok, Sologub—and I'm only talking about poets of his generation (why doesn't Bely ever fit?)—who among them, in what hour of final prostration, could have uttered this "dreams — are oxen"? And if it had been "will" instead of "oxen," the poem would have been formulaic.

( )

A poet of willpower. An act of will, even if short-lived, is limitless at the given moment. Will is of this world, all here, all now. Who else held sway over real live people and fates like Briusov? Balmont? People were drawn to him. Blok? People were infected with him. Vyacheslav? People heeded him. Sologub? People conjectured about him. And people listened spellbound to them all. Everyone obeyed Briusov. There was something of the Stone Guest in his appearances at the Don Juan feasts of young poetry. The wine froze in glasses. People bent under Briusov's palm, not loving him, and his yoke was a hard one. "Magician," "Sorcerer" — you never heard this about the bewitching Balmont, nor the magical Blok, nor the born alchemist Vyacheslav, nor the alien Sologub — only about Briusov, about this dispassionate master of verse. What was this power? What kind of spells? The power was un-Russian and the spells were un-Russian: willpower, unusual in Russ, supernatural, a marvel in a magical kingdom where, as in a dream, everything is possible. Everything except naked will. And the marvelous magical kingdom of the Soul — Russia — was captivated, worshiped it, and bowed to this naked will.* To the Roman will of a Moscow merchant's son from somewhere near Trubnaya Square.

— Isn't this a fairy tale?

( )

It seems to me that Briusov must never have dreamed in his sleep, but knowing that poets dream, he replaced undreamed dreams with invented ones.

Isn't this — the inability to simply dream — the source of the sad passion for narcotics?

Briusov. Brius. (A Moscow black magician of the 18th century.) Per-

---

*A generation of poets is, after all, that very same Russia, and not the worst of it . . . (M.Ts.)

haps it's already been noted. (Knowing that I was going to write, I didn't read my predecessors in Briusov — not out of a fear of coinciding, but out of a fear that if they upbraided him, then I would overpraise him. Briusov. Brius. The assonance isn't accidental. Rationalists, seen by their contemporaries as black magicians. (*Enlightenment,* which in Russia transforms into *black magic.*)

(())

Briusov's fate and essence are tragic. The tragedy of loneliness? The tragedy created by all poets.

. . . Und sind ihr ganzes Leben so allein . . .
(Rilke on poets.)

Here, a tragedy of desired loneliness, of an artificial gap between you and all that is alive, a fateful desire to be a monument — in your own life-time. The tragedy of a proud man, with the sad satisfaction that at least it's his own fault. His whole life he fought doggedly to be a monument in his lifetime: not to love too much, not to give too much, not to deign.

I would like to not be Valery Briusov —

is only proof that he wanted nothing else his entire life. And so, in 1922, an empty pedestal, surrounded by the hoots and howls of the ne'er-do-wells, good-for-nothings, don't-give-a-damners. The best — fell away, turned away. With the infallible instinct of baseness sensing — great-ness — the boors to whom he bowed in vain spat on him ("he's not one of us! Too good for us, he is!"). Briusov was alone. Not alone *above* (the dream of an ambitious man), but alone — *outside.*

"I want to write in the new way — and I can't!" I heard this admission with my own ears in Moscow in 1920 from the stage of the Great Hall of the Conservatory. (About this evening — later.) *I can't!* Briusov, whose whole meaning was "I can," Briusov, who, in the end, could not!

(())

In this exclamation there was — a wolf. Not a human being, but a wolf. Briusov the human being always made me think of a wolf. For so long — unpunished! From 1918 to 1922 — hunted. By whom? By the very same poetic scum that screeched at the dying Blok (he died a month later): "Don't you see that you're dead? You're a corpse! You stink! Into the grave with you!" By the poetic scum: cocaine addicts, speculators of scandal and saccharine with whom he, the master, the Parnassian, the power, the spellbinder, fraternized. Whose coats he held with whining obsequiousness in the foyer of his apartment.

(( ))

Briusov was able to spurn his friends and colleagues, his *contemporaries*. The hour was not theirs. Matters of affection — he transgressed. But he couldn't make do without those who called themselves the "new poetry": the hour was *theirs!*

(( ))

A passion for fame and glory. This, too, is Rome. Who of those named — Balmont, Blok, Vyacheslav, Sologub — wanted fame? Balmont? Too in love with himself and the world. Blok? That knot of pure conscience? Vyacheslav? He'd outgrown it by a millennium. Sologub?

I won't sit in the sled in the moonlight —
And I won't travel anywhere at all!

Sologub with his magnificent disdain?

A Russian views glory-seeking during one's lifetime either with disdain or with ridicule. Love of fame: is self-love. Since time immemorial, the Russian poet has left glory to the military and paid homage to this glory. And what about Pushkin's poem "The Monument"?* Insight, nothing else. On lifetime fame:

Take praise and slander with indifference
And don't dispute a fool,

and remain indifferent to the most important foundation — the quantitative — of fame. I can't help quoting the cry of the best contemporary Russian poet: "O, with what joy I would declare my own mediocrity for all to hear, if only they would let me live and work in mediocrity!"

*Briusov has a poem "Monument" as well. Whoever has read it — remembers. (M.Ts.)

The cry of every poet — especially of a Russian poet: the greater the poet — the louder the cry. Briusov alone craved fame. The whisper behind the back: "Briusov!"; the lowered or staring eyes: "Briusov!"; the hand growing chill in the hand: "Briusov!" This Stone Guest was — a fame seeker. This is not our greatness, for us — it's a ridiculous greatness, if I said it in Russian, it would sound like a translation: une petitesse qui ne manque pas de grandeur.

(( ))

"Briusov was the first, Annensky wasn't the first" (the words of the same poet). Yes, incomparable poet, you are right: the only one is never first. First is a *degree,* after all, the last step of a ladder whose first step — is the last. The first is relative, dependent, in a line. The unique one — is outside. There is never a second inimitable.

Two types of poetry.

A common cause, created separately.

(The creative work of isolated individuals. Annensky.)

A personal affair, created together.

(Cliquishness. Briusov's Institute.)

(( ))

There was one vice that Briusov didn't have: their pettiness. All of his vices, beginning with that very same pettiness, are *en grand.* One would like to believe that in Rome they would have been virtues.

(( ))

Fame? Billions love you. Power? Billions fear you.

Briusov didn't love fame, but power.

Everyone — has his own verb, which defines his deeds. Briusov's was — to harass.

(( ))

There is a certain baseness in laying out poet's cards this way, in front of everyone. There's no cliquishness (it's despicable!), but there is a round robin of responsibility. Everyone can make a judgment about an artist — at least, that's what's usually thought and done. But only artists — I maintain — may judge an artist. An artist should be judged either by a court of peers or a supreme court — either by colleagues in craft, or by God. Only they and God know what it means: to create the other world — in these worlds. The philistine is no judge of the poet, no matter what he was like in life. His sins — are not yours. And his vices are preferable to your virtues.

Avoir les rieurs de son côté — is too easy, the effect is too cheap. I, de mon côté, would like to have not les rieurs, but les penseurs. And the only purpose of these notes — is to force *friends* to think about it.

(( ))

The purpose of V. Ya. Briusov's arrival on earth — was to prove to people what can and can't, but mostly can, be done — by willpower.

(( ))

Three words reveal Briusov: will, ox, wolf. A trinity not only of sound, but of sense: will — is Rome, and the ox — is Rome, and the wolf — is Rome. Valery Briusov was a Roman thrice over: as will and the ox in poetry, as a wolf (*homo homini lupus est*) in life. And my unjust heart, which nonetheless craves justice, will not rest until there is in Rome — at least in some far-flung suburb — in what, if not marble? — a statue:

TO THE SCYTHIAN ROMAN FROM ROME

II

First Encounter

My first encounter with Briusov was indirect. I was six years old. I had just started Zograf-Plaksina's music school (an old white house on Merzliakovsky Lane, at Nikitsky Gates). The day I'm talking about was my first performance on stage, a piece for four hands (the first in the Lebert and Stark anthology), and my partner was — Evgeniya Yakovlevna Briusova, the pearl of the school and my love. The oldest student and the youngest. For one, all the musical trials were over — the other was a blank page. After a triumph (of an amusing sort) I went over to my mother. She was in the audience with an unknown older lady. Mother's conversation with the lady about music, children, the lady's tale of her son Valery (my sister's name was Valeriya, which is why I remembered), "so talented and spirited," who wrote poems and had had a misunderstanding with the police. (Apparently that student business of '98–'99? Whether Briusov was a student at this time, and what misunderstanding he had — I don't know, I'm simply telling it the way I remember.) I remember that my mother sympathized (because of the poems? That was certainly no less a misfortune than a misunderstanding with the police). They said something about hotheaded youth. My mother sympathized, the other mother complained and commended. "So talented and spirited." "He's so spirited because he's talented." The conversation went on. (It was intermission.) Both mothers complained and commended. I listened.

"The police — why get involved with politics? — and that's why he's so spirited."

III

The Letter

The first indirect encounter — was at six years of age, the first face-to-face — at sixteen.

I went to buy books at Wolf's, on Kuznetsky — to buy Rostand's *Chanteclair,* which they didn't have in stock. At sixteen, an unreceived book that you've gone to buy is the same as an unreceived letter to general delivery: you wait — and it isn't there, you could be carrying it — but all you've got is emptiness. I was standing, looking for a substitute, but Rostand at 16? There is none. Even now, sometimes — he is irreplaceable, so I was standing no longer looking for a substitute, when suddenly, behind my left shoulder, where angels are supposed to be — came a staccato bark never before heard and instantly recognized:

"*Lettres de Femmes* — Prevault. *Fleurs du Mal,* Baudelaire, and *Chanteclair,* I suppose, though I'm not an admirer of Rostand."

I raise my eyes, my heart stops: Briusov!

I stand there, having already found a substitute, I browse through the books, my heart is in my throat, for minutes like these — even now! — I'd give my life. And Briusov, with an insistent, methodical bark, biting the words off and spitting them out: "Although I'm not an admirer of Rostand."

My heart in my throat — twice. Briusov himself! Briusov of the Black Mass, Briusov of Renata, Briusov of Antony! — And — not an admirer of Rostand: Rostand of *L'Aiglon,* Rostand — of Melissande, Rostand — of Romanticism!

While I let the impact of the last word sink in, an impact that could not be felt completely, for the word was — the soul, Briusov left, shutting the door with a dry click. I left as well — not to follow him, but to meet him: I went home to write him a letter.

(()

Dear Valery Yakovlevich,
(I reconstruct from memory.)

Today, in Wolf's shop, ordering *Chanteclair* from the clerk, you added: "although I'm not an admirer of Rostand." You said it not once, but twice. Three questions:

How could you, a poet, announce your dislike of another poet — to a clerk?

Second: how could you, who wrote Renata, not love Rostand, who wrote *Melissande?*

Third: — and how could you prefer Marcel Prevault to Rostand?

I didn't speak to you then, in the store, from fear that you would take it as an ambitious desire "to talk with Briusov." You are free not to answer this letter.

Marina Tsvetaeva

I didn't include my address — so it wouldn't be easy to answer. (At the time I was in the 6th year of gymnasium, my first book came out only a year later; Briusov didn't know me, but he was certain to know my father's name and could answer, if he so desired.)

About two days later, if I'm not mistaken — a sealed card arrived at the address of the Rumiantsev Museum, of which my father was director (we lived in our own house on Trekhprudny). Not a postcard—insufficiently attentive, not a letter—too attentive, *die goldene Mitte,* a way out—a sealed card. (Briusov's "not to give too much.") I opened it:

"Gracious Mademoiselle Tsvetaeva,"

(NB! I addressed him as—Dear Valery Yakovlevich, and he was twenty years older than I!)

I don't remember the beginning. Regarding the poet and clerk there was simply no answer. Marcel Prevault evaporated. On Rostand, literally the following:

"Rostand was progressive in the movement from the XIX to the XX century and regressive from the XX century to our days" (this was in 1910). "I didn't take to Rostand, because I didn't happen to fall in love with him. *For love—is a matter of chance*" (underlined).

A few more words, indicating either the desire to meet, or perhaps correspond further, but not clearly, otherwise I would have remembered. And—his signature.

Naturally I didn't answer this letter (because I passionately wanted to).

For love—is a matter of chance.

(())

This letters survives; it's preserved with my other papers with friends, in Moscow.

The first letter remained the last.

IV

Two Little Verses

My first book, *Evening Album,* came out when I was 17—poems written at 15, 16, and 17. I published it for reasons unrelated to literature, but akin to poetry—as a substitute for a letter to a person with whom I had no opportunity to communicate otherwise. I never did become a true literati, the beginning was portentous.

At that time it was easy to publish a book: collect the poems, take them to the printer's, select a cover, pay the invoice—and that was it.

That's what I did, without telling anyone, as a VIIth-year schoolgirl. When the printing was finished I took all 500 copies of the book to the warehouse of Spiridonov and Mikhailov's godforsaken store (why?) and calmed down. I didn't send a single copy for review, I didn't even know that it was done, and if I had known — I wouldn't have: to ask for a review! My book couldn't be found anywhere except Spiridonov and Mikhailov's, but reviews appeared nonetheless — well-wishing ones at that: a big article by Max Voloshin that laid the foundation of our friendship, one by Marietta Shaginian (I mention those I valued) and, finally, a review by Briusov. Here's what sank in:

"Miss Tsvetaeva's poems possess a kind of horrible intimacy, which at times becomes embarrassing, as though one had accidentally glanced into the window of a stranger's apartment." (I thought: a house, not an apartment!)

I omit the middle — about the complete mastery of form, the absence of influences, an originality of themes and their expression unusual in a beginner — since I don't remember the exact words. And, at the end: "We won't hide the fact, however, that there are feelings more piercing and concepts more vital than:

No! The Pharisees arrogance is hateful to me!

But when we find out that the author is only seventeen years old, we're at a loss for words."

This approach was unusual for Briusov. I repeat, people congratulated me on the review. And I, of all the pleasant remarks, naturally remembering only the unpleasant, made a joke of it: "More vital concepts and piercing feelings? Just wait!"

A year later my second book, *Magic Lantern,* came out (1912 then a break until 1922; I wrote, but didn't publish) — and the following poem was in it —

> To V. Ya. Briusov
> You may smile into my "window,"
> Or among the clowns account me —
> You will change me not a whit
> "Piercing feelings," "vital concepts"

Were not granted me by God.
One must sing that all is drear,
That black dreams hang o'er the planet.
—Tis the custom now I fear.—
But those feelings and those concepts
Were not granted me by God!

In a word, the troops crossed the border. On a certain day, at a certain hour, I, a nobody, opened hostilities against — Briusov.

The poem isn't brilliant, but it's beside the point; the point is Briusov's reaction to it.

"Unfortunately, Miss Tsvetaeva's second book, *Magic Lantern,* didn't live up to our hopes. The excessive, ruinous facility of the verse." A series of unpleasant things I don't remember, and, at the end: "For that matter, what else can one expect from a poet who admits that God granted her no piercing feelings and vital concepts." The words from his first review, which I had put in quotation marks, as *his* words, were presented without quotation marks. I looked like an idiot. (Valery Briusov, *Far and Near,* a collection of critical articles.)

The riposte was instantaneous. Almost immediately after *Magic Lantern* I published a small collection from the two first books, called just that, *From Two Books,* and in that collection, in black on white:

To V. Ya. Briusov
I forgot that your heart — is no more than a night light,
Not a star! I forgot!
That your poetry comes out of books,
Your critique comes from envy. Old man now in looks —
Once again, for a moment — I thought
That your place was among the great poets.

It's curious that this poem arose not after the review, but after a dream about him with Renata, a magical dream he never knew about. The point of the poem — is its end, and in Briusov's place, I would have seen only the last two words. But Briusov was a poor reader (of souls).

(( ))

This time no printed review followed, but "in the mountains" (of his steep soul) "the rebound" lasted — his whole life.

(())

I'm not flattering myself. Briusov in the experience of my feelings, more precisely: in the youthful experience of enmity, Briusov meant incomparably more to me than I did — to his world-weary experience. First of all, for me, he was Briusov (a solid entity), who didn't like me; for him I was — X, who didn't like him and meant something only because I didn't like him. I didn't like Briusov, but he didn't like one of these young poets, a woman for that matter, and he disdained women in general. I felt no disdain for him — neither then, when he was at the summit of his fame, nor later, when he lay under its ruins. I know this because of the excitement with which I now write these lines, an infallible excitement, communicated to us only by greatness. I was brash — yes, I was brazen — yes, disdainful — no. And, perhaps, I was both brash and brazen only because I didn't know how else (didn't want?) to display my own sense of rank, which I feel very strongly. In a word, if I were to carry our encounter into the walls of a school, I was brazen to the director, the rector, but not to the teacher. There was a certain reverence in my brashness, in his offendedness — only irritation. The significance of enmity corresponds directly to the significance of the object. For that reason, in this non-love affair the winner (for the only prize any of our feelings may claim — is their own maximum) — was I.

V

"The Family of Poets"

That same winter of 1911–12, between one rhymed attack and the other, I was invited to read somewhere — at the "Society for Free Esthetics" I think it was. (All the young poets of Moscow were supposed to read.) I remember a green room, not the main one, but the one where everyone waited to go on stage. A thick black male group of poets, and, a head above them, actually heading them up — Briusov.

"And this is the poetess Marina Tsvetaeva. But since 'we're all friends in the family of poets,' we can dispense (a turn to me) with the hand shakes."

(Didn't this presage the Soviet "handshakes are canceled"; for the Soviets — it was because of scabies, but what was Briusov's reason?)

Targeting the only person I knew in the entire group — Rubanovich, I approached and shook his hand in greeting, then moved on to his closest neighbor: "Tsvetaeva," then to the neighbor's neighbor, then to the neighbor's neighbor's neighbor and so on in a circle until I had greeted all of them — except Briusov. This took a certain amount of time — after all, there were about twenty people — particularly since, though quick by nature, I transformed the pro forma into feeling, a routine into a rite. "Silence reigned" in the room. I introduced myself: "Tsvetaeva." Briusov waited. Shaking the twentieth hand, I humbly left the circle and stood to one side, innocently, almost like a schoolgirl. The staccato of Briusov's broad-muzzled bark sounded simultaneously.

"Now, gentlemen, may we begin?"

( )

What did Briusov want with his "family of poets"? Were we such good friends that it wasn't worth shaking hands? Did he want to free me from twenty alien hands in my one hand? Himself — from five minutes of inaction? Was he trying to spare the beginner her supposed shyness?

Perhaps it was one of the above, or perhaps everything together, but more likely it was his subconscious dislike of close, human (and, therefore, obligating) acquaintance through the palm of the hand. A wolf's leap back upon spying another breed. A nose for difference. Instinct.

So from then on it was an exchange of nods. Each time it became later and later for the hand. You have to admit that having greeted one another dryly for ten years in a row, it's rather awkward, even indecent, to suddenly up and shake hands.

I never did find out what kind of palm Briusov had.

VI

Prize Puppy

Il faut à chacun donner son joujou.
— *E. Rostand*

It was Christmas Eve of 1911 — a blizzardy Moscow night, with stars in the eyes and stars falling on the eyes. That morning I found out from Sergei Yakovlevich Efron, whom I would soon marry, that Briusov had announced a competition on the following two lines of Pushkin:

But Jenny never will abandon
Edmond, even in heaven.

"What if you took the prize — how amusing! I can just imagine how moved Briusov would be! If Briusov is Salieri, do you know who his Mozart is?"

"Balmont?"

"Pushkin!"

A prize given to me by Briusov for a poem presented at the last hour of the last day (the final deadline was Christmas Eve) — that was a tempting idea! But — a poem on a theme!* A poem — on commission! A poem — at Briusov's behest! And the second stumbling block, the hardest — was that I didn't have the slightest idea who Edmond was, a man or a woman, a boyfriend or girlfriend. If it was in the genitive case: "whom-of what" — then Edmond was a man, and Jenny would never abandon *him;* if it was the nominative case: "Who-what" — then Edmonda was a woman and would never abandon her girlfriend Jenny. The block was removed easily. Someone, laughing, incredulous at my innocence, opened Pushkin's *Feast in Time of Plague,* thus confirming *Edmond's* masculinity. But the time had passed: Christmas Eve crept over Moscow in stars and snowflakes.

In the darkness, just before the lighting of the trees, I stood on the corner of Arbat Square and handed an envelope to a gray-haired messenger in a red hat; inside that envelope was another, inside which there was yet another envelope. On the outside one was Briusov's address, on the second one (with the poem) a motto (the competition was anony-

---

*Now I think differently. (M.Ts.)

mous, the author's name revealed only when the prizes were awarded), on the third — the same motto, with a note: the name and address. It was something like the kingdom beyond the seas and the story of Kashchei's Death in the Egg. I sent the "missive" to Briusov's house on Tsvetnoi Boulevard as a present for the Christmas tree.

What was the motto? From Rostand, of course:

"Il faut à chacun donner son joujou"* — E. Rostand

What was the poem like? It wasn't on the theme, of course, it wasn't written about Edmond at all, but six months earlier, about my own Edmond, a poem not only not on the theme, but its opposite, and fitting in its oppositeness.

Here it is:

But Jenny never will abandon
Edmond, even in heaven.

My shoulders are sore bowed with recollections,
I'll cry about this earth in heaven too.
Old words and feelings I won't hide,[†] when
We meet anew.
Where there are hosts of angels sleekly flying,
Where harps and lilies lull a children's choir,
Where all is restful, calm — restless then,
I'll seek your gaze.
Smiling, I'll bid farewell to heaven's visions,
Alone among aloof and faultless maids,
I'll sing, terrestrial, a stranger,
The earth's refrain!
My shoulders are sore bowed with recollections,
I'll not conceal the tears that flood my eyes,
Not here, nor there — I need no visitations,
And not for visits will we wake in paradise!

I took this poem from *Magic Lantern,* which had already been type-set and would appear in print before the prize ceremony, but after the jury's decision. (*Magic Lantern,* p. 75.)

*NB! A competition to Briusov, for example. (M.Ts.)
†"Won't repeat" would have been better. (M.Ts.)

A month later — I had just gotten married — my husband and I happened to drop by to see the publisher Kozhebatkin.

"Congratulations, Marina Ivanovna!"

I, thinking about marriage:

"Thank you."

"You got the first prize, but when Briusov found out that it was you he decided to give you the first of two second prizes, since you're so young."

I burst out laughing.

The prizes were awarded at the "Society for Free Esthetics." The details have faded. I remember only that when Briusov announced: "No one received the first prize, the first of two second prizes was received by Miss Tsvetaeva," a certain perplexity spread through the hall, and a grin over my face. Then the poems themselves were read, by Briusov himself it seems, and after those of the "prizewinners" (Khodasevich, Rafalovich, me) — were poems worthy of "honorable mention," I don't remember whose. The distribution of the actual prizes took place not on the stage, but at the entry table, behind which sat Briusov's wife, Zhanna Matveevna, who kept writing in something and writing out something; a sweet, shy woman who was always smoothing over things as much as possible and thus came off extremely well against the background of Briusov's cruelty.

The prize — a gold coin engraved with our names, sporting a black Pegasus — was handed out by Briusov himself. Not exactly a handshake, but our hands did meet! Threading it through the chain of my bracelet, I asked in a loud, jolly voice:

"So this means I'm a prize puppy now?"

There was answering laughter from the hall and — kind — sudden — wolflike — a smile from Briusov. The word "smile" — is just a convention, it was simply a sudden exposure and disappearance of the teeth. Not a smile? Yes, a smile! Only not ours, a wolf's. (A grimace, a grin, a gnashing.)

That's when I first guessed that Briusov — was a wolf.

( )

If I'm not mistaken, that same evening I saw the poetess Lvova for the first (and only) time. Not very tall, dressed modestly in blue, black eyes-eyebrows-head, vivid rosy cheeks, very much the student from a young ladies' institute, a real girl. A lifting to meet Briusov's bowing. The perfect vision of a man and a woman: to her head-flung-back pride in him — the condescension of his own pride in *himself.* A happiness restrained all round with difficulty.

He — was circling her, pursuing.

PART TWO

THE REVOLUTION

I

Lito

My youthful episode with Briusov ended with the prize puppy. From 1912 to 1920 I lived outside of literary life — and we didn't meet.

It was the year 1919 — the most plagued, blackest, deathly of all those years in Moscow. I don't remember who it was, perhaps Khodasevich, who advised me to take a book of poems to Lito.* "Lito doesn't print anything, but they buy everything."

I: "Wonderful."

"Briusov runs it."

I: "Wonderful, but less so. He can't stand me."

"You, but not your poetry. I promise you, they'll buy. After all, it will be at least five days of bread."

I copied out *Youthful Poems* (1913–16, still unpublished) and *Mileposts I* (published by Gosizdat in 1922) and, taking my then five-year-old daughter Alya in my right hand and the manuscript in my left, I went to try my luck at Lito. On Nikitskaya St., was it? Briusov wasn't there; someone was, and I handed the manuscript over to him. I handed it over and everything vanished — the poems and I.

About a year passed. I went on living, the poems lay there. I remem-

*Literary Department. (M.Ts.)

bered them with invariable hostility, as one remembers something loaned, not requested in time, and therefore — no longer mine. Nonetheless I somehow pulled myself together. I went to Lito: it was empty: Budantsev was there. "I came to find out about two books of poems submitted approximately a year ago." A slight embarrassment and, helping him out: "I would really like to get the manuscripts back — after all, nothing worked out, did it?"

Budantsev, joyously: "It didn't work out, didn't work out, between you and me — Valery Yakovlevich was *very* much against you."

"Here even a little is enough. But the manuscripts still exist, don't they?"

"They exist, they exist, just a minute I'll return them."

"Marvelous. These days that's more than a poet can ask."

And so, home again with the manuscripts. At home I open them, leaf through them, and — oh surprise! — the second Briusov autograph in my life! Three entire lines of review — in his own handwriting!

"M. Tsvetaeva's poems, as they weren't published in time and do not reflect the corresponding contemporaneity, are useless." No, there was something else, as always, I remembered the high note — the end. I have the visual impression of precisely three lines of Briusov's cramped, miserly, anxious handwriting. What could have been in those other one and a half lines? I don't know, but it wasn't any worse. This review, together with some of my other papers, is with friends in Moscow. The continuation of Briusov's Roman formula was the spacious Russian statement (this time typed) of his admirer, follower and adherent — S. Bobrov. "Nauseatingly gushy verbiage on the subject of her own death." This is about *Youthful Poems,* about *Mileposts* I remember only one word, and even then not exactly; I can see it written, but I can't read it, something like "gnosiological," but referring to the meter. "The poems are written in a heavy, indigestible, 'gnosiological' iambs." Briusov set the theme, Bobrov digested it, and in the end — I had the manuscript in hand.

In 1922, Gosizdat, in the person of the communist censor Meshcheriakov, turned out to be more tractable and more magnanimous.

( )

(Having written the word "censor," I suddenly realized: how well the very Roman sound of the word corresponds to Briusov! Censor, mentor, dictator, Cerberus .)

(( ))

Later, when I ran into Budantsev, he begged me, fervently and touchingly, to return the reviews:

"You weren't supposed to read them, it was my oversight, they'll make me pay for it!"

"Forgive me, but this is my *titre de noblesse,* Tiutchev's patent of nobility, an honorary ticket everywhere poetry is honored."

"Copy them and return the originals!"

"What? How could I give up a Briusov autograph? The autograph of the author of *Fiery Angel?* (Pause.) Give it away, when I could sell it? I'll go abroad and sell it there — you can tell Briusov that!"

"And the Bobrov review? At least give Bobrov back!"

"I'll keep Bobrov for company. Three lines of Briusov — cost such and such, and they get four pages of Bobrov into the bargain. You can tell that to Bobrov."

I made a joke of it and remained intransigent.

II

An Evening at the Conservatory

*Notes of My Daughter Alya, Then Seven Years Old**
8 Nikitskaya St.
An Evening in the Great Hall of the Conservatory

A dark night. We're walking down Nikitskaya St. to the Great Hall of the Conservatory. Marina is going to read there and a lot of other poets. Finally, we got there. We wandered around a long time and looked for the dinky poet V. G. Shershenevich. Finally, Mama comes across an acquaintance who brings us into the little room where everyone who was going to read was already sitting. The old man Briusov was sitting there

---

*These notes were not changed by a single letter. (M.Ts.)

with a stony face (after the reading I slept under his coat). I asked Marina to play the piano, but she hesitated. Soon after we came in I began to recite Mama's poems to Briusov, but she held me back. Some man with curled hair and a blue shirt came up to Mama. He looked quite full of himself. He said: "I was told that you are planning to get married . . ." "Tell those who are so well informed that I sleep and in my dreams I dream I'm seeing Seriozha, Alya's papa."* He went away. Soon the first bell started ringing. Budantsev came up to Mama and went on stage with her. I went with her. The platform looked like a stage. There was a row of chairs. Marina sat there and a lot of other people. The first time Briusov came out. He read an introduction, but I didn't listen to anything because I didn't understand. Then the Imaginist Shershenevich came out. He read about a head, and on the head stood a botanical garden, on the botanical garden stood a circus dome, and I sit on it and look into a woman's womb as into a chalice. The poor cars, they look like a flock of geese, that is, like a triangle. Spring, spring, the automobiles enjoy spring. And stuff like that. Then Briusov started to read poems. After him there came a little woman with slightly buck teeth. She was in a torn padded jacket, with a gentle face. She definitely didn't have wings, or wool, or even sheepskin. She held her thin body in her arms and couldn't tame it or let it go. Finally they called Mama. She sat me down on her seat and went up to the reading table. Looking at her everyone started laughing. (Probably because she had a purse.)† She read poems about Stenka Razin. She read clearly, without any foreign words. She stood like an angel. All the people in the hall looked at the reader like a hawk or an owl at a defenseless bird. Some Imaginist said: "Look over there. The 'loners' are sitting in the upper boxes. They're keeping together." She didn't read very loud. One man even stood up and came closer to the platform. Stenka Razin, three poems about how he loved the Persian girl. Then his dream, how she came to him for her shoe, which she had dropped on the ship. Then, when she had finished, *she bowed,*‡ which no one else did. Her applause didn't last long, but

---

*My husband had been in the army since 1917. (M.Ts.)

†An officer's field pouch. (M.Ts.)

‡Underlined in the original. (M.Ts.)

everyone clapped. Marina sat back down on her seat and put me on her lap. After her, a dark young man who was sitting next to us started to read a drama. The beginning: under the ceiling in the circus a dancer hangs from a thin string, and under her in the arena is a hunchback who praises her. "Alya! Let's go! This is going to go on a long time." "No, Marina, let's see what happens." Marina asked and I finally agreed. We left and went into the secret room. No one was there, except some woman who had recently moved from the countryside. I sat down on a chair with a completely bleary look and Mama suggested I lie down until people came. I was glad. I lay down. The country woman suggested covering me and Marina spread someone's coat over me. Soon after I lay down, the whole crowd of poets barged in. There were only four chairs in the room. People sat on the tables, on the windowsills, and though I dimly heard them even sitting on the piano, I just stretched out my legs. Mama and the thin poetess perched near the bent armrest. "She's sleeping." "No, her eyes are open." "Alya, are you sleeping?" "Nnoo." White spots, heads, horses, men, children, houses, snow. A round garden with a gray vegetable patch. A black iron fence. A gray circus dome with a cross. And under the botanical garden a red triangular chalice. I was dreaming the poem of that crazy Shershenevich. Waking up, I threw off the blanket of a wolf-fur coat. Mama was completely suffocated by my legs. The poets walked around, sat on the floor. I sat on the sofa. Mama was happy that I could give a seat to others. Two people stood by the table. One in a short summer coat, the other in a winter fur-lined fur coat. Suddenly the short one rushed to the door through which a thin man with long ears* entered. "Seriozha, dear, sweet Seriozha, where have you been?" "I haven't eaten anything for eight days." "Where were you, Seriozhenka?" "They gave me half an apple. They don't even celebrate Sunday. There wasn't even a piece of bread. I barely got out. It was cold. Didn't take off my underclothes for eight days. Oh, I'm so hungry!" "Poor guy, how did you get out?" "Someone made a fuss." Everyone crowded around and started asking questions. Soon Mama got her 10 Soviets and we started getting ready to leave. I began looking for my mittens and hood. Finally we were dressed and we left.

*Sergei Esenin. (M.Ts.)

We went out through some winding back entrance and came out in the dark courtyard of the Great Conservatory. We went out. There are lamps* all along Nikitskaya St. Somewhere a primus stove was burning in a window. A dog barked. I kept falling and we walked along talking about Briusov. The store windows with dolls and books are lit up.† I said: "Briusov is a stone. He looks like the grandfather of Lord Fauntleroy. Only a creature like Fauntleroy could love him. If they took him to court, he would tell lies like the truth, and truth like a lie."

(())

Moscow, the beginning of December 1920.

A few days later, reading *The Jungle Book*.

"Marina! Do you know who Shere-Khan is? Briusov! He's also lame and lonely, and he also has an Adalis there." (She reads): "'And old Shere-Khan walked around and openly accepted flattery.' I really recognized Briusov in that! And Adalis was a stray, one of the young wolves."

(())

I'll fill in the blanks. Entering the room with me, and having recognized Briusov immediately from my descriptions, Alya lived for him alone. So all the offers to play the piano — were exclusively for him, to keep him scared: what if I began to play? Briusov made an effort not to look, clearly wary, sensing that there was more here than met the eye, and not knowing what might happen (*telle mère, telle fille*). One doesn't engage with seven-year-olds (and given her Soviet malnourishment, she looked five years old), so if something happened, his position was extremely awkward. (I'm convinced that Briusov took two-year-olds into account!)

A second note. The declamation of my poem to Briusov — to Briusov himself — was impromptu, and sent chills through me. The feeling that the room had suddenly become crowded — not a room but a cage, and not only is there a wolf in it — but I'm in there with him! Exactly the feeling of being locked up with a wolf, with that same awkwardness of both animal and human in the first seconds. But there was something

*But they aren't lit. (M.Ts.)

†At night — from thieves — windows of the secondhand stores.

else as well. Here, in this closeness, almost brow to brow — in front of so many witnesses! — to hear from a seven-year-old child — with such marvelous eyes! — the bravado of her not-so-long-ago-seventeen-year-old mother. To hear with his own ears! If Briusov had been profound, if he had had feelings more piercing than: Briusov! (vital concepts he had aplenty) — had he been able to get over himself, he would have appreciated the uniqueness of the phenomenon.

I forgot that your heart — is no more than a night light,
Not a star! I forgot!
That your poetry — comes out of books.

I stopped her on the first line, she stopped on the third. But in this challenge there was, aside from revenge for me, *the infatuation of enmity* inherited from me, and which I immediately recognized. And, if the poem didn't suddenly end with a kiss — it was due solely to shyness. (This breed is shy in affection, not on the attack.)

What did he think? A badly behaved child? No, she was well behaved. Prompted by me? Clearly not, he saw the purity of my fright. Nor could he have helped but like her physical appearance (Vyacheslav Ivanov: "She opens your heart and walks right in"). I think that the only thing he thought was: "The sooner they leave." And — o horrors! — he's on the stage, she (with me) — is following him! We're sitting almost next to each other. What else is in store? What other "impromptu?"

To his credit I will say that he didn't remove his wolf coat from her while she slept, though he was in a hurry. He kept clearing his throat. In my own defense, I'll say that I didn't choose *his* coat specifically. It's just that — it was fur! It's good to sleep under fur! Alya can say: "I slept under the enemy's hide."

About the hand, that didn't remove it:

If I die, and they ask me, "Pray tell,
What good deed did you do then to charm?"
I shall answer: "My thoughts on that day in May's dell
Wished the butterfly come to no harm."
(Balmont)

III

An Evening of Poetesses

They didn't do much sewing there
Their strength was not in sewing . . .

In the summer of 1920, late in the evening, someone . . . something . . . a female voice in a huge hat, dropped by unexpectedly. (There was no light, there was also no face.)

Accustomed to unexpected visits — the front door didn't lock — accustomed to everything in the world and having developed the habit over the Soviet years of never speaking first, I waited, my face turned aside.

"Are you Marina Tsvetaeva?"

"Yes."

"This is the way you live, without light?"

"Yes."

"Why don't you order it to be repaired?"

"I don't know how."

"To repair or to order?"

"Neither."

"What do you do at night?"

"I wait."

"For it to turn on?"

"For the Bolsheviks to leave."

"They'll never leave."

"Never."

A brief burst of double laughter filled the room. In speech the voice was drawn out, almost to the point of song. The laughter indicated intelligence.

"I'm Adalis. You haven't heard about me?"

"No."

"All Moscow knows."

"I don't know all Moscow."

"Adalis, with whom — who is . . . All Valery Yakovlevich's recent poems are dedicated to me. You really don't like him, I hear?"

"Nor does he like me."

"He can't stand you."

"That's fine with me."

"And me. I'm endlessly grateful to you that he never liked you."

"Never."

More laughter. The wave of mutual goodwill grows.

"I came here to ask you if you would read at an evening of poetesses."

"No."

"I knew it, and I told V. Ya. so right away. Well, but would you read with me?"

"With you by yourself, yes."

"Why? You don't even know my poetry."

"You are smart and witty and couldn't write bad poetry. Much less read it."

(In an ingratiating voice.) "And with me and Radlova?"

"The communist?"

"Well, female communism."

"I agree that male monarchism is better." (Pause.) "Don monarchism. But jokes aside, is she a Party member or not?"

"No, no, of course not!"

"And the evening is completely unrelated."

"Completely."

"You, Radlova, and I."

"You, Radlova, and I."

"Will they pay?"

"You'll be paid."

"Oh, don't be so quick! People like me, but they don't pay me."

"Briusov doesn't like you, and he'll pay you."

"It's a good thing that Briusov doesn't like me!"

"I tell you, he can't stand you. Do you know what he said when he got your manuscripts? 'I hold her in high esteem as a poet, but I as a woman I can't abide her, and she'll get nowhere with me!'"

"But the poems were offered by a poet, not a woman!"

"You know, that's what I said — others said it, too — but we couldn't change his mind. What happened between the two of you?"

Laughing, I told her what the reader already knows. Adalis: "Oh, he's vengeful and holds grudges."

"I never considered him a Christian or a Slav."

"And sometimes he's excessively petty."

"For 'excessively' I forgive him."

(( ))

If the poetess Adalis and I didn't exactly become good friends, we nonetheless struck up a friendly acquaintanceship. She would often drop in to see me, mostly at night, always excited, always hungry, always unexpected, invariably witty.

"V. Ya. is jealous of you, I'm always talking about you."

"On purpose or not?"

"Both. His face darkens at the very sound of your name."

"Why darken obscure things? He's not exactly fair anyway."

Briusov's appearance. First: inflexibility, rigidity, down to the very bristle of hairs spurting from his skull (a "crew" cut). The inability to bend (the impossibility of humor, fancy, *imprévu* — of everything that relates to mental grace). Mustaches like tusks, the typical French *en croc*. The mustaches of an attacker, which twitched when he was angry. A cone-shaped head, tilted upward, chilly gaze and challenge, invariably from on high. A willful, Napoleonic, *completely natural* — a gesture of focused will! — crossing of the arms. Arms down along the body — wasn't Briusov. Either a pen, or a cross. In the slant of the eyes and high cheekbones — a resemblance to Lenin. Rough-hewn looks, with an ax, not a chisel. Not powerfully, but precisely. Given the inadequacy of what was given — the strongest *gift* (it wasn't given to him, so he gave it himself).

Here, as in his work, Briusov made everything of himself that he could.

(( ))

And his eyes were yellowish brown, a wolf's.

(( ))

(After writing these lines. In answer to my question, what was his face like? An acquaintance of mine said with the brilliance of female directness: "I don't know . . . sort of . . . shodden.")

◯ ⟩

Adalis's face was fair, I saw her in daylight in her light-filled attic room in the Palace of Arts (corner of Povarskaya and Kudrinskaya, the house of Count Sologub). A marvelous brow, marvelous eyes, the whole top filled with light. And the poems were good, not Briusovian at all, rather more Mandelstamian, obviously Petersburgian (Briusov is completely outside the elementary, but in some respects correct division of Russian poetry into Moscow and Petersburg).

"Everyone says that Briusov fixes them for me," she complained, "but I assure you."

"You don't need to assure me. Briusov is lucky with his poetesses, and if something needs fixing, then at the moment he's not the one to fix yours."

"What do you think about his poems?"

"What do I think? Many things. What do I feel? Nothing."

"But he's a great master."

"But he's a great master."

◯ ⟩

Here's one of Adalis's stories about Briusov. A story that makes my heart ache.

"V. Ya. has a ward, a four-year-old boy whom he loves dearly, tenderly; he takes him out for walks himself, and especially loves explaining everything to him along the way. 'This is called a pediment. Repeat after me: pediment.' 'Pediment.' 'And this is a column — a Doric column. Repeat after me: Doric.' 'Doric.' 'And this one, with the curlicues, is the Ionic style. Repeat!' 'Ionic.' And so on and so on. Then, not long ago — he told me himself — they passed a dog with some kind of strange tail, all curled up. And the boy asked Briusov: 'And that dog — what style is it? Ionic or Doric?'"

◯ ⟩

My joint performance with Adalis took place more than six months later; I think it was in February 1921. I can't say that I was particularly inspired by the blue posters reading "An Evening of Poetesses" — a list of nine names—with introductory remarks by Valery Briusov. We had talked about three, here there were three times three, instead of a performance—it was an exhibition. I had already turned down one such women's show in 1916, feeling that in poetry there are more essential distinctions than belonging to the male or female sex, and having an inborn aversion to everything bearing the stamp of female (mass) separatism, namely: women's courses, suffragism, feminism, the Salvation Army, the famous woman's question, with the exception of its military resolution: the fairy-tale kingdoms of Penthesilea—Brunhilde—Maria Morevna—and the no less magical Petrograd women's battalion. (I support sewing schools, however.) In creative work there is no women's question; there are women's answers to human questions, namely: Sappho—Joan of Arc—Saint Teresa—Bettina Brentano. There are delightful women's cries (*Lettres de Mlle de Lespinasse*), there is women's thought (Maria Bashkirtseva), there is a woman's brush (Rosa Bonheur), but these are all isolated individuals who weren't aware of the women's question, and who, through this unawareness, decimated (destroyed) it.

But Briusov, this man in poetry par excellence, this fancier of a sex outside of the human, this nonfancier of souls, this: right-left, black-white, man-woman, was naturally attracted to such divisions and effects. Just recall *Nelly's Poems*—an anonymous book in woman's name, which belied its author precisely by its soullessness—and the surprisingly meager-hearted introduction to Karolina Pavlova's poems. And he wasn't only attracted to the man-woman division—but to all kinds of divisions, limitations, classifications, to everything that could be subjected to figures and graphs. The guardian of a forty-four rank cemetery—that was Briusov's interpretation of the free brotherhood of poetry and his role in it. For Briusov, a poet without an "ist" wasn't a poet. Thus, in 1920 I think it was, to the question why neither Khodasevich nor I was invited to an evening of all the poetic movements (a "literary quadrille"), his answer was: "They are nobodies. What group would I put them in?" (I think that for Khodasevich, as for me, being this kind of "nobody" amounts to another *titre de noblesse*).

Briusov was inquisitive about women his entire life. He was attracted, inquisitive, and didn't love. And the secret of his striking lack of success in everything related to female Psyche lies precisely in this excessive inquisitiveness, in the further classification of that which has already been tragically classified, in the removal of woman from the human circle, in this artificial isolation, in this enchanted circle of hers, which he created himself. Willpower won't work here, and the wonderful translation of an utterly mediocre poet involuntarily comes to mind:

> They asked: "How can we make those beauties sigh,
> Heed passion's speech; without the goblet's charms
> Fall willingly into our arms?"
> "Love them!" the women did reply.

(( ))

Briusov had everything: the goblet's charm, and will, and passionate speech, he simply didn't have one thing—love. And Psyche—I'm not talking about living women—passed him by.

(( ))

The evening of poetesses was held in the Great Hall of the Polytechnical Museum. I remember the waiting room—cement, with a lone bench and an empty space from a bathtub that seemed to have been recently removed. The poetesses, corresponding, according to the poster, to the number nine (I only just guessed—nine Muses! Ah, pseudoclassicist!) turned out not to be nine, but three times as many. Under the pressure of emotion, perfume, raised temperatures (many were coughing), gossip and cocaine, the freezing cement relented and began to sweat. Steam filled the little room. Through the steam there were pale blots—faces, red smudges—lips, black circumflexes—eyebrows. The poetesses, for all the variety of types, looked remarkably alike. By name and appearance I remember Adalis, Benar, the poetess Malvina and Poplavskaya. The fifth—was myself. The rest evaporated in the steam. From one of them, however, a raspberry-colored beret survived, which cut off precisely half of the face in its flight from the temples to a décolleté that was maximally descended on one shoulder. In the parallel asymmetry of the beret and the décolleté there was an unpleasant symmetry: the symmetry of two warpings. With the exception of Adalis (who wore something closed and dark), the poetesses were dressed according to the themes and meters of their works—that is, freestyle, and, for 1921, quite luxuriously. I can see one of them—tall, feverish, dancing all over—with her petite shoe, fingers, rings, sable tails, pearls, teeth, and cocaine in her pupils. She was horrid and enchanting, with that tenth-rate kind of charm you can't help being tempted by, which people then feel ashamed of being tempted by, and which I shamelessly, in everyone's earshot—declare myself tempted by. Of visual impressions, other than the red beret and consumptive furs, there remains with me as well the gaminish outline of the poetess Benar—a little Gavroche head on the free stem of the neck; and, thirties style, accentuated—out of place—the intolerably innocent vision of the poetess Malvina—"fashionable" down to the blue glass beads gracing the unclouded half-sphere of the forehead.

To all appearances, the exhibition promised to be successful, Briusov hadn't miscalculated.

(( ))

To fail to mention myself, having more or less dissected all the others, would be hypocritical. And so: on that day I appeared "To Rome and the World" in a green, cassocklike thing—you couldn't call it a dress (it was a paraphrase of a coat that had seen better times)—that was honestly (i.e., tightly) belted, not even with an officer's belt, but a Junker's, the 1st Peterhoff Ensigns' School. A bag over my shoulder, this time an officer's (brown leather, for field binoculars or cigarettes), which I felt it would be a betrayal to remove and which I took off only on the third day after I arrived in Berlin (1922), and even then only at the ardent request of the poet Ehrenburg. My feet were in gray felt peasant boots, and although they weren't men's, but were my size, surrounded by all those patent leather pumps they looked like elephant pillars. The entire outfit, by virtue of its monstrousness, relieved me of any suspicion of ostentation ("ne peut pas qui veut"). The slenderness of my waist was praised; no one mentioned the belt. All in all, I have to say that I was met with kindness in the alien world of the professional women of narcotic poetry. Women, in general, are kinder. Men forgive neither starving children nor felt boots. I'm convinced that that very same Poplavskaya would have immediately taken her sable from her shoulders if I had told her that my child was starving. A mere gesture? Yes. And more complete than the gesture of St. Martin, royally tossing half (o irony!) of his cloak to a beggar from the height of his steed. (The most worthless, most wretched, most shameful of all gestures of giving!)

The beret, the sable, the '30s part of the hair, Gavroche, my cassock (more on Adalis separately) — if Briusov hadn't miscalculated, neither had the audience.

In the process of copying this out, I remembered two more: a Georgian princess, very pretty, with, I think, not bad poems, and a certain Susanna — a beauty — completely without poems.

The stage. The stage is a visible place. There's visibility in the very sound: "Stay! Enjoy!" The stage is a plaza raised off the ground, and your sense of self on it — is the sense of self on a beachhead, of a cavalry officer facing the crowd. The passions of the stage — are military. The very fact that you are physically higher than everyone else creates friends and enemies. What is tolerable and even endearing in a room ("no technique, but a lot of feeling," "no meter, but there is feeling," "no voice, but a lot of feeling"), is criminal on the stage. Rising — even by three inches — above the average level of the floor, you are obligated to rise three miles above the average (salon) level in your art. The stage has its own scale: merciless. It's a place where there are no half measures. One against all (early Scriabin, for instance), or one for all (late Blok, for instance), in these two forms — is the formula of the stage. Everyone else should sit at home and amuse friends.

The stage of the Polytechnical Museum isn't a stage. It's a place from which people read — the bottom of the sea. The performer — is a drowned man (drowning), on whom the entire human sea weighs; or a victim strangled by the ringlike movements of a boa constrictor (the amphitheater). The viewer tumbles over the performer. The voice of the performer — is a cry from the depth of the seas, a scream for help, not a cry of victory. If he is booed, that's the end, for there isn't even the purely physical comfort of standing above — that the booing is coming from below. Someone booed on stage falls only to the mid-level (of the viewer), someone booed in the Polytechnical Museum — falls lower than low, into a bottomless pit. The entire human 'above' boos you, the very idea of above. The empyrean booing the abyss. And not only boo-ing. Whether it's the attraction of the abyss, or an expression of power and ease, the heights dispose to the throwing of objects. The herd in-stinct of impunity, the individual feeling of a hierarchical-topographical superiority, which immediately results in an exceeding of rights. The Polytechnical Museum — is an unsurpassed place for herdish impu-dence, and a deadly one — for an author's timidity. Max Voloshin once (in his lecture on Repin) heroically overcame it.

I finally realized: the stage of the Polytechnical Museum is simply an arena, with the sole difference that the tigers and lions are up above.

So, an arena. Freezing. And with a gradual raising of the eyes — as if praying to the audience! — the half-chain, necklace, Chinese lantern gar-lands of faces. (By the way, why is it that faces, bloodless in our time, in 1920 downright green — invariably seem pink from the stage?) I glance at the poetesses: they're blue. It's three degrees below zero in the hall and not one of them will put on a coat. There you have it, the heroics of beauty. By the coarseness of the crowd's hum and the strong smell of boots, I conclude that the audience is young and military.

While Briusov waits for the silence that has not yet fallen, I savor the thought that it is from here, from this very place where I stand (a laugh-ing stock), from the depths of this very well that Blok's voice rose not so long ago. And how the entire hall, holding its breath, waited. And how the entire hall, forestalling a stutter, cued him. And how the entire hall — exhaling — exploded! And the broken dam — current — avalanche — of love of the all toward the one who was one for all!

"Comrades, I will begin."

Woman. Love. Passion. Woman, from the beginning of time has known how to sing only of love and passion. The only passion of woman — is love. Every love of a woman — is passion. Outside of love, woman — in creative work, is nothing. Take passion away from woman . . . Woman . . . Love . . . Passion . . .

These three words, always in the same sequence, recurred after every next three, recurred where expected and unexpected, like numbers on a taxi meter, with the difference that the numbers are new, the words were always the same. My ears, already tired of the mechanics, pricked up under my hair. As for the audience, it was appalling, the constant din obliged the speaker to resort to an ever greater staccato of sound and meaning. It was as if the audience was giving a lecture that Briusov was interrupting with isolated shouts. A double shame arose in me: to read to *those people! these* poems! with *those* poets! A triple shame.

And so: woman: love: passion. There have, of course, been other attempts — the poetess Ada Negri with her scholarly issues. But this is an exception and doesn't count. (I'm quoting almost verbatim.) "The best example of the one-sidedness of female creativity is . . . is . . ." — Pause. — " . . . Is . . . comrades, you all know. Is the famous poetess" (with an irritated entreaty). "Comrades, the most famous poetess of our days. Is the poetess . . ."

I, behind his back, under my breath, distinctly:

"Lvova?"

A twitch of the shoulders and — almost shouting:

"Akhmatova! Is the poetess — Anna — Akhmatova . . ."

" . . . Let us hope that the social changes taking place in the whole world, and which have already taken place in Russia, will also be reflected in women's creative work. But so far, I maintain, they have not yet been reflected, and women are still writing about love and passion. About love and about passion."

Under my hair, my ears quite definitely stood up. I hurriedly flipped pages and marked poems with matches in my black ledger book.

"Now, comrades, you will hear nine Russian poetesses, perhaps different in details, but in essence identical, for, I repeat, woman does not yet know how to sing of anything except love and passion. The reading will be in alphabetical order." (He ended as he broke off, and, turning slightly toward the nine muses:) "Comrade Adalis?"

Adalis's quiet voice: "Valery Yakovlevich, I won't begin."

— "But."

"It's pointless, I won't begin. Let Benar begin."

Briusov, to Benar, quietly: "Comrade Benar?"

And the tiny, ringing, gaminlike voice: "Comrade Briusov, I don't want to go first . . ."

There was laughter in the hall. Briusov turns to the third, the fourth; the answer, with variations, was the same: "I won't begin." (Variations:

"I'm afraid," "It's best not to be first," "I'm not used to going first," "I've forgotten my poems," etc.) The situation was desperate. The negotiations were getting lengthy. The audience was already roaring with laughter. I was waiting for what I knew would happen from the first second: Briusov's one-billionth of a millimeter turn in my direction. Anticipating the request, I said in a simple, friendly tone of voice. "V. Ya., would you like me to begin?" That marvelous wolflike smile (the second—to me—in my life!) and, with an emancipated bark:

"Comrades, the first to read will be" (an emphatic pause) *"the poet* Tsvetaeva."

I stood, as I always do on stage, my myopic eyes lowered to a notebook held high—very calm—waiting for the silence (which fell immediately). And with the most distinct diction, with the most earnest voice:

> Survivors—will die. But the dead—will awaken.
> Descendants, recalling the past that is gone:
> "Where were you?" Their question will rumble like thunder,
> The answer, like thunder, will rumble: the Don!

> "What did you?" "Endured tribulation and torment.
> Then slept, in exhaustion, our countenance wan . . ."
> In dictionaries, right above the word: Duty,
> Their pensive great-grandsons will write the word: Don.

A second of waiting and—applause. Stopping them with a wave of the hand, I continue. After the Don—Moscow ("The Kremlin's Flanks" and "Grishka-the-Thief"), after Moscow—André Chenier ("André Chenier climbed the scaffold"), after André Chenier—Yaroslavna, after Yaroslavna—"The Swan's Encampment," all in all, seven poems in a row (more on the seventh shortly). I must say that after every poem there was a perplexed second of silence (is that really what I heard?) and then (no, obviously not!) it broke—and they applauded. The applause saved me each time, like the Hunch-Backed Horse saved the Tsar's son in the fairy tale. Moreover, it confirmed my deepest conviction that the first time, especially read aloud, the meaning of poems doesn't get through at all. I'd even say: for most people meaning is not the most important thing in poetry; and — I wouldn't be exaggerating to say that at this evening of poetesses poetry was completely beside the point. Here, after Briusov's introduction (even if they didn't listen — they heard it!) I could allow myself absolutely everything — *le pavillon* (Briusov with his love and passion) *couvre la marchandise* (myself, for instance, with my White Guard). Doing something so obviously insane, I had two, no, three, four goals: 1) seven women's poems without love and the pronoun 'I'; 2) to verify the meaninglessness of the poems for the audience; 3) contact with even a single person who understood me (even a cadet!); 4) and most important: the discharge here, in Moscow, 1921, of a *duty of honor*. And beyond any goals, the goal-less — greater than goals! — simple, extreme feeling: — well, and what if?

Speaking, or rather just about to speak certain lines: ("Yes! Hurrah! Hurrah! And Long Live the Tsar!") I felt as though I was about to fly off a mountain. I hadn't yet said it, but in just a moment — it's no longer my will, but the poem's — I will say it. I have spoken the words. It's irrevocable.

The poem that turned out to be the final one was for me at that moment — the wife of a White officer standing before Red Army soldiers, communists, cadets — my final truth.

> *The women cried hurrah*
> *And threw their bonnets in the air*

Hand on heart an oath I swear,
I am not a highborn lady fair,
Rather, rebel — gut and brow — that's me.

People in the square confirm —
I've never been on friendly terms
With my genealogical tree.

Kremlin! Black! You've blackened me!
But — no secrets, now — key
To my heart are Grishka's ashes.

If I hurl my bonnet high,
Isn't this how boys the whole world wide
Cheer on city squares and plazas?

Shout "Hurrah!" Marvelous morn
Of all entrances since time was born.
Yes! Hurrah! Hurrah! Long Live the Tsar!

Flying, cap surpasses spire,
Skirts the idol's wreath of bronze — heads higher —
Charting passage straight on to a star!

This poem was my alliance with the audience, with all the audiences and town squares of the world, my last confidence — covering all divisions — the flight of all caps — whether Phrygian or familial — above all fortresses and prisons — it was me — my very own true self.

"Miss Tsvetaeva, that will be enough," came Briusov's commandingly pleading whisper. In a half turn to Briusov: "Quite enough," a bow to the audience — and to the side, yielding the road —

"Now Comrade Adalis will read."

(( ))

Comrade Adalis definitely should not have been reading on that particular evening, more precisely, in that particular month of her life, and her performance, like every act of disregard for possible, unavoidable sneers — was a form of heroics. Sneers there were, and also, clearly, jeers. But, as always, the voice (and it isn't always there) had its effect: the audience was drawn in, began to listen. (It's not a matter of the voice's resources: "on a toujours assez de voix pour être entendu.") A — Adalis, B — Benar. Benar's poems, I remember, seemed ultracontemporary and cheaply topical: whorl-world, glass-glad, cloud-flouting, with artificial, purely visual rhyming that gives the ear nothing and works only in Akhmatova (who first introduced it) — for whom everything works. Themes and comparisons from the world of cement, subtle sounds without subtle meanings. I don't think that the poems were terribly valuable — they were far too terribly contemporary. With a nod to the audience, Benar stepped aside.

In Benar's place — the elegiac appearance of Malvina. She had an album, and poets wrote poems in it — not just any poets and not just any poems — I had the luck to open it to the simple, sophisticated dedication by Vyacheslav. (I say "Vyacheslav" not to be abrupt with the poet and not from a behind-the-back familiarity — it's just that this name doesn't need a surname any more than Balmont needs a first name. Vyacheslav covers Ivanov the way Balmont covers Konstantin. Ivanov after Vyacheslav is like Romanov after the monarch — revolutionary protocol.) And thus, the elegiac, streamy, willowy Malvina faced an audience that was beginning to enjoy itself. What were the poems about? About streams and about willows, it seems, about the abstract yearning for spring. (Briusov, Briusov, where are your famed love and passion? I read about the White Guard, Adalis read something descriptive, Benar — about cars, Malvina — about streams; moreover no one, except me, did so on purpose! Are not you yourself that very woman in the singular, and won't you be obliged, to justify your words, to perform after the ninth muse — as the tenth?)

I didn't hear the poems of the fur-covered beauty — but I doubt that cocaine was conducive to love. Having listened to the cooing of Malvina's streams, I went to check on Adalis, who disappeared right after her performance. When I came in, Comrade Adalis was lying down on the bench, wrapped from the sharp point of her patent leather shoes to the sharp point of her chin in something like a fur coat. She looked shaky and somber. "Well?"

"They're still reading."

"And V. Ya.?"

"He's listening."

"And the audience?"

"It's watching."

"A total embarrassment?"

"A bride inspection."

We lit cigarettes. Comrade Adalis's teeth chattered. Suddenly, throwing off the coat: "You know, Tsvetaeva, I think it's starting."

"It's your imagination."

"I tell you, it's starting."

"And I tell you that you're imagining it."

"How do you know?"

"It's too dramatic: an evening of poetesses — and . . . Something like Pope Joan. It happens in history, but it doesn't happen in life."

We laugh. And a minute later, Adalis, in a singsong voice: "Tsvetaeva, I don't know if it's starting or not, but could you do me a great service?"

I, sensing something: "Yes!"

"Go and tell V. Ya. that I'm asking for him — and it's urgent."

"And interrupt the reading?" "Well, that's up to you."

"Adalis, he'll have a fit."

"He won't dare, he's afraid of you, especially after today."

"Are you serious, this is what you want?"

"Sérieux comme la mort."

I enter during the applause for Sable-Tails, call Briusov aside and say, quietly and distinctly, eye to eye: "Comrade Briusov, Comrade Adalis asked me to tell you that it seems to be starting." Briusov's eyebrows: "?" "I don't know what is starting, I'm repeating what I was told, she asks you to come quickly: it's urgent."

Briusov exits abruptly, I don't follow, but listen to the next poetess, one of the ones who dissolved in the mist. (By the way, the un-Russianness of the first names and surnames: Adalis, Benar, Susanna, Malvina, the Pole Poplavskaya, the Georgian princess ending in "ili" or "idze." The un-Russianness, that in this instance coincided with the inorganic quality of the poetry. A coincidence by no means a priori: Mandelstam, for example, is not only a Russian poet, but derives from a specific Russian poetic tradition. In 1916 I was the first to christen him Derzhavin:

> What good is my ill-mannered verse,
> To you, my youthful Derzhavin!

Briusov himself, the merchant's son, is a Muscovite who reflects neither Moscow, nor Russia, nor the land. Nationality is not nothing, but it's not everything.)

After four stanzas Briusov reappears; this time he says to me: "Miss Tsvetaeva, comrade Adalis asks you to come . . ." Also quietly and distinctly, also eye to eye. I go in: Adalis is powdering her nose in front of the mirror. "What a horrible man, he doesn't believe anything."

I: "Especially when 'it's starting' every day."

Adalis, pouting: "How do I know? It could be, after all it will start sooner or later! . . . I send him for a cab — he won't go: 'My place is on the stage.'" "And mine is above. Do you want me to go get one?"

"Tsvetaeva, dearest, I don't have a kopeck for a cab, but I really don't feel well."

"Should I get the money from Briusov?"

She, terrified: "No, no, God forbid!"

Both of us shake out the contents of our purses — it's hopeless, there's not enough for a quarter of a cab.

Suddenly — there's a gust of wind, perfumed, garrulous, and alarmed. Sable-tails flies in, accompanied by a young man in a jacket and a fur hat with earflaps. The pearls on her stringed neck rattle, the sable tails fly, and so do the deer's ears: "Je vous assure, je vous assure, je vous jure . . ." Absolutely pure French with that incomparable, pearly "r" — in the throat or in the palate? no, nestled in the ages and in the blood — which stirs the whole Slavic soul. "Mais ce que je voudrais bien savoir, Madame," this is the ears gasping, "si c'est vous ou votre mari qui m'avez vendu?" Blind, obsessed, they don't hear, don't see. The young man is in the last stage of rage, the woman is restrained, you just hear the tap of patent leather on cement. (If she were a snake, the very end of the tail would be tapping.) "That's N." Adalis whispers in my ear, forgetting all about the cab; "she's a baroness, recently married a baron, and the young man . . ."

The young man and the woman are now talking simultaneously, not listening, not answering, not pausing — lengthy roulades of "r's," each of them repeating the same thing, each his or her own: "Je vous assure, je vous assure, je vous jure." "Je le saurai, Madame!" The words "*Tschéka, fusillé, perquisition*" recur. The pearls are in grave danger: any second now she'll break them, they'll spill, roll around with the same rattling scatter of guttural roulades: "Je vous assure, je vous assure, je . . ."

The heroine's eyes are light, unseeing, transcending the interlocutor and life. On the lunatic face, only the mouth is alive, unclosing, relentlessly throwing out roulades, cascades, myriad "r's." My eyes are already drooping from the "r's," in a drowsy stupor, as though from thousands of burbling brooks. A scene from a novel? Yes. From cheap, gutter fiction? Yes. Only the outpost rivals the gutter in bloodiness. But the situation has changed; now it's the woman who's attacking, overtaking, hurling insult after insult in his face, and the man has shrunk, like his own ears under the fur ones, he's slunk off, shriveled down to nothing at all — nothing! Sable-tail has cornered Deer-ears!

"The Devil can take this woman's poetree! No box office in it! Only cadets and coquettes. I told V. Ya., and he told 'feminine leerics, feminine leerics . . .' and here's your leerics — a room and some perfume!"

The actual impresario entered, the organizer of the evening, an eastern type, with an "idze." (He was the author of the witticism making the rounds in Moscow at the time regarding the now deceased writer Gershenzon, after a reading that was unprofitable for Idze: "How could I think that the Writers Union would put out such an idiot?")

I said:

"Under Ludwig XIV the poet Gilbert went mad from lyrical poetry and swallowed the key to his manuscripts; in the XVIII century the Englishman Chetterton — I don't remember exactly what happened — but it was from lyrical poetry; André Chenier — lost his head. It's dangerous stuff, lyrical poetry. Just be glad that you got off so cheap."

"You're talking about the gentlemen poets themselves — it's their business they want to choose such a profession — but what's it got to do with me, Miss Poetess?"

"You loiter around lyrical poetry. You want to get rich off lyrical poetry!"

"That's what you think. Just who you think organized Igor Severianin's evening? Your humble servant. And I made good money off that Igor, and he came out none the worse. The problem's not poetree, but . . ."

"Broads. There's a moral for you: don't get involved with women — it will always end in woe."

"You think it's funny, Miss Poetess."

"It's laughable. Selling women's souls! Like Chichikov! You'd be better off selling their bodies!"

"Idze", not listening:

"You'll get your honorarium and" (suddenly stopping): "what is this disaster now?"

We all run out: the impresario, the warring lovers, N., Adalis, and I.

A dam broke? The ceiling didn't hold? The Polytechnical Museum decided it was Vesuvius? Or Moscow is collapsing—for its sins?

On the stage, with the sweetest, most luminous, most raspberry-colored of smiles—was Red Beret!

A short digression. We were all applauded—Adalis, Benar, the poetess in pearls, Malvina, I—just about equally: within the limits of a fully satisfied curiosity. This, however, was—success. (Success in advance and on credit, for she hadn't yet uttered a single word, but—do words really matter?)

And so, still silent, gradually, the way the sun as it rises illuminates ridge after mountain ridge, Red Beret was greeting the amphitheater. She must have recognized someone in the first row—there was a nod to the first row, and someone in the third as well, because she nodded to the third, and in the fifth, and the fifteenth; and each got a different, an individual, not a standard nod—but a sly nod, a short nod, a nod with a sudden toss of the beret from one ear to the other, a superficial nod, a memorable nod. How lovely she was, how simple in her joy, how humble in her triumph. The applause persisted; not satisfied with hands, the audience had already engaged its feet—soon it would start throwing things! And the smile grew wider still, stretched into infinity, transcended the boundaries of the lips and the possible, the raspberry beret was cocked further and further back, completely upward into the heavens, to paradise, to the balconies. And—strangely enough—the audience wasn't oppressed by this expectation, wasn't hurrying events or rushing things; the audience didn't want poems, the audience was happy—just like that.

"Comrade X, begin!" But Comrade Beret didn't hear, she had her own affair with the audience. "Come now, begin, Comrade X!" In Briusov's voice one could almost hear irritation. And naturally enough, because of the entire mirage—to see only the back and the crown of the cocked beret!

Nearby, "Idze's" exclamation:

"Now if you just put this one out all by herself! A girl like that wouldn't flop!"

( )

Poems? Were there any? I don't remember any words or ideas. Ideas and words dissolved, were lost, flowed out in the smile, raspberry-colored and wide like the dawn. Even if she'd been a genius in a woman's being, she couldn't have said more about it than this smile of hers. This was not a smiling face — there are many of those, they are easily forgotten; it wasn't a mouth — the mouth was lost in the smile, there was nothing but the smile: an endless extension of the lips, which had already been washed away by it! A smile — and nothing but, the dissolution of the world in a smile, the smile itself: a smile. And if I'm asked about the earth on another planet — what I saw there, what I remember most, sorting through things and leaving much aside — I'll smile.

But, from the planets to the stage. This performance was the decisive triumph of red — not a bloody, banner, comradely red, but, with a correction for the feminine (the tint of the face, the coloring, the outfit), the triumph not of a plaza or street red — but of a battle red — a feminine-battle red.

Thus, if not in creative work, then at least in the personality of this poetess, Briusov's assertions regarding the sources of female creativity — were confirmed.

( )

Red Beret's performance dragged on. The restless Adalis and I sat in the cement room awaiting fate (money). "Will they pay or not?"

"They'll pay, but how much? They promised thirty each."

"That means ten each."

"That means three each."

The tower of Babylon boomed anew — obviously Beret was leaving her post. Babylon booms, booms, booms. Cries penetrate even our cement coffin.

"Red Devil! Red De-eevillll! De-e-vi-il!"

Frightened, I ask Adalis: "Could they really be calling her that?"

Adalis, laughing: "No, it's the name of one of her poems, her farewell to the audience, her grand finale. When she's finished, that's the end. Let's go."

We catch the last fling of the raspberry beret. All effects at the end! And yet another unforeseen fling (effect) — the broad gesture with which the poetess, passing by, instantaneously and just for an instant — sincerely, in an excess of emotion — wraps Briusov in her cheery, striped, voluminously rustling, hospitable skirt.

This final gesture marked the final end of the evening. Nine muses girdled the stage — for rhyme and reason I'll get rid of one of us — "eight girls, and me at the pearly gates." The last, by now utterly bestial, howls, calls, the bows in response, shortened by the upcoming versts home, the thunder of the amphitheater, which was dispersing, scattering like a bunch of grapes; the barrier is down, the audience goes to the barrier, the stage into the audience.

(( ))

The upshot: not thirty, not ten, but not three either — nine. And the tenacious arm of the willowy streamy Malvina, digging into my steel arm. The '30s feet, mistaking the century, not waiting for a carriage, couldn't handle icy Soviet conditions, and given the lack of more pleasant support, I ended up having to direct them along the sidewalk glaciers of Moscow, early February 1921.

(( ))

There you have the whole truth of my encounters with Briusov. "And that's all?" Yes, life in general hasn't given me many such encounters. Blok — twice. Kuzmin — once, Sologub — once. Pasternak — a lot — five times, Mayakovsky — as many, Akhmatova — never, Gumilyov — *never.*

One real conversation with Vyacheslav in my life. (There have been lucky moments, but faced with the bitterness of everything not taken . . .)

I always skirted the great ones in life, I *orbited* them, as a planet does another planet. Add the mountain of my own love to their everyday cares and psychic burden? Because, if not for love — why bother to meet? For other things there are books. And if it's not a mountain (I take it in all its dimensions) — then is it really love? In this mixture of protection and pride, in this most natural step backward at the sight of greatness — lies the key to many bypassings (not only my own, but of humans in general, that's why I mention it).

Protect oneself? From what you came into this world to do? No, in my vocabulary "protection" is always — to protect someone else.

And perhaps that's the way it should be — further on. To see further, so as to see more, so as to see with more. And my lot — the distances between myself and the suns — is noble.

Thus, to the question: that's it? My answer: "Yes — but how!"

(( ))

And, turning to the most polar of the suns, my polar opposite sun — to Briusov, I can see it. I could have loved Briusov, if not like every other poet — Briusov was manifest not in poetry, but in the will to it — then like every other *power.* And, listening very attentively, I can prove: under the sincere guise of hatred I simply loved Briusov, only in this type of love (repulsion) I loved him with greater strength than had I loved him in the simplest form — attraction.

Briusov himself — so stiff-hearted, didn't detect this and sincerely detested first "that girl," then — "that woman," whose entire meaning and purpose — I maintain — was love, and not hatred, hymns and not epigrams.

Should Briusov hear this, either from the heights of his lowly Roman heaven, or from the depths of his high Gothic inferno, the sound of his name will cause me less pain.

IV

Briusov and Balmont

> *But I don't think about my poems*
> *And, truth be told, I don't compose!*
> *— Balmont*

> *And since your carefree childhood,*
> *You have been searching for the words.*
> *— Briusov*

Balmont and Briusov. One could write an entire book about this — a poem has already been written: Mozart, Salieri.

By the way, has even one critic noted the stubborn predominance of the letter B in the generation of the so-called Symbolists? — Balmont, Briusov, Bely, Blok, Baltrushaitis.

Balmont, Briusov. People who grew up in those years never named one of them without naming (at least mentally) the other. There were other poets, no lesser, and they were named individually. With these two — it was as if they'd made an arrangement. These names came in a pair.

Paired names are not new: Goethe and Schiller, Byron and Shelley, Pushkin and Lermontov. The fraternity of two powers, two heights. There's no mystery in this pairing. But "Balmont and Briusov" — what is the mystery?

It is in the polarity of the two names — of the gifts — of the personalities, in the extreme expression in each of one of two basic types of creativity, in the naturally arising juxtaposition, in their *mutual exclusivity*.

Everything that is not Balmont — is Briusov, and everything that is not Briusov — is Balmont.

Not two names — but two camps, two personages, two races.

Balmònt.* Briusov. Just listen to the sound of the names. Balmont: openness, wide open — flung abreast. Briusov: tightness ("iu" is a half vowel, rather like his sealed card to me back then), miserliness, self-contained egoism.

Briusov is crowded. Balmont is spacious.

Briusov thuds, Balmont: rings.

Balmont is an open palm — tossing; in Briusov — there's the scrape of a key.

Balmont. Briusov. Both of them reigned back then. In other worlds, as you see, unlike our world, diarchy is possible. To take it further: the only sign of a thing's belonging to another world is its impossibility —

---

*I ask that the reader, in accord with the bearer of the name, place the stress on the last syllable. (M.Ts.)

intolerableness — impermissability — here. The Balmont-Briusov diarchy presents us with an unprecedented example — historically unimaginable — of a beneficent diarchy, not simply not of friends — but of enemies. As you see, one can learn something not only from poets' *poems*.

(( ))

Balmont. Briusov. Two poles of creativity. The creator-child (Balmont) and the creator-worker (Briusov). (The child as *der Spieler,* the player.) Nothing of the worker — in Balmont; nothing of the child — in Briusov. The creativity of play and the creativity of muscles. Almost as in the fable "The Dragonfly and the Ant," and in 1919 it came to life, except that the dragonfly in *my* fable even then, when he was dying of hunger, *felt sorry for* the ant.

God save us, who write, from insults to craft. May no one be deaf to one particular line of the linguistically uneven *International*. But may the gods save us even more from Briusov's institutes, in short: may craft become an inspiration, and not inspiration a craft.

The pluses of both poles are clear. Let's look at the minuses. The creativity of a child. The minuses — it's haphazard, accidental, a matter of "following the hand." The creativity of the worker. Its minuses — it's not haphazard, not accidental, no question of "following the hand," that is: the minus of the second — is the absence of the minus of the first. Between them, Balmont and Briusov precisely divided the proverb: "Place your hopes in God" (Balmont), "but don't botch things up" (Briusov). Balmont's hopes were not in vain, and Briusov in his own "no botching up" didn't botch anything. I'll explain: in talking about Balmont's creative play, I am not by any means suggesting that he didn't work on his creations. Without work the child cannot build his sand castles. But the secret of work of the child and of Balmont lies in its (work's) concealment from them, in their unawareness of it. A mountain of gravel, bricks, clay. "Are you working?" "No, I'm playing." The process of work is concealed in play. Exertion is transformed into ecstasy.

(( ))

Work-blessing (Balmont) and work-curse (Briusov). God's work in paradise (Balmont, innocence), man's work on earth (Briusov, guilt).

No one would call Balmont guilty and Briusov innocent, Balmont knowing and Briusov unknowing. Balmont is — insatiability for all kinds of apples, except for the apple of good and evil; Briusov is — a pursed mouth from all of them except the serpent's. For Balmont — the snake, for Briusov — the serpent. Balmont admires the snake; Briusov learns from the serpent. And even if Balmont were to glorify the serpent in ten thousand lines, it is Briusov, not he, who is kin to it.

Briusov is sinful through and through. You simply can't escape the feeling of his sinfulness. And since reading is participation, reading Briusov — is criminal complicity. He is sinful because he knows; he knows because he is sinful. Sin (ashes) is extraordinarily tangible in him. And the heaviness of his verse — is the heaviness of sin (ashes).

In the absence of asceticism — a full sense of the sinfulness of the world and oneself. Sin without joy, without pride, without bitterness, with no way out. Sin as a normal state of being. Sin as sojourn. Sin as a dead end. And, perhaps the worst thing in sin — the *boredom* of sin. (They don't let people like this into hell; they don't burn them.)

Sin-love, sin-joy, sin-beauty, sin-motherhood. It's sufficient to recall his vile poem "To Young Women," which begins:

> I saw a woman. Twisted, and by pain unbound,
> Without a hint of shame, she spread her body open.
> And when she moaned she made a savage sound.

And ends:

> O girls! O butterflies aloft in freedom's hour,
> A ringing waltz does lure you to the ball.
> You fill our lives like the magnolia flower,
> But each of you eventually will fall,
> Contorted, back upon the bed's white pall,
> You'll all turn into beasts, all of you, all!

This is about motherhood, *which cleanses* everything!

The word "reprobate" sticks to Briusov as to no other. Dour and hopeless, like the howl of a wolf on the big road.

And, a realization: among animals the reprobate is indeed — the wolf!

(( ))

Balmont — is a reveler. Briusov — a reprobate.

The merriment of revelry — is Balmont. The dourness of the reprobate — is Briusov.

And he is not an enchanter but a lecher.

(( ))

But, returning to his work, his cleansing:

There's the labor of God in paradise (Balmont) and the labor of man on earth (Briusov). Enraptured by the former, we pay our respects to the latter.

(( ))

Yes, the way children play and nightingales sing — rapturously! Briusov does it — you can't find a resemblance in nature, although the woodpecker does come to mind, he hammers away like a stonecutter — reductively. The happiness of submitting (Balmont). The happiness of surmounting (Briusov). The happiness of giving away (Balmont). The happiness of grabbing (Briusov). Flowing with the current of one's own gift — Balmont. Battling the current of one's own lack of gift — Briusov.

(The inaccuracy of the last comparison. Lack of gift, an absence, can't be a current, a presence. Moreover, the very concept of lack of gift obviously contradicts the concept of flow. Lack of gift is a wall, a barrier, inertness. What is inert cannot flow. It's more like — butting up against the wall of his own lack of gift: Briusov. I leave the mistake as something useful for readers and writers.)

And, as a formula: like a child, Balmont plays even when he's working; like a tutor, Briusov works even when he's playing. (The arduousness of his rondeau, rondelet, ritornello — of all the poetic games of the pen.)

Briusov: impromptu is excluded a priori.

(( ))

The victoriousness of Balmont is the victoriousness of the rising sun: "I am and therefore I conquer." Briusov's victoriousness — you can't find a resemblance in nature — is the victoriousness of the warrior, who, pursuing his own goals and by his own will, stops the sun.

As figures (poetic evaluation aside) they are worthy of one another.

(())

Balmont. Briusov. Their only connection — their otherlandishness. Two exotic kings ruled a generation. It's not the time and place to go into it, I'll just give the milestones (let the reader *dig!*). After the "most Russian" Chekhov and the super-Russo-intelligentsian Nadson (God forbid they should be seen as equals! a generation is to blame for their dual reign) — after moods and dispositions, disorders, disintegrations — after repressions, confessions — suddenly — "Let's be like the sun!" says Balmont; "To Rome and the World," says Briusov.

No, Balmont is not Russian, Balmont, despite the Vladimir guberniya, "in Russian nature there is a tired tenderness"(a description whose very precision reveals the foreigner), despite Russian spells and sorcery, despite the convincingness of themes and feelings — he's a not-Russian, Balmont, he's from abroad. In the Russian fairy tale Balmont isn't Ivan Tsarevich, he's the overseas guest who showers the Tsar's daughter with the gifts of the sands and seas. The overseas guest is by no means the least character in the fairy tale! But — I'm asking, not asserting — isn't Balmont's very not-Russianness — a sign of his actual Russianness? The pre-Russia, fairy-tale longing of Russ — for the sea, for lands beyond the sea. The pull of Russ — to get out of Russ? And, listening closely — no. If that were the case, his longing would speak Russian. I always have the feeling that Balmont speaks some foreign language, I don't know which one — Balmontian. Here we come up against a mystery. Organic poetry in a nonorganic language. For, I insist, Balmont's language, in the folk sense, is not organic. How strong must be the inner, personal (individual) organicity to get through in words, despite the linguistic nonorganicness. I would say of Balmont what one teacher at the Paris Alliance Française said in response to one of my French poems, "Vous êtes surement poète dans votre langue."

At birth Balmont discovered a fourth dimension: Balmont! A fifth element: Balmont! A sixth sense and a sixth continent: Balmont! And he lived in them.

His love of Russia — is the infatuation of a foreigner. There's no way, for all my love of him, that you can call him a national poet. A one-time innovator of the Russian language, without followers — yes. I want to say: Balmont is a phenomenon, but not in Russia. A poet in the world of poetry, but not in the country. Air — in the air.

A nation — exists in the flesh, a national poet cannot be incorporeal (merely a poet — can). And Balmont — even if he heaped the Himalayas on top of the Andes and elephants on top of ichthyosauruses — is always, a priori, charmingly weightless.

> I'm a guest of the universe,
> Everywhere I find a feast.

A vice or an advantage? A country is bigger than a home, the earth is bigger than a country, the universe is bigger than the earth. The not-Russianness (Russianness as a component) and Russianness of Balmont — is his universality. He wasn't born in Russia, but in the world. It is only in Pushkin — the sole Russian poetic genius (genius, which, after range, is also a question of balancing the effect of various forces. Other than this, Lermontov is no less than Pushkin) — and so, only in Pushkin is the world present without detriment to the home (and vice-versa). In Balmont — the world dominates. The enchanted traveler never returned to the home he left on entering the world! All of his returns home — are simply quick visits. In saying "Balmont," we say: water, wind, sun. (Less or more than Russia?) Saying "Balmont" we (geographically and roughly) say: Tahiti — Ceylon — Sierra, and, perhaps, most of all: Atlantis, and perhaps, less than anything — Russia. His "Moscow" — is his longing. Longing for what cannot be, for the place one cannot live. The unattainable dream of a foreigner. And anyway, in the end, everyone has the right to choose his own homeland.

(( ))

Pushkin — Balmont. There is no direct connection. Pushkin — Blok. The connection is direct. (Blok's last poem, dedicated to Pushkin, was not an accident.) I'm not talking about the inner kinship of Pushkin and Blok, but about the similarity of our love, which makes them kin.

Like first love,
The heart of Russia will not forget you.

After Pushkin — this all Russia could say only to Blok. The gift isn't the point — Balmont is also gifted; death isn't the point — Gumilyov died too; the point is the incarnated longing — dream — grief — not of an entire generation (Nadson is a horrifying example), but of an entire fifth element — of Russia. (Less or more than the world?)

The Pushkin-Blok line bypasses the island of Balmont. And, combining Balmont's foreignness and his oceanness, and his paradiseness, and his unattachedness: *a floating island!* — finally, there's a name for it.

(( ))

Where is Balmont's poetic clan? In the world. He's a brother to those he translated and loved.

(( ))

Just as Balmont himself is Russ's longing for lands beyond the sea, so our love for him — is a self-same longing for the same.

(( ))

Balmont and Briusov's incapacity for Russian song. For a poet to compose a folk song, the people must inhabit the poet. A folk song is not a rejection of self, but the organic coincidence, coalescence, consonance of a given "I" with the people's. (In our day, I insist, it's not Esenin, but Blok.) Balmont is too Balmont for folk song, even if it's with the last word of the last word — he will Balmontify it! . . . This is incapacity not from a lack of organicity (he's entirely organic!) — but from the peculiarity of this organism.

On Briusov and Russian song . . . If Balmont is too Balmont, Briusov is in no sense the people.*

*For a Russian, Balmont's language is too personal (individual). Briusov's language, for a Russian, is too general (nationally impersonal). (M.Ts.)

(The tempting juxtaposition of Balmont and Gumilyov. The exoticism of the one and the exoticism of the other. The presence in Balmont and, with rare exceptions, the absence in Gumilyov of the theme "Russia." The un-Russianness of Balmont and the utter Russianness of Gumilyov.)

( )

Balmont will remain thus in Russian poetry — an overseas guest who lavished gifts on poetry, enchanted her, entranced her — in one fell swoop — and disappeared without trace.

( )

Balmont on Briusov. On the 12th of Russian June 1920, Balmont left Bolshoi Nikolo-Peskovsky Lane in a truck to move abroad. I have a separate entry on this departure — flight — but I'll limit myself to two exclamations, the penultimate — to the Imaginist Kusikov: "Don't make friends with Briusov!" — and the last, from the truck as it drove off — to me:

"And you, Marina, tell Valery Briusov that I *do not* send my regards!"

( )

(I didn't pass along the nonregards — Briusov had gone very gray.)

( )

Balmont made another remark about Briusov that I remember. We were returning home, I no longer recall from what, some Soviet entertainment or ordeal. (Balmont and I, as luck would have it, shared the difficulties more often than the joys of life — perhaps in order to transform them into joy?)

We were talking about Briusov, his "occasional almanacs" (in other words: impromptu poetry evenings). About Briusov's Poetry Institute (in other words: about its closed food stores), about the hourly appearances (with whom!) and introductions (to what!), and I — Balmont would forgive me taking first place, but the flow of the sentence demands it — I was talking about the tragic nature of such humiliations,

Balmont—about the baseness of such tragedy. I don't remember the context, but I can clearly hear the following exclamation in my ears:

"That's why I don't forgive him!"

"You don't forgive him because you treat him as a human being, but you must understand he's a wolf—a poor, shedding, graying wolf."

"Wolves aren't only pitiful—they're villainous!"

You have to know Balmont's tender heart to appreciate such an exclamation coming from his lips.

❨❩

Balmont, on learning that Briusov published his own complete works with notes and a bibliography:

"Briusov imagines that he's a classic and he's already croaked."

❨❩

I—to Balmont:

"Balmont, do you know Koiransky's remark about Briusov? 'Briusov is an example of lack of talent overcome.'"

Balmont, in a flash:

"Not overcome."

❨❩

A conclusion is called for.

If Briusov is an example of talentlessness not overcome (that is, the failure to acquire in oneself, by any kind of labor, "a born, not created" gift), then Balmont is an example of a gift not overcome.

Briusov couldn't conjure the demon.

Balmont couldn't cope with him.

v

Last Words

When Briusov died, there was nothing to get used to.

I don't know what Briusov died of. And it isn't strange that I didn't try to find out. It's rude to look at the human end of a life, not a human life lived. A posthumous assault permitted only to reporters.

I want to think that he departed without a struggle. Conquerors die quietly.

I only know that this death didn't surprise anyone — didn't upset anyone didn't soften anyone. The proverb "de mortuis aut bene aut nihil" is superficial, or else the people who created it are no match for us. The proverb "de mortuis aut bene aut nihil" was created by Rome, and not by Russia. Here it's the other way around, because he's dead — he's right, because he's dead — he's sacred, the opposite of the Roman warning is the Russian affirmation: "you don't beat someone who's lying down." (And who lies quieter or lower than a dead man?) The inhumanity with which we Russians, both here and over there, have met this death, only speaks to the inhumanity of the human being.

（ ）

It's neither the time nor place to speak of Blok, but: in Blok all our humanity mourned for him; in Briusov, mourning — and I stop, struck by the disjunction of the name and the verb. It is possible to pity Briusov with two types of pity: 1) as a first-class brain mechanism that broke down (not he himself, but about him), 2) as a wolf. With pity-disappointment and pity-irritation, that is, with two compound feelings that together don't yield a simple whole.

This simple whole is: love, with all its components, which Briusov did not seek and did not earn.

Blok's death — was a thunderbolt to the heart; Briusov's death — was the silence that falls when a machine suddenly stops.

（ ）

One often comes across accusations that Briusov sold his pen to the Soviets. But I will say that of all those who crossed over or crossed half way, Briusov is perhaps the only one who did not betray and did not sell out. Briusov was precisely where he belonged — in the USSR.

What regime and what worldview could better correspond to this hero of labor and willpower than a worldview whose cornerstone was will, and a regime that not only threw the slogan

> Labor will become master of the world

into its anthem, but — just as Bonaparte established an order of Heroes of Honor — established an order of Heroes of Labor.

And recall Briusov's abstractness, his passion for schematization, for mechanization, for systematization, for stabilization, recall — so long before Bolshevism, his utopia "The City of the Future." Finally, his genuine areligiosity. No, no and no. Briusov's service to the communist idea is not forced: it's affectionate; in the USSR Briusov feels like a student looking at a painting by Repin — "what expanses!" (Breadth — for his narrownesses, for his crampednesses — space.) Simply: birds of a feather.

Neither Mayakovsky, with his obviously Russian, cobblestone thundering, nor Esenin, who, if not "the last village bard" is still not the least, nor certainly Boris Pasternak, an innovator in the kingdom of the Spirit, will remain emblematic of the new soulless communist soul forcibly imposed on Russ, something Blok so feared. All the above-mentioned are higher (and perhaps — broader, and perhaps — deeper) than the communist idea. Briusov alone saw eye to eye with it.

(( ))

(I'm speaking about the communist ideal, not about Bolshevism. There are plenty of Bolsheviks in poetry, for example — I don't know their political convictions — Mayakovsky and Esenin themselves. Bolshevism and communism. Here, more than elsewhere, you have to look at the root (big — comm —). A signifying and tribal difference of roots that defines the difference of the concepts. The Third International has already emerged from the latter, the former may yet produce Nazional-Russianism.

And if, as the rumor has it from his posthumous papers, Briusov turned out to be not only not a communist, but a die-hard monarchist, his monarchism and counterrevolution are only on paper. In Briusov there was nothing counter, nothing of the revolutionary in the revolution — i.e., of the monarchist. Like a genuine lover of power, he willingly and immediately submitted to the regime that promised him *power* in one or another sphere. (There is a certain point at which Bonapartism converges with ideal communism: "*la carrière, ouverte aux talents*" — Napoleon.) In the realm of Smolny and Catherine's institutes

"Briusov's Institute" — would be more than problematic. Communism, the reign of specialists, with its principle of using everything and everyone, appreciated it (Briusov's Institute) and implemented it.

The communism of Briusov and the anarchy of Balmont. The plebeian qualities of Briusov and the aristocratism of Balmont (Briusov, like Bonaparte is a plebe and not a democrat). Balmont's regality (an islander's) and Briusov's Caesarism.

Balmont, like a genuine revolutionary an hour after the revolution, in the first hour of *stabilité,* turned out to be *in opposition.* Briusov, the very same hour and for the same reason, turned out to be *for.*

Here, as in everything other than otherlandishness, they were mutually exclusive.

If Balmont is not a monarchist, then it's because he is by nature revolutionary.

If Briusov is a monarchist, then it's because he was personally ignored by the communists.

Briusov's monarchism — is like Arakcheev's settlements.

Balmont's monarchism — is a Ludwigo-Wagnerian palace.

Balmont — is hatred of communism, then of communists.

Briusov — could hate communists, never — communism.

( )

Briusov — is a bureaucrat-communist.

Balmont — is a revolutionary-monarchist.

( )

Revolutions are made by Balmonts and supported by Briusovs.

( )

(The first sign of a passion for power — is the willing subjugation to it. Honoring the very idea of power, of rank. Power lovers are not revolutionaries, just as revolutionaries, for the most part, are not power-loving. Marat, Saint Juste, up to their necks in blood, are innocent of avarice. Their passions may be personal, but their cause is suprapersonal. The fearsome power that consecrates the hearts of the crowd and the minds of individuals to them exists only in the purity of the dream.

Marat would never say "in my name," despite all the monstrous exceeding of rights, just as Bonaparte would not say "in your name," despite all the sacrifice of serving the idea of power. A warring power is "in your name."

The young Bonaparte's distaste for revolution. Watching the execution of Louis XVI from the height of some building, it wasn't softheartedness that made him exclaim: "Et dire qu'il ne faudrait que deux compagnies pour balayer toute cette canaille-là."* The weapon of power lovers is a properly conducted war. Revolution only as an extreme and *not* ethically distasteful means. For that reason, power lovers are less frightening to the state than dreamers. It's a matter of knowing how to use them. In the most extreme case — a love of power of the inhuman, Bonapartian variety — you just have a new regime. The idea of statehood in the hands of a lover of power — is in good hands.

In the communists' place, posthumous paper revelations notwithstanding, I would include Briusov among the already existing roster of saints.)

(( ))

A few more words about Briusov's profound a-nationalism (yet another *correspondence* to the Soviets). Specifically about a-nationalism, a worldview, and not about a lack of kinship, the native feeling for Russianness, of which there is no trace in Briusov.[†] Blok is without kin, Briusov is a-national. Whether filial devotion or orphanhood — Briusov did not live by feelings (or at least — "emotions"). For love of one's country he substituted inquisitiveness not only about other countries, but: lands, planets. And not only planets: the anthill — the hive — the infusorial seething in a drop of water.

> I love my brain so keen, and eyes' bright shining gleam,
> My heart's strong beat, blood coursing through my veins
>   like treasure.
> I love myself; of nature and humanity I dream,
> And want to give myself to them in fullest measure.

*N.B. Distaste for revolution in him, at this moment, equaled only distaste for a king who lost his head in *this way*. (M.Ts.)

[†]Joylessness, hopelessness, indivisibleness, immeasurableness, boundlessness, termlessness, irrevocableness — all of Russia in *less* and lack. (M.Ts.)

(What a chilly "I love" and what a chilly "I want." Wanting and love for exactly four well-rhymed lines. To give oneself—is not a Briusovian verb. If instead of the verb "to give oneself"—it was "to harass"—o, how different it would sound! Briusov didn't want things the right way—when he wanted!)

But whether a microscope or a telescope, infusorial seething or the universe teeming with other worlds—it is the very same dispassionate, evaluating, inquisitive gaze. A microscope or a telescope—but Briusov didn't have a plain human (with the unaided eye) look: it wasn't given to him.

( )

In confirmation of my words about a-nationalism, I refer the reader to his early—and all the worse for being early—poem "Moscow," in memory of the city that didn't survive (*Moscow,* an anthology compiled by M. Kovalensky, pub. "Universal Library," last page. Perhaps it's in *Youthful Poems.* Date of writing, 1899).

( )

Briusov will remain in the world, not as a poet, but as the hero of an epic poem. Similarly, Salieri remained—by virtue of Pushkin's creative will. No one will learn to write poems by reading Briusov (there are better sources even than—Pushkin! The music of all the world, as yet unheard, but which should be heard). Through Briusov they'll learn to want—want what?—just to want, without defining the object: everything. And, perhaps, least of all—to want to write poems.

Briusov will be included in the anthologies, not under "Lyric poetry," but in the section—and there will be such a section in Soviet anthologies: "Willpower." In this section (of trailblazers, overcomers, surmounters) his name, I'd like to believe, will be one of the first among Russian names.

And my unjust heart, which nonetheless craves justice, will not rest in peace until a sculpture is erected on Moscow's most prominent plaza—in granite: a sculpture of inhuman height is:

TO A HERO OF LABOR OF THE U.S.S.R.

Prague, August 1925

NOTES

Citations of Russian texts are transliterated according to the Library of Congress system; elsewhere in the book, that system has been adapted for the convenience of nonspecialist English readers.

Introduction

1. Marina Tsvetaeva, *Sobranie sochinenii vsemi tomakh, tom 4* (Moscow: Ellis Lak), 621. This statement comes from Tsvetaeva's answer to a biographical questionnaire that Boris Pasternak sent her in 1926. It has often been quoted by scholars and biographers, but *evreistvo* (Jewry) was read as *geroistvo* ("heroic action"), due to the difficulty in deciphering Tsvetaeva's handwriting. The mistake was repeated in volume after volume of her works until scholars gained access to her archives and examined the original handwritten copy. The correction is important for properly understanding Tsvetaeva (whose husband, Sergei Efron, was Jewish) and for avoiding misinterpretations of scenes in works like "Free Passage" and "My Jobs" as anti-Semitic. Except for the word "Jewry," the translation of this passage is taken from Viktoria Schweitzer, *Tsvetaeva* (New York: Farrar, Straus and Giroux, 1993), 11.

2. Ibid., 60.

3. Valerii Briusov, *Sobranie sochinenii vsemi tomakh* (Moscow, 1975), vol. 6: 365–66.

4. Simon Karlinsky, *Marina Cvetaeva: Her Life and Art* (Berkeley: University of California Press, 1966), 197. A second, revised edition of Karlinsky's book, still the most useful English biography of Tsvetaeva, and an excellent introduction to her poetry, was published by Cambridge University Press in 1985.

5. This is perhaps the best known episode in Tsvetaeva's life. See *Letters, Summer 1926: Pasternak, Tsvetayeva, Rilke,* 2d enlarged ed., eds. Yevgeny Pasternak, Yelena Pasternak, and Konstantin M. Azadovsky, preface by Susan Sontag, translated by Margaret Wettlin, Walter Arndt, and Jamey Gambrell (New York: New York Review of Books, 2001).

6. Quoted in Schweitzer, *Tsvetaeva,* 241.

7. Ibid., 329–30.

8. Marina Tsvetaeva, *Pis'ma k Anne Teskovoi* (Prague, 1969); quoted in Schweitzer, *Tsvetaeva,* 347.

9. Quoted in Schweitzer, *Tsvetaeva,* 347.

10. Efron was shot on October 16, 1941.

11. Mariia Belkina, *Skreshcheniia sudeb* (Moscow, 1988), 258; my translation.

12. Ibid., 282.

13. Schweitzer, *Tsvetaeva*, 378.

14. A Russian émigré writer, later the editor of *Novyi Zhurnal.*

15. Other renderings of *Zemnye primety* have included "Terrestrial Indicia," "Signs of Earth," and, most often, "Omens of the Earth." I have chosen the perhaps more prosaic "Earthly Signs" because it retains the simple adjective-noun structure of the Russian title, which contains an implied opposition with "heavenly signs." The Russian *primeta* — a word often heard in everyday conversation — is far less marked or exotic than the English *omen,* and does not always convey foreboding or refer to the supernatural.

16. All three excerpts are from "Pis'ma M. Tsvetaevoi k Romanu Guliu," *Novyi Zhurnal* 58 (1959): 169–89, reprinted in *Marina Tsvetaeva: Izbrannaia proza v dvukh tomakh,* ed. Alexander Sumerkin (New York: Russica Publishers, 1979), vol. 1: 445–46. All translations are my own, unless another source is indicated.

17. See Karlinsky, *Marina Cvetaeva,* 127.

18. "New March" refers to the Gregorian calendar, which the Soviet Union adopted shortly after the Revolution. Before the Revolution, Russia used the Julian calendar.

19. A Russian literary critic who emigrated from the Soviet Union in 1920.

20. Black Hundreds was a far-right, anti-Semitic organization responsible for pogroms in Odessa and other cities and for assassinations of Russian liberals in the years between the Russian revolutions of 1905 and 1917. The group was banned after the February Revolution of 1917.

21. Quoted in Karlinsky, *Marina Cvetaeva,* 128.

22. Feliks Edmundovich Dzerzhinsky (1877–1926), founder of the Soviet secret police.

23. "My Jobs" was first published in the USSR in 1989, but this episode was omitted by the censor.

24. The writer Vladimir Aleksandrovich Giliarovsky (1853–1935) was widely admired for his stories, essays, reports, and sketches of prerevolutionary Moscow life, which were published in newspapers and journals. His first collection, *Slum People* (*Trushchobnye liudi,* 1887), was forbidden by the censor, and all but two copies of the print run were destroyed. Giliarovsky is best known for *Moscow and Muscovites* (*Moskva i Moskvichi*), a collection first published in 1926.

25. Joseph Brodsky, "A Poet and Prose," in *Less Than One: Selected Essays* (New York: Farrar, Straus and Giroux, 1986), 178–79.

26. In the song, Stenka Razin marries a Persian princess only to throw her overboard from his boat when his Cossacks disapprove. Stenka hears the grumbling of his men the morning after his wedding feast.

27. In Russian: "Moi Razin (pesennyi) belokur, — s ryzhevtsoi belokur. (Ksta-
ti, glupoe uprazdnenie bukvy d: belokudr, belyi kudri: i buino i belo. A belokur —
chto? Belye kury? Kakoe-to beskhvostoe slovo!). Pugachev cheren, Razin bel. Da
i slovo samo: Stepan! Seno, soloma, step'. Razve chernye Stepany byvaiut? A: Ra —
zin! Zaria, razliv, — razi, Razin! Gde prostorno, tam ne cherno. Chernota — gu-
shcha."

28. In Russian: "Sten'ka Razin, ia ne persiianochka, vo mne net dvuostrogo ko-
varstva: Persii i neliubiashchei. No ia ne russkaia, Razin, ia do-russkaia, do-
tatarskaia, — dovremennaia Rus' ia — tebe navstrechu! Solomennyi Stepan, slushai
menia, step': byli kibitki i byli kochev'ia, byli kostry i byli zvezdy. Kibitochnyi
shater — khochesh'? gde skvoz' dyru — samaia bol'shaia zvezda."

29. *Letters, Summer 1926: Pasternak, Tsvetayeva, Rilke,* 359. In the original, Tsvetaeva includes the following footnote following "dichten": "To sing, to tell, to
compose, create? — it doesn't exist in Russian."

Earthly Signs

OCTOBER ON THE TRAIN

"Oktiabr' v vagone" was first published in the Prague journal *Volia Rossii* 11–12 (1927). This translation first appeared in *Partisan Review* 54, no. 4 (Fall 1987): 517–26.

1: *S. is talking about Vladivostok.* In many of the diaries Tsvetaeva refers to her husband, Sergei Yakovlevich Efron (1893–1941), by the initial S.

1: *I read* Yuzhny Krai. The newspaper, *Southern Land.*

2: *The Kremlin, Tverskaya Street, the Arbat, the Metropol Hotel, Voznesensky Square.* All places in Moscow where battles took place during the October Revolution.

3: *Something of an affectionate Pugachev.* Emelian Ivanovich Pugachev (ca. 1740–75), a Don Cossack who led Russian peasant uprisings of 1773–74 and was captured and executed by order of Catherine the Great. Pugachev became a legendary folk hero and was extolled by many Russian writers. In 1937 Tsvetaeva wrote an essay called "Pushkin and Pugachev."

5: *Boris and Gleb Lane.* Now Ulitsa Pisemskogo, no. 6. Tsvetaeva and her family moved into the house in the fall of 1916, and she lived there until she emigrated in 1922. The building is now occupied by the Tsvetaeva Museum.

7: *The enormous, almost physically burning joy of Max V.* The Russian poet and artist Maximilian Voloshin (1877–1932). Tsvetaeva met Voloshin in late 1910. They immediately became fast friends, and it was at Voloshin's house in Koktebel that she met her future husband, Sergei Efron, in May 1911. Tsvetaeva wrote an essay on Voloshin after his death in 1932. "Zhivoe o zhivom" ("The Living about the Living").

8: *Breshko-Breshkovskaya's a bastard too!* Ekaterina Breshkovskaya (1844–1934), one of the founders of the Socialist Revolutionary Party, known as the "grandmother of the Russian Revolution."

9: *Across from me, on the bench, sleeps a downcast, emaciated, prudent Vikzhel.* Presumably a railroad employee. Vikzhel was the acronym of the All-Russian Administrative Committee of The Railroad Workers Union, founded in August 1917. It did not support the October Revolution and was disbanded for counterrevolutionary activities in January 1918.

FREE PASSAGE

"Vol'nyi proezd" was first published in the Paris journal *Sovremennye Zapiski* 21 (1924).

13: *Dame of the St. Catherine Order.* An honorary society for noblewomen founded by Catherine the Great.

13: *Free passage — transport — of 1 1/2 poods.* One pood equals 36.11 pounds.

17: *Terror, as if faced with* oprichniks. The *oprichniks* were the special secret police of Ivan the Terrible; Triumphal Square is in Moscow.

20: *And on all this brownness — the last blue tint of a late, woman's summer.* The Russian expression "woman's summer" is the equivalent of the English "Indian summer."

23: *The mother-in-law: a former seamstress, a dauntless, garrulous matchmaker from Zamoskvoreche.* Zamoskvoreche is a merchant neighborhood across the river from the Kremlin.

26: *And to the murdered Uritsky.* Moisei Solomonovich Uritsky (1873–1918), a member of the Central Committee of the CPSU from July 1917 and head of the Petrograd Cheka. He was assassinated by Leonid Kanegisser (1897–1918), a poet and member of the Socialist Revolutionary Party.

26: *Also Jewish (addressing the host, politely) — the same last name as you: Kaplan.* Fania Kaplan (the pseudonym of Feiga Efimovna Roidman, 1890–1918), a member of the Socialist Revolutionary Party, attempted to assassinate Lenin on August 30, 1918. Lenin was wounded; Kaplan was reportedly executed in September 1918.

27: *You are now at the requisition base, Usman Station, at the home of an active member of the RCP.* RCP is the Russian Communist Party.

28: *Stenka Razin. Two St. George Crosses.* Medals of the Order of St. George, founded in 1769, for military excellence.

28: *Esenin, but without the pettiness.* The poet Sergei Esenin (1895–1925).

30: *They talk about fasting, but their tongues lick meat and milk thoughts off their lips.* In the Russian Orthodox Church it is forbidden to eat meat or dairy products on fast days.

30: *What do they write in those books? Marx, for instance, and the Gracchus brothers?* The Gracchus brothers, Tiberius and Gaius, second century b.c., were from a famous plebeian Roman family. According to the *Great Soviet Encyclopedia,* "They tried to bring about democratic land reform in order to ameliorate the plight of the peasants. They died in the struggle with the Senate which opposed reform."

31: *I bet they're all foreigners: your tongue twists just saying the names, and there's no patrimony.* "Razin" appears to confuse otechestvo (meaning "fatherland"), with otchestvo ("patronymic") — a confusion that would have appealed to Tsvetaeva.

32: *I recite him the poems: "To the Tsarevich," "To the Tsar on Easter," "Purebred Steeds."*

The three poems Tsvetaeva mentions here are from the cycle *Lebedinyi stan* (The Swans' Encampment): "Za Otroka — za Golubia — za Syna" ("For the Boy — for the Dove — for the Son"); "Tsariu — na Paskhu" ("To the Tsar on Easter"); and "Krovnykh konei zapriagaite v drovni!" ("Hitch the Purebred Steeds to the Wood Sledge"). Tsvetaeva did not publish *Lebedinyi stan* during her lifetime; but it was one of the prepared texts she deposited in Basel, Switzerland, before she returned to the Soviet Union in 1939. The collection was published for the first time posthumously, in Munich in 1957, by Gleb Struve. It was translated into English by Robin Kemball and published as *The Demesne of the Swans* (Ann Arbor: Ardis, 1980).

32: *"Slop/stall." They'd really give it to him for that stall bit, wouldn't they?* The rhyme "Razin" refers to — "slop/stall" (or stables), in Russian, "poila/stoila" — is from the poem "Krovnykh konei."

32: *Shall I recite you a poem about Stenka Razin?* The following are the first three lines of Tsvetaeva's three-part poem "Stenka Razin," written in the spring of 1917. In the third part, subtitled "Son Razina" (Razin's Dream), the chiming of bells is compared to silver drops of liquid, prefiguring the fairy tale that this "Razin" tells Tsvetaeva in "Free Passage."

33: *And there's yat, just like a church with a dome.* Yat' is a letter of the prerevolutionary Russian alphabet that was discarded as part of Bolshevik reforms but that Tsvetaeva continued to use.

33: *I won't give away my Pomoga.* Pomoga appears to be the name of the town.

35: *"M.I., clear out — and we're off!"* Tsvetaeva's name and patronymic, Marina Ivanovna.

36: *Now fancy that, I wouldn't have thought.* I.e., that Tsvetaeva is Jewish, as the first and last names she gives indicate.

38: *Moscow, Execution Place — it's a little square where they used to execute tsars — Brute St., Trotsky Lane.* "Lobnoe mesto" (Execution Place) is on Red Square, but Tsvetaeva invents the other street names.

39: *Worse than sand: the complete works of Steklov!* Yury Mikhailovich Steklov (Nakhamkis), 1873–1941, historian, journalist, prominent Soviet official, member of the Bolshevik Party from 1893; in 1917 he was named editor of *Izvestia;* he was executed in 1941.

MY JOBS

"Moi sluzhby" was first published in *Sovremennye Zapiski,* no. 25 (1925).

44: *My lodger flew in, X, a communist.* Henryk Sachs (1880–1937), a Polish Communist, who was secretary to Feliks Dzerzhinsky.

44: *And at Narkomnats.* The People's Commissariat on Nationalities (Narodnyi komissariat po delam national'nostei), which functioned between 1917 and 1924), was headed by Stalin. The building Tsvetaeva worked in later became the headquarters of the USSR Writers Union.

44: *In the first Cheka building.* The Cheka (Chrezvychainyi Komitet), or Extra-ordinary Committee, was the precursor to the KGB. It was founded and headed at the time by Feliks Dzerzhinsky.

46: *I rephrase Steklov, Kerzhentsev.* On Steklov, see notes to "Free Passage." Platon Mikhailovich Kerzhentsev (1881–1940) was a journalist and an activist in the Soviet government and Communist Party.

48: *If foreign governments would leave the Russian people in peaces.* The typographical error in Russian is: "ostavili v *pomoe* russkii narod," i.e., "in the garbage," in-stead of "v pokoe," "in peace."

49: *To Butyrki, I'm bringing a package.* Butyrskaya prison, in central Moscow.

49: *The former town governor, D-sky.* Vladimir Fedorovich Dzhunkovsky (1865–1938?).

49: *Wi(pi)r we(pe)erde(pe)n.* Tsvetaeva is speaking to her sister in German "pig Latin."

53: *It smells of damp and Bonivard.* The reference is to François Bonivard (1493–1570), the hero of Byron's *The Prisoner of Chillon.*

53: *Like Pan in the Tretyakov Gallery.* Tsvetaeva is referring to the painting *Pan,* by Mikhail Vrubel (1856–1910), in the Tretyakov Gallery in Moscow.

55: *At my elbow—Mamontov, on my knees—Denikin, near my heart—Kolchak.* Kon-stantin Konstantinovich Mamontov (1869–1920), lieutenant-general in the White Guard who fought in the armed forces of the Russian south during the Civil War. Anatoly Ivanovich Denikin (1872–1947), one of the primary leaders of the White Army and commander of the armed forces of the Rus-sian south; emigrated in 1920. Aleksandr Vasilevich Kolchak (1873–1920), admiral of the Black Sea Fleet who fought against the Bolsheviks and estab-lished a provisional White regime in Siberia, the Urals, and the Far East; ex-ecuted in 1920.

58: *I rake up the draft of Casanova.* At the time, Tsvetaeva was writing a play called *Casanova's End (Konets Kazanovy).*

58: *9/23 of January (Central Executive Committee News.)* Tsvetaeva gives the dates of both the Julian and Gregorian calendars. Russia switched to the Gregorian calendar after the Revolution.

58: *Someone reads: Kornilov's son, Georgy.* Lavrenty Georgievich Kornilov (1870–1918), one of the organizers of the White Guard Voluntary Army, killed in battle near Ekaterinodar.

63: *A swarm of snow-white maidens! One, two, . . . four.* This stanza describes Tsar

Nicholas II's daughters in their white dresses. Tsvetaeva saw them in 1913 when her father opened the Alexander III Museum of Fine Arts (now the Pushkin Museum). Tsvetaeva quotes the same poem when describing this episode in "Museum Opening" ("Otkrytie muzeiia").

64: *Those poor Sollogubian Elzevirs!* Books published by the seventeenth-century Dutch publishing family Elzevir, presumably from Count Sollogub's library.

64: *The library commission is headed by Briusov.* On Valery Yakovlevich Briusov (1873–1924), see "A Hero of Labor."

68: *I remember Stakhovich.* On Aleksei Aleksandrovich Stakhovich (1856–1919), see "The Death of Stakhovich."

69: *What's soap going for at Sukhareva?* There was a large flea market at Sukhareva Square in Moscow.

69: *Instead of Monplenbezh.* Tsvetaeva is apparently referring to Tsentroplenbezh, the "Tsentral'naia kollegiia po delam plennykh i bezhentsev" (Central Collegium on Affairs of Prisoners and Refugees).

72: *Yesterday I gave a reading of* Fortuna. *Fortuna* was a play that Tsvetaeva wrote in early 1919.

73: *In addition to me the readers were: Lunacharsky.* Anatoly Vasilevich Lunacharsky (1875–1933) was head of Narkompros (People's Commissariat of Education) at this time. Tsvetaeva was quite taken with Lunacharsky, as is evident from her description here.

73: *A certain Dir Tumanny.* Pseudonym of the poet Nikolai Nikolaevich Panov (1903–73).

73: *I chose Fortuna because of the monologue at the end.* Simon Karlinsky has the following to say about *Fortuna:* "Armand Louis de Gontaud Biron, Duc de Lauzun (1747–93). Lauzun was an aristocrat who lent his support to the French Revolution and died by the guillotine during the Jacobin terror. . . . The final scene of *Fortuna* shows Lauzun awaiting execution at the hands of the revolutionaries whose cause he had supported and for whom he had fought against the peasant insurgents of the Vendée (for Tsvetaeva, the Vendée was always the equivalent of the White Army). Lauzun's long soliloquy in this scene is clearly meant as topical commentary on the plight of many Russian liberals and Socialists who were then being put to death by the revolution they had helped to bring about" (Simon Karlinsky, *Marina Tsvetaeva: The Woman, Her World, and Her Poetry* [Cambridge: Cambridge University Press, 1985], 90–91).

73: *The whole of No. 2 Lubianka!* The address of the secret police headquarters.

74: *Three days later I found out from B.* Konstantin Dmitrievich Balmont (1867–

1942), Russian poet and lifelong friend of Tsvetaeva; he emigrated to France in 1920.

ATTIC LIFE

"Cherdachnoe (Iz moskovskikh zapisei 1919–1920)" was first published in *Sovremennye zapiski*, no. 26 (1925). This translation first appeared in *Partisan Review* 53, no. 4 (1986): 499–508.

75: *I know nothing of S.* Sergei Efron.

75: *I live with Alya and Irina.* Tsvetaeva's daughters, Ariadna Sergeevna Efron (1913–75) and Irina Sergeevna Efron (1917–20). At the end of November 1919, Tsvetaeva placed her daughters in a children's home in the Moscow suburb of Kuntsevo, hoping that they would receive more food she could provide them. Alya soon contracted malaria, and Tsvetaeva brought her back to Moscow in early January, where she nursed her with the help of her friend V. A. Zhukovskaya and Vera Efron, her sister-in-law. Irina died at the children's home in early February 1920, apparently of starvation or malnutrition. See Karlinsky, *Marina Tsvetaeva*, 81–82, and Anna Saakiants, *Stranitsy zhizni i tvorchestva (1910–1922)* (Moscow, 1986), 213–21.

82: *But there's no Gogol.* All the names mentioned in the preceding paragraph are characters in Gogol's novel *Dead Souls*.

83: *Is there presently in Russia—Rozanov is dead.* Vasily Vasilevich Rozanov (1856–1919), writer and philosopher. Rozanov knew Ivan Vladimirovich Tsvetaev, the poet's father, and wrote his obituary. Tsvetaeva, who had read Rozanov, wrote to the philosopher in 1914 after her sister, Anastasia Ivanovna, began a correspondence with him.

ON LOVE

"O liubvi: Iz dnevnika, 1917" was first published in the Berlin newspaper *Dni*, December 25, 1925.

87: *"O, l'Amour! l'Amour!"—of Sarah.* Tsvetaeva is referring to Sarah Bernhardt in the role of Marguerite Gautier in Dumas fils' *Camille*.

89: *"Just live!" I dropped my hands.* This poem is from *Versty II*, which Tsvetaeva published in Moscow in two editions (the first contained many typographical errors, which she corrected in the second). The first came out in 1921, the second in 1922.

90: *The parlor is the field, yesterday's Smolny student.* The Smolny Institute in St. Petersburg was a school for daughters of the nobility. Founded in 1764, it was closed after the Revolution.

92: *And a red maple leaf was placed.* Tsvetaeva is quoting Anna Akhmatova's poem

"Under the Frozen Roof of an Empty Dwelling" ("Pod kryshei promerzshei pustovo zhil'ia," 1915).

93: *Pavel Antokolsky: "The Lord had Judas."* Pavel Grigorevich Antokolsky (1896– 1978). Poet, critic, actor, onetime director of the Vakhtangov Theater and recipient of the Stalin prize. See Schweitzer, *Tsvetaeva*, 386.

95: *Antokolsky: "But fatherhood is a big 0, that is, nought, zero."* The Russian word for "fatherhood," *ottsovstvo*, begins and ends with the letter "o," hence the association with zero.

96: *The trial of Admiral Shchastny.* Aleksei Mikhailovich Shchastny (1883–1918) was an admiral in the Imperial Navy and later commander of the Red Baltic Fleet. He was convicted of treason by a revolutionary tribunal for not following Trotsky's orders; his execution in June 1918 was the first official death sentence carried out after the death sentence had been abolished by the Soviet government.

97: *When she was two, Alya would say: camhill.* In Russian *gorbliud,* a compound word constructed from *gora* (mountain) and *verbliud* (camel). "Koshka na moei grudi delaet verbliuda. (Alia, dvukh let, govorila: gorbliud!)."

98: *A letter about Lauzun.* Through Antokolsky, Tsvetaeva came into contact with the Third Studio experimental group of the Moscow Art Theater. The description that follows relates to Yury Zavadsky, an actor of the Third Studio, with whom Tsvetaeva was infatuated, and on whom she based the character of Lauzun in her play *Fortuna.*

THE DEATH OF STAKHOVICH

"Iz dnevnika. Smert' Stakhovicha (27 fevralia 1919 g)" was first published in the Paris newspaper *Poslednie novosti,* January 26, 1926.

101: *Aleksei Aleksandrovich Stakhovich.* Stakhovich (1856–1919) was an actor in the Moscow Art Theater (MKhAT) and taught at MKhAT's III Studio.

103: *M[chede]lov came up to me.* Vakhtang Levanovich Mchedelov, (real name Mchedlishvili (1884–1924), a director and acting teacher.

106: *The hold that the bold word "Khudozhestvenniki."* I.e., actors of MKhAT (Moskovskii Khudozhestvennyi Akademicheskii Teatr).

107: *Kameneva and someone else were there. Nemirovich-Danchenko simmered.* Olga Davydovna Kameneva (1883–1941) was head of the theater section of the People Commissariat of Englightenment from 1918 to 1919. V. I. Nemirovich-Danchenko (1858–1943) was a director and playwright.

111: *Kachalov received a poem from you, unsigned.* Kachalov, the pseudonym of Vasily Ivanovich Shverubovich (1875–1948), an actor in the Moscow Art Theater.

ON GRATITUDE

"O blagodarnosti (Iz dnevnika 1919)" was first published in the Brussels journal *Blagonamerennyi,* no. 1 (1926). This translation first appeared in *Formations* (Winter 1988).

EXCERPTS FROM THE BOOK *Earthly Signs*

"Otryvki iz knigi *Zemnye primety*" was first published in the Prague journal *Volia Rossii,* nos. 1–2 (1924).

130: *Lazarus — glassy eyes —* Glas. The Russian for "eyes" is *glaza.*

ON GERMANY

"O Germanii" was first published in *Dni,* December 13, 1925.

150: *Since she died at the age of 34.* In a nearly identical passage in "Excerpts from the Book *Earthly Signs,*"Tsvetaeva writes that her mother died at the age of thirty-six. In fact, Maria Alexandrovna was born in 1868 and died in July 1906.

FROM A DIARY

"Iz dnevnika" was first published in *Poslednie novosti,* December 25, 1925.

A HERO OF LABOR

"Geroi truda (Zapisi o Valerii Briusove)" was first published in *Volia Rossii,* nos. 9–10, 11 (1925).

170: *Valery Yakovlevich Briusov.* Russian poet (1873–1924) and one of the founders of Russian Symbolism. After the Revolution, he established the Higher Literary-Artistic Institute. Briusov died in Moscow on October 9, 1924. Tsvetaeva was living in Prague at the time she wrote this essay. She mentions it in a letter to A. A. Teskovà on September 9, 1925: "It came out, as always, five times longer than I thought, instead of anecdotal notes on Briusov-the-man — an evaluation of the poetic and human figure with numerous accompanying thoughts. I wonder how you will like it. It was a difficult job: despite the repulsion that he inspired in me (and not in me alone), to give an idea of his peculiar greatness. To judge, without passing judgment, although the sentence — it would seem — was a foregone conclusion. Unfortunately, I was writing without sources, quoting from memory. But perhaps that was better — it could have been an entire volume" (M. Tsvetaeva, *Pis'ma k Anne Teskovoi* [Prague: Academia, 1969], 32).

170: *His Fiery Angel. The Fiery Angel* (1907–08) is a historical novella set in sixteenth-century Germany. The heroine, Renata, dies, convicted by the inquisition for witchcraft.

170: *Adelaida Kazimirovna Gertsyk* (1874–1925), a Russian poet with whom Tsvetaeva was friendly.

In Russian, the word "poetess" can be used merely to indicate gender, since Russian nouns are either masculine, feminine, or neuter, and adjectives must agree with nouns in number and gender. Generally speaking, however, "poetess" has much the same pejorative connotation in Russian that it does in English; "poetesses" belong to a lesser order of being than poets.

Tsvetaeva always referred to herself as a poet, and never wrote of Anna Akhmatova or Karolina Pavlova, for instance, as anything but poets. For her, a poet is a quality of soul, spirit, and verse, unconnected to gender: "the poems were offered by a poet, not a woman," she says to Adalis in this essay. Tsvetaeva elaborates her own, radical "inborn aversion to everything bearing the stamp of female (mass) separatism" at some length here. "In creative work," she explains, "there is no women's question; there are women's answers to human questions . . ."

Tsvetaeva chose her words scrupulously, and thus her frequent use of the word "poetess" in this essay is deliberate (it is not used in any of the other pieces in this book). The "punch line," so to speak, is the moment in the scene "The Evening of Poetesses" when Briusov introduces Tsvetaeva alone among twenty-some readers, as the "*poet* Tsvetaeva."

175: *The* Egyptian Nights *that Briusov finished.* In 1914–16, using Pushkin's drafts, Briusov resurrected and completed Pushkin's long, unfinished poem *Egyptian Nights.*

176: *Isn't this — the inability to simply dream — the source of the sad passion for narcotics?* According to Khodasevich's memoirs, Briusov regularly used morphine. See Vladislav Khodasevich, *Nekropol'* (Brussels: Les Editions Petropolis, 1939), 21, 60.

176: *Briusov. Brius. (A Moscow black magician of the 18th century.)* Yakov Vilimovich Brius (1670–1735) — a Russian count, statesman, scholar, and military man, one of the compilers of "Briusov's calendar," which presented astronomical tables and predictions.

177: *I would like not to be Valery Briusov.* Tsvetaeva quotes from Briusov's poem "L'ennui de vivre" (1902) inexactly. The quote should read "I would not desire to be."

178: *The cry of the best contemporary Russian poet.* Tsvetaeva means Boris Pasternak.

180: *Three words reveal Briusov: will, ox, wolf.* In Russian, *volia* (will), *vol* (ox), *volk* (wolf).

180: *To the Scythian Roman.* A reference to Alexander Blok's poem "The Scythians,"

in which the Russian people are described as a semi-Asiatic horde alien to
Western European culture.

180: *Evgeniya Yakovlevna Briusova* (Kaliuzhnaya) 1882-?. Taught at the Moscow
conservatory.

181: *Valeriya Ivanovna Tsvetaeva* (1882–1966). Tsvetaeva's half-sister.

181: *Apparently that student business of '98-'99?* Student uprising of 1898–99 at
Moscow University among the history faculty, where Briusov was a student.

181: *Edmond Rostand* (1868–1918). French poet and playwright. Rostand is best
known for his play *Cyrano de Bergerac*.

182: *Renata, Antony.* Characters in Briusov's work: Renata, whose tragic love is the
center of the story *Fiery Angel,* and Marc Antony, from the poem "Antony"
(1905).

182: *Rostand of L'Aiglon, Rostand — of Melissande. L'Aiglon* (1910), a play by Rostand;
Melissande, an Eastern princess of the twelfth century, the hero of Rostand's *La Princesse Greuze* (1895).

182: *I went home to write him a letter.* As the eminent Tsvetaeva scholar Anna
Saakiants shows in her book *Marina Tsvetaeva: Zhizn' i tvorchestvo (Marina
Tsvetaeva: Life and Work* [Moscow, 1997]), some of Tsvetaeva's memories of
her early literary career and her attitude toward Briusov are disingenuous.
Tsvetaeva's memory of her initial letter to Briusov is also rather different in
tone; furthermore, she did, in fact give Briusov her address. Anna Saakiants
quotes the original letter, dated March 15, 1910, Moscow, in her *Zhizn' i
tvorchestvo:* "Most Esteemed Valery Yakovlevich, Just now at Wolf's you
said: ' . . . although I am not an admirer of Rostand.' . . . I immediately
wanted to ask you, why? But I thought that you would take my question as
idle curiosity or as an ambitious desire 'to talk with Briusov.' When the door
had closed behind you, I was sad and I began to regret my silence, but in the
end comforted myself with the thought that I could put the question to you
in written form. Why don't you like Rostand? Could it really be that you see
in him only a 'virtuoso verbalist,' could it really be that his endless nobility,
his love of great deed and purity escape you? This is not an idle question. For
me, Rostand — is a part of my soul, a very large part. He comforts me, gives
me the strength to live alone. I think that no one, no one knows, loves or
values him as I do. Your passing phrase saddened me. I began to think: all
the poets I love should feel close to Rostand, Heine, Victor Hugo, Lamartine, Lermontov — all of them would have loved him. He shares with Heine
a common love of the Roman king, of Melissande, the Tripolian princess;
Lamartine could not have loved this 'amant du Rêve'; Lermontov, who
wrote *Mtsyri,* would immediately have recognized a brother in the author of

L'Aiglon; Victor Hugo would have been proud of such a pupil. Why then is Briusov, who loves Heine, Lermontov, who values Victor Hugo, so indifferent to Rostand? If you, dearly respected Valery Yakovlevich, find my question worthy of an answer — please write me about this. My sister, 'the little girl with big eyes,' who pursued you last spring on the street — often thinks of you. Yours with sincere respect, M. Tsvetaeva [Postscript:] Address: Here, Trekhprudny Lane, private house, Marina Ivanovna Tsvetaeva" (Saakiants, *Zhizn' i tvorchestvo,* 11).

184: *I didn't send a single copy for review.* As Saakiants further points out, eighteen-year-old Marina did indeed send out review copies of her first book to a number of writers, including Briusov and the poet Maximilian Voloshin (whose favorable and insightful review marked the beginning of an important, lifetime friendship), which explains in part why this first effort by an unknown poet was so widely reviewed. In addition to Briusov and Voloshin's comments, reviews appeared by Nikolai Gumilyov, Aleksei Tolstoi, and Marietta Shaginian, among other literary figures. Briusov's review, which provoked such an extreme reaction, was in fact, as Tsvetaeva says, quite positive. In a detailed survey of sixteen new books by young poets published in 1911 (among them Aleksei Tolstoi and Ilya Ehrenburg), Briusov wrote: "Marina Tsvetaeva presents a rather sharp contrast to I. Ehrenburg. Ehrenburg continually turns in an imaginary world that he himself has created, in the world of knights, chaplains, troubadours, tournaments; he more willingly speaks not of those feelings he actually experienced, but of those he would like to experience. The starting point of Marina Tsvetaeva's poems, in contrast, is always some real fact, something actually lived. Not afraid to bring everyday life into poetry, she takes the features of life directly, and this gives her poems a terrible intimacy. When you read her book, at times it becomes embarrassing, as though you'd peered impolitely through a half-closed window into someone else's apartment and witnessed a scene that outsiders should not see. However, this immediacy, appealing as it is in the more successful pieces, turns into a kind of 'domesticity' on many pages of this thick collection. What you then have are not poetic creations (whether bad or good, is another question), but simply the pages of a personal diary, and for that matter rather insipid pages. The latter is explained by the youth of the writer, who refers to her age several times. [']While/All life is like a book for me,['] — Marina Tsvetaeva says in one place; in another she applies the epithet 'not grown-up' to her verse; in yet another she speaks directly of her 'eighteen years.' These confessions disarm the critic. But if in Miss Tsvetaeva's next books her favorite heroes again appear — Mama, Volodya, Seryozha, little Anya, little Valenka — and the same favorite places — the dark parlor, melting ice-skating pond, the dining room four times a day, the lively Arbat and so on, we hope that they will become synthetic images, symbols of the human, not simply fleeting portraits of near and dear and memories of her apartment. We will also expect that the poet find in her soul feelings more piercing than the charming trifles that take up a lot of space in *Evening Album,* and concepts more vital than repetitions of the old truth: 'The Pharisees' arrogance is hateful.' Undoubtedly talented, Marina Tsvetaeva may give us a genuine poetry of intimate life and may, given the ease with which she appears to write verse, waste her entire gift on unneeded, though perhaps elegant baubles (Briusov, *Sobranie sochinenii,* vol. 6, pp. 365–66, my translation).

198: *Adalis.* The pen name of Adelina Efimovna Efron (1900–69; no relation to Tsvetaeva's husband), a Russian Soviet poet and translator.

199: *Anna Dmitrievna Radlova.* Russian Soviet poet (1891–1949).

199: *"I agree that male monarchism is better." (Pause.) "Don monarchism.* Tsvetaeva here is referring to the "monarchism" of the men (like her husband) fighting with the White Army on the Don River. This "monarchism" she saw as a matter of honor and loyalty to Russia and its traditions, rather than blind devotion to any given monarch or regime. Similarly, when Adalis says "female communism," just above, she implies a personal interpretation of communism rather than strict adherence to the Party line.

201: *My joint performance with Adalis took place more than six months later.* The reading was held on December 11, 1920 (and not in February 1921, as Tsvetaeva writes). According to the posters, nine women poets were to read: Adalis, Natalia Benar, Feiga Kogan, Natalia Poplavskaya, Nadezhda Vol'pin, Nadezhda De-Gurno, Vera Il'ina, Tsvetaeva, and Mal'vina Marianova.

202: *Maria Morevna.* The beautiful, kind heroine of a Russian folktale.

202: *Maria Konstantinovna Bashkirtseva.* An artist (1860–84), the author of "A Diary."

204: *Rome and the World.* The title of the second volume of Briusov's three-volume collected poems (1908).

205: *The stage is a visible place . . . There's visibility in the very sound: Stay! Enjoy!* In Russian: estrada (stage); zdravstvuite (hello); raduites' (be joyful).

207: *Ada Negri.* An Italian poet (1870–1945).

208: *The Don.* This poem, written in 1918, and the others listed were included in the collection *The Demesne of the Swans,* trans. by Robin Kemball (Ann Arbor: Ardis, 1980). The poems in "Hero of Labor" are my translations.

209: *The women cried hurrah.* A quote from Griboedov's *Woe from Wit.* This poem was apparently never included in any collection and is known only from this essay.

217: *Gumilyov never.* Nikolai Gumilyov, Acmeist poet and husband of Anna Akhmatova, was executed for antirevolutionary activity in 1921.

219: *Jurgis Kazimirovich Baltrushaitis.* Lithuanian poet and translator (1873–1944).

220: *May no one be deaf to one particular line of the linguistically uneven* International. Tsvetaeva is most likely referring to "Kto byl nichem, tot stanet vsem." ("We are but naught we shall be all," literally "He who was nothing, will become everything.")

221: *Briusov's poem "To Young Women."* The actual title of this poem is "Woman" (from the cycle "Sonnets and Terzinas," 1901–03).

223: *Let's Be Like the Sun.* The title of a collection of poems by Balmont (1903).

223: *Despite the Vladimir guberniya.* Balmont was born in the Vladimir guberniya.

224: *I'm a guest of the universe.* A paraphrase of Karolina Pavlova's poem "The Poet" (1839): "On vselennoi gost',/emu vsiudu pir."

227: *Alexander Arnoldovich Koiransky.* A Russian writer and artist (1884–1968). But the quote is from Yury Aikhenvald, who, writing on Briusov's version of *Egyptian Nights,* concluded that "Briusov is not foreign to the greatness of talentlessness overcome" (cited in *Marina Tsvetaeva: Sobranie sochinenii v semi tomakh* [Moscow: Ellis Lak, 1994], vol. 4, p. 642).

229: *"City of the Future."* Apparently Briusov's poem "The World" (1903) is meant here.

SUGGESTED READING

Works by Marina Tsvetaeva in English translation:

After Russia (with facing Russian text), translated by Michael Naydan. Ann Arbor, Mich.: Ardis, 1992.

Art in the Light of Conscience: Eight Essays on Poetry, translated by Angela Livingstone. Cambridge: Harvard University Press, 1992.

A Captive Spirit: Selected Prose of Marina Tsvetaeva, translated by J. Marin King. Ann Arbor, Mich.: Ardis, 1980; rpt., with a preface by Susan Sontag, London: Virago Press, 1984.

The Demesne of the Swan, translated by Robin Kemball. Ann Arbor, Mich.: Ardis, 1980.

Letters, Summer 1926: Pasternak, Tsvetayeva, Rilke, 2d ed., eds. Yevgeny Pasternak, Yelena Pasternak, and Konstantin M. Azadovsky, preface by Susan Sontag, translated by Margaret Wettlin and Walter Arndt, with new material translated by Jamey Gambrell. New York: New York Review Books Classics, 2001.

Poem of the End: Selected Narrative and Lyric Poetry (with facing Russian text), with an introduction by Laura Weeks, translated by Nina Kossman. Ann Arbor: Ardis, 1998.

Ratcatcher: A Lyrical Satire, translated by Angela Livingston. Evanston: Northwestern, 2000.

On Tsvetaeva

Joseph Brodsky, "A Poet and Prose" and "Footnote to a Poem," in *Less Than One: Selected Essays.* New York: Farrar, Straus & Giroux, 1986.

——. "A Footnote to a Commentary," in *Rereading Russian Poetry,* ed. Stephanie Sandler. New Haven: Yale University Press, 1999.

Lily Feiler, *Marina Tsvetaeva: The Double Beat of Heaven and Hell.* Durham: Duke University Press, 1994.

Simon Karlinsky, *Marina Tsvetaeva: The Woman, Her World, and Her Poetry,* London: Cambridge University Press, 1985.

Viktoria Schweitzer, *Tsvetaeva.* New York: Farrar, Straus & Giroux, 1993.

Jane A. Taubman, *Life Through Poetry: Marina Tsvetaeva's Lyric Poetry.* Ohio: Slavica Publishers, 1989.

RUSSIAN LITERATURE
AND THOUGHT